Religion and Political Power

Religion and Political Power

edited by
Gustavo Benavides and M. W. Daly

State University of New York Press

Published by
State University of New York Press, Albany

© 1989 State University of New York

Printed in the United States of America

For information, address State University of New York
Press, State University Plaza, Albany, N.Y., 12246

Library of Congress Cataloging-in-Publication Data

Religion and political power.
    This book originated from a seminar on "Religion and
Nationalism" held at the University of California,
Santa Barbara, 1986.
    Includes index.
    1. Religion and politics—Congresses. 2. Religion
and state—Congresses. 3. Power (Social sciences)—
Congresses. I. Benavides, Gustavo. II. Daly, M. W.
    BL65.P7R432   1989   322'.1   88-24861
    ISBN 0-7914-0026-3
    ISBN 0-7914-0027-1 (pbk.)

10 9 8 7 6 5 4 3 2 1

Contents

Preface

This book has its origins in a seminar on "Religion and National-ism" held under the auspices of the National Endowment for the Humanities at the University of California, Santa Barbara, June–August 1986. Directed by Professors Phillip E. Hammond and Ninian Smart, both of the Department of Religious Studies, the seminar explored the role played by religion in the emergence and the political life of modern states. From India and Sri Lanka to the Islamic Republic of Iran, to the resurgence of religious fundamentalism in the United States and its persistence in Israel, the members of the seminar discussed the many forms that the tension between religion and the modern state assumes. However, the thread running through most of our discussions proved to be something more general than the state, although it is the state that now embodies it. That theme is the exercise of political power: more precisely, the exercise of political power in a context that mobilizes religious representations. The essays that follow explore this issue. Two essays, those of Professor Bennigsen and Professor Feuchtwang, who did not participate in the seminar, were commissioned separately.

As editors we wish to acknowledge the essential support of the National Endowment for the Humanities: without its Summer Seminar program our discussions could not have taken place. The University of California, Santa Barbara also deserves our thanks. It is a splendid setting for such a venture, and its resources and those of the other universities of the State of California were open to us. Professors Smart and Hammond have added to their early encouragement by contributing essays; we thank them for their collaboration. While we much appreciate the roles of individuals and institutions in making this volume possible, responsibility for its contents rests with its authors and editors.

Gustavo Benavides
M. W. Daly

— 1 —

Religious Articulations of Power

Gustavo Benavides

I

A meaningful discussion of the relationship between religion and power requires a certain degree of agreement as to the meaning of the terms under consideration. In this essay, "power" will be broadly understood, following Weber's definition, as the chance to impose one's will against the resistance of others.[1] Whether this imposition is exercised by those who already are in a position of power, or whether an attempt is made to impose one's will against established groups, the central characteristic of power remains the same: power is a tension between interests, ideologies, classes, or individuals, and is always defended and contested, using all the weapons—physical and ideological—at the group's disposal. At the same time, this give and take takes place not in a vacuum but within structures that are themselves constituted by power relations.[2] Indeed, individuals, groups, classes, and nations engage in activities aimed at maximizing their prestige, wealth, etc., in a space structured hierarchically, that is, according to preexistent relations based on unequal access to goods, status, ritual purity, or anything that a group defines as desirable. Power without structure would be as difficult as movement unencumbered by some physical laws, whereas structure without the tension provided by contested power would either collapse upon itself or persist eternally without any possibility of change whatsoever.

It is beyond the scope of this essay to examine the current controversies surrounding the concept of power; therefore, we will not discuss the possible difference between "power" and "domination," nor the problem concerning the conscious or unconscious way in which power is exercised.[3] An issue that will be considered is the extent to which a given religion or, more generally, a given culture determines the way in which power or resistance to it are exercised. Surely it would be presumptuous to believe that a specific—in this case

1

a late twentieth-century, Western—conception of power allows us to understand power relations in other cultures. On the other hand, it would be no less dangerous to become imprisoned by an extreme cultural relativism that would lead us to believe that certain societies function in a manner that, for example, makes power and wealth, or ritual purity and political position, totally independent of each other.[4]

The case of India is instructive in this regard. Louis Dumont maintains that Western scholars, imprisoned by an all-encompassing ideology built upon individualism and economism, are largely incapable of gaining an adequate understanding of an Indian ideology that is founded on community and on the opposition between purity and impurity.[5] In *Homo hierarchicus,* Dumont develops a theory of caste based on the ideological opposition between purity and impurity, an opposition which is "ideological" in the sense that its function is merely a classificatory one, without any explicit or implicit economic function.[6] However, an examination of the literature on caste and particularly on the untouchables shows that, as a group, untouchables are not just ritually polluting but also poorer and less educated than so-called caste Hindus. The ritual avoidance surrounding polluting untouchables does not merely segregate them in "ritual" occasions, but, in a society such as the Indian in which the distinction between "sacred" and "profane" is nonexistent,[7] it affects their access to land, irrigation water, education, jobs, etc. (if this were not the case, the current Indian system of education and employment quotas in favor of "scheduled castes" would be quite unnecessary).[8] Indeed, one does not have to be imprisoned by an ideology based on individualism and economism to recognize that the apparent disjunction between ritual status and economic/political power may be the price dominant groups pay to regulate general access to wealth and power. When some attempt to defend the *sui generis* character of the *jāti* system by pointing out that in India one finds both rich untouchables and poor Brahmans, they forget that what counts is, on the one hand, the relative economic position of the *jātis* and, on the other, the attempts to improve the ritual position of a given *jāti* when its economic/political position has improved. If the disjunction between status based on ritual purity and economic/political power were as absolute as Dumont claims, there would be no need to try to match them. Positions such as Dumont's assume the existence of a monolithic ideology, in this case a Brahmanic one, accepted both by those who benefit from it as well as those who suffer under it (in the language of Indian mythology we could say that, according to Dumont, those who emerge from the mouth and the arms of Purusha are as satisfied with their fates as those who emerge from the thighs and the feet). The validity in India and elsewhere of the "dominant ideology thesis," however, is far from certain. In India, the emergence of new religions such as Jainism, Buddhism and Sikhism, conversion to Islam, and the appearance of *Bhakti* movements[9] (not to mention the existence of materialist schools in Indian philosophy), indicate that the dominant ideology is not accepted uncritically by all members of the society.[10]

More recently, Lucien Pye has attempted to give an overview of the cultural dimensions of power in Asia. He argues that in Asian cultures there is the tendency to disassociate power from responsibility, wealth, and purposeful activities. According to Pye, Asian notions of power are based on the phenomenon of dependency, which itself depends on certain patterns of child-rearing and paternalism that seem to be pan-Asian. We will not review Pye's psychologist theories, except for a few words about his views on the religious-cultural causes for one of the main components of the struggle to maintain or defend power, namely violence. Discussing Islam, he writes: "The potential for otherwise peaceful and disciplined Believers to become violent results in no small measure from the sharp line drawn by Islam between good and evil, between purity and pollution, between virtuous and abominable behavior. Muslim standards of personal conduct seem so unattainable to the common people that they are driven to compensate for personal failings by expressing righteous indignation toward superiors who appear to them to be violating the spirit of Islam."[11] That this interpretation of sudden outbursts of violence is inadequate becomes clear when we remember the current violent confrontations between Hindus and Buddhists in Sri Lanka (or Hindus, Sikhs, and Muslims in India). Would our understanding of these conflicts be increasd by claiming that "the potential for otherwise peaceful Hindus to become violent results in no small measure from the sharp line drawn by Hinduism between good and evil, between purity and pollution, between virtuous and abominable behavior"? Surely, Hindus are no less concerned than Muslims with ritual pollution, but it is not realistic to use those concerns as an explanation for developments whose causes lie elsewhere. Likewise, psychological explanations of violence based on the frustration felt by believers for their personal failings are also inadequate. After all, in Theravada countries, nirvana is generally believed to be attainable only by monks, a belief that does not seem to compel lay Buddhists to engage in random acts of violence against their rulers. Furthermore, legitimation of violence and warfare, and of political power in general, are not unknown in the history of Buddhism, both in Theravada and in Mahayana countries.[12]

II

To provide even a working definition of "religion" is an almost hopeless task. Of course, it is always possible to use Durkheim's reference to the sacred and to things set apart, or Tylor's belief in spiritual beings, or Geertz's pan-symbolic definition.[13] But in all these cases, religion somehow appears as something that exists in itself, when in fact it might be better to consider the term "religion" as a label which, because of our unavoidable cultural prejudices, we tend to apply to certain not always overlapping processes. Consider, for instance, certain cultures' attempts to regulate for no clearly discernible reason what is edible and what is not.[14] This classificatory activity, common among Muslims, Orthodox Jews, Hindus, and others, but almost non-existent now among Christians, should certainly be considered as belonging to the realm of the "religious" in Judaism, Islam, and Hinduism. Now one could possibly argue that from the point of view of a religion that considers the regulation of food as central, Christianity is for all practical purposes not a religion. It is true that this would have been accepted without great trepidation by Barth and his followers (for whom, as is well known, Christianity is not a religion), but such an extreme view is unlikely to satisfy anthropologists, historians, religionists, and indeed most Christians. Nevertheless, no one seems to be particularly surprised when some understand as religion a corpus of practices and particularly beliefs centered around the relationship between mankind and an eternal, omnipotent, omniscient, creator god, an understanding which would restrict the use of the term religion to Christianity, Islam, and Judaism. Similarly, an understanding of religion such as the one common to perhaps most Christians, at least in industrialized countries, namely, one which privileges the personal relationship between the believer and God, and which attempts to eliminate most of its ritual and social components, would be unable to deal with most "religions" of mankind through most of their history.

To avoid this impasse, the most common alternative is to resort to expressions such as "absolute" and "ultimate concern." But, then, the semantic range of "absolute" is zero, whereas that of "ultimate concern" is potentially so vast as to preclude any meaningful delimitation of its use.[15] Another, more radical, alternative would be to conclude, as Leach has done recently, "that anthropologists who study primitive societies had best avoid the use of the category 'religion' altogether."[16] However, Leach's proposal, even in the unlikely case of its adoption, would not solve the problem concerning non-"primitive" religions. Should one, then, abandon the category "religion" altogether? The solution, which can not be explored in depth in this essay, is to be found in the context of the issue of power and structure. In effect, what is central to every ideological system identified by the label "religion" is the problem of difference or, to be more precise, the creation of difference: its absolute maintenance, its absolute overcoming, and the paradoxical formulations that result from the attempts to deal with the tension between identity and difference. Difference in a "religious" context deals with the distinction between god and creature, permissible and non-permissible, priest and non-priest, man and woman, edible and non-edible (more abstract distinctions, such as I and non-I, unity and plurality, are generally the concern of systems known as mystical). These differences, validated—sanctified—in a way that places them beyond discussion,[17] constitute the models which, by analogy and by contiguity, that is, metaphorically and metonymically, are used to regulate further distinctions within the world. Thus difference—the precondition of any type of structure, social, linguistic, cognitive—and the power required to enforce it are at the very center both of any socially constructed world and of what is traditionally identified as religion.

The difference between difference-systems in a religious and in an ideological but non-religious context is the apparent absoluteness of the former, an absoluteness that may act as a surplus, necessary to compensate for the expenditure that takes place as a result of the metaphorical and metonymic displacements mentioned above. The magnitude of these displacements will depend on the complexity of the society under consideration; the more homogeneous a society, the less pronounced the displacement, and consequently, the less visible the distinction between religious and non-religious spheres. In more hierarchical groups, particularly in societies where the state has already appeared, the displacements will be of such magnitude that a religious realm with its priestly hierarchies, canon, and sacred language will be clearly distinguishable.[18] What is significant in these "religious" realms is not their specific contents, but rather their delimited status, and the fact that this separation has to be maintained. Therefore, whereas understanding religion as a thing-in-itself would necessarily lead us to accept Leach's suggestion concerning the absence of religion is small-scale societies, an approach based on difference allows us to identify the 'religious' fault-lines which are used to organize a society, while at the same time warning us against reifying realms, inhabited by gods and supposedly recognizable only by those who have undergone an irreducible religious experience.[19]

Metaphorical and metonymic displacements, however, go in both directions: supernatural, divine, sacred sructures validate social formations, but the inhabitants of these formations, insofar as they reject such arrangements, can always attempt to take control of the process of symbolization and create counter-symbolic systems. If the process stops with the creation of symbolic systems, without attempts at political implementation, what is likely to emerge is vague utopian, esoteric, or quietist groups. If, on the contrary, symbolic manipulation does not remain purely symbolic, we are likely to encounter millenarian, utopian revolutionary, or counterrevolutionary movements, such as the ones discussed in some of the contributions that follow. In any event, rather than constituting two realms that come together only sporadically, or at best only in "archaic" societies, religion and power are inextricably linked.[20] A religion, like a language, organizes the world, but by creating not *a* system of symbols which contributes to formulate conceptions of *a* general order of existence, as Geertz would have it, but by contributing to the formulation of multiple, in fact competing, systems of symbols. Religions as symbolic structures of existing or desired power relations are not, then, mere mirrors of reality, nor static models for it. They are fields—ideological battlefields—to which one gains access by using metonymic and metaphorical chains as ladders, and in which multiple mirrors and models are in constant competition. The function of legitimation has to be approached not simply from the point of view of those who have already managed to legitimize their claims by, for example, developing mythologies that sacralize kingship or the state,[21] but also from the point of view of those engaged in attempting to reorganize the world— bearing in mind that this reorganization is not undertaken for purely cognitive, rhetorical, or spiritual reasons.[22]

It is true that in most advanced industrial societies (with the clear exception of the United States) the realm of the religious has not only become clearly delimited but has also shrunk almost to the level of insignificance, even if in economic terms the reign of difference has certainly not disappeared in those societies. But even in some of those countries—for example, Holland and Ireland—the existence of separate versions of Christianity can still be used to articulate political, linguistic, and ethnic differences, while it is not unlikely that attempts by the Spanish right to regain power and of the French right to exploit the issue of North African Muslim immigrants might lead to a resurgence of religious politics. In Europe, religious articulations of political and economic grievances are currently taking place in Northern Ireland, in Poland, in some Muslim areas of Yugoslavia (and, although unlikely, it is not beyond the relam of possibility that changes in Soviet society brought about by *perestroika* and *glasnost* might lead to a shift in the role of the Russian Orthodox Church).

III

The contributions to this volume exemplify the issues discussed above. In Sri Lanka, Buddhism, "a religion stressing peace, non-violence, rationality and friendship," could nevertheless become involved in political violence by functioning, as Smart puts it, as "a cultural matrix for the majority of the Sinhalese." Here again, what is fundamental is not the rationality or the "content" of Buddhism, but its dominant position—which made it not only the main source of identity for the majority of the population, but also in a sense for the Hindu Tamilians, for whom Buddhism defines what they are not. In India, on the other hand, Hinduism—perhaps more than other "religions" an umbrella term—manages through a peculiar combination of social ritual rigidity—the *jāti* system—and an extremely flexible belief system to function as the ideology within which most of the various groups that share the sub-continent can function. This pluralism has its limits, however, since Hinduism has been able to assimilate neither the Muslims nor the Sikhs (and other smaller goups). Since independence in 1947, India has seen the limits of its pluralism put to the test, first through partition and the exchange of population with Pakistan, and then through continuous acts of violence involving not only Muslims and Sikhs, but also the untouchables, against whom violence is endemic, if largely invisible to the rest of the world.

The case of the Sikhs is particulary grave. Having originated as a kind of compromise between Hinduism and Islam, Sikhism is the religion of one of the most enterprising groups in contemporary India. Sikks, found mostly (but not exclusively) in the Punjab and identified not only by their religion but also by their language, Punjabi, and their physical appearance, have not been able to see their economic status matched by political power. If they were Hindus, it would have been possible for them to raise the position of their caste, but their non-Hindu status precludes that solution.[23] The solution advanced by radical Sikh groups (apparently not shared by the majority of Sikhs) and explored in Lina Gupta's essay, defines religious rights in terms of political rights and tests the limits of India's pluralism in the process.

Stephan Feuchtwang deals with the relationship between religion *(zongjiao)* and superstition *(mixin)* in the People's Republic of China, and shows how inextricably related these concepts are to the ever-changing economic measures taken by the Chinese political leadership. Feuchtwang shows quite clearly how the difference between religion and superstition is fundamentally one of definition: religious are those activities that are institutional (and therefore easy to control), do not interfere with the State, and involve organized and systematic belief. Superstition, on the contrary, includes random, non-controllable activities that interfere with the policies of the State. Feuchtwang demonstrates how the economic changes that encourage, for example, independent household production and marketing are likely to encourage feasting, ancestral memorialism and rituals, that is, activities which before the current economic changes would have been considered as superstitious, but which now have to be redefined and tolerated. We can assume that if the current policies were changed and another cultural revolution were to take place, much of what is now understood as religion would again be defined as superstition. The limits of state power constitute also the limits of religion; the rest, as in Christendom until at least the eighteenth century, is a created category: superstition (or heresy).

A similar situation, discussed by Alexandre Bennigsen, is found in the Muslim areas of the Soviet Union. In Soviet Central Asia, the State recognizes and deals with official Islam, and accepts the existence of a personal religion that leaves the political realm—the realm of power—to the State. It does not recognize parallel, sufi, out-of-mosque Islam, which by not relegating religion to the personal realm competes with the State in the political sphere. It is important to note that against common prejudices about the function of mystical movements and of "mysticism" in general, the role of the sufi *tariqas* in Soviet Central Asia is fundamentally a political one. The Sudanese situation, examined by M. W. Daly, is quite different. Here, Nimeiri's attempt to spread Islam, the use of Arabic, and finally the *Sharia* in the non-Muslim southern region exemplifies the legitimizing use to which religions are usually put. The imposition of Islam in the non-Muslim south would exclude southerners from the full rights of citizenship, and would place this region totally under the control of culturally alien northerners.

The issue dealt with by Shahin Gerami involves a difference that has been sacralized by most religions: that of gender. In her contribution Gerami examines from the angle of gender relations an issue we have encountered in previous chapters: the distinction between the public sphere—the realm of politics, business, work and men—and the private sphere—that of home, family, and women. The difference, absolute according to the ideology of the Islamic Republic of Iran, should be seen as a central component of the attempt to create a universe structured according to Islamic values and as a rejection of the old non-Islamic order imposed by the Pahlavi dynasty and its ally, the United States. The strict division of the world in terms of gender is meant to redress the moral chaos produced by Westernization, and as such its centrality in the ideology of the Iranian clergy is beyond doubt.[24] If contemporary Iran constitutes one of the clearest examples of the issue of power and structure discussed earlier in this essay, Israel offers another. In his contribution, William Batkay examines the monopoly exercised by Orthodox rabbis in the religious life and in the self-definition of the country, a monopoly which includes determining who is to be considered as a Jew, and in consequence who is able to enjoy the considerable benefits of full citizenship.[25] Batkay discusses the tension between the Orthodox on the one hand and the non-orthodox on the other, coming to the conclusion that the Orthodox version of Judaism seems to have been explicitly accepted as Judaism *tout court,* even if this is not the form of Judaism followed by most Israeli (and non-Israeli) Jews.[26] To his discussion we could add that the determining factor in the privileged status of Orthodox Judaism is the perceived need to delimit the Jewish character of Israel as against its Muslim neighbors (and also against its Muslim minority). In a sense, the rigid ritual standards of Orthodox Judaism, with its emphasis on endogamy, ritual purity, strict observance of holidays, and its dependence on foundation myths (all of this having its parallels in the *jāti* system) cannot be understood apart from a context in which rigidity is seen as the price one has to pay to maintain the difference that creates a religiously legitimized identity, which in turn is used to validate territorial claims.

The role of religion in the establishment of an American identity and in the validation of American interests is beyond dispute. From John Winthrop's "citty vpon a hill" to Ronald Reagan's "shining city upon a hill," American military and economic enterprises, and indeed the very existence of the United States, have been surrounded with an aura of moral necessity. In his contribution, Warren Vinz examines this phenomenon by focusing on the career of Russell Conwell, an early twentieth-century preacher who embodies the tensions inherent in any attempt to harmonize the reality of imperialist politics grown out of increasing economic and military power with the desire to perceive these enterprises as exercises in moral leadership. Conwell's position is less extreme than Albert J. Beveridge's ideal of imperialist annexation, and closer to that of William Jennings Bryan[27] and to the formulator of American civil religion, Robert Bellah. A proper discussion of the concept of civil religion cannot be attempted here, but nevertheless it should be pointed out that in an American context the spectacle of sociology as *ancilla theologiae* is not particularly surprising, being one more example of the need to sacralize the limits of "Americanness," that is, the difference between what is American and what is not. What is interesting about Conwell, Bryan, Bellah, and others is the tension between their perception of the uniqueness of what is American and their messianic conception of the potentially universal nature of Americanness. This moral imperialism has been expressed quite clearly by Bellah when he writes that "a world civil religion could be accepted as a fulfilment and not as a denial of American civil religion."[28]

Spencer Bennett's contribution is precisely an attempt to widen the concept of American civil religion by incorporating an "ethnic" element: the Mexican-American faith of César Chávez. Bennett examines the role of religious symbols, particularly the Virgin of Guadalupe, in the articulation of ethnic identity and resistance against economic exploitation. He also stresses the contribution that a tradition of harmony with the natural world can make to an ideology of manifest destiny concerned only with the domestication and control of the wilderness and which has led to the devastation of natural resources and pollution of the environment. In his essay, Phillip Hammond characterizes Conwell's career as "an instance of a vibrant civil religion in operation." Hammond, however, takes issue with Bennett's understanding of the religious articulation of the political activities of the United Farm Workers, which, he maintains, cannot be considered as a form of civil religon "unless the transcendent theory encompasses, and is embraced by, otherwise contending factions." According to Hammond, what can make the farm workers' ideology a part of American civil religion is not any distinctive religious symbol—the Cricifix or the Virgin of Guadalupe—but the very quest for civil righteousness and justice. It should be pointed out, however, that the assumed identity between any quest for justice and the ideals of *American* civil religion, would lead us to understand, for example, American Indian resistance to white settlers—the original carriers of American civil religion—as an episode in the universal unfolding of *American* civil religion.

The last essay deals with the role played by religion in the process of conquest, domination, and resistance to that domination in Peru. Several issues are examined briefly: the articulation of the Spanish conquest in terms of the ideology of Christendom, the partial adoption of Christian themes by the conquered population and their use in the rebellions against the new order. Against this historical background, and in the context of a discussion of the relationship between power, religion, and symbolic appropriation, two contemporary developments are studied: the coming into being of Liberation Theology and the emergence of Shining Path, both movements in which it is possible to identify certain millenarian components.

IV

Although the number of developments involving the connection between religion and political activities examined in this book is necessarily limited, it is hoped that the inextricable connection between religion and political power and the role played by religiously grounded difference in the structuring of social reality has been made visible. In some of the cases examined—Sikhism, the United Farm Workers, Liberation Theology—what we encounter are variations of the quest for the transcendent legitimation of the demands of a specific ethnic group or social class: the Sikhs, Mexican-American Catholic farm workers, the poor of Latin America. Religious legitimation of already present, and expanding, power is found in the cases of Buddhist Sri Lanka, Iran, Israel, and the United States. The situation in the People's Republic of China and in the Soviet Union is more complex; what we find there is an attempt to define the limits of what constitutes permissible religious activities in such a way that they do not interfere with the power of the state. Other cases having to do with the religious legitimation of empire, involving the elaboration of a civil religion-political mythology, include South Africa; whereas in the Philippines we find the development of an Asian version of Liberation Theology.[29]

We hope that the following essays contribute in some measure to the development of an interdisciplinary approach to the study of what is likely to continue to be called religion, an approach that goes beyond the repetition of pious statements about meaning and the sacred, and which does not protect itself by considering anything other than crypto-theology as reductionism. In fact, the very concept of "meaning"—unless we use this term as the tautological ground of all that is—implies classification and therefore difference, and difference requires the capacity to place and to maintain in place the signifying components of the world. This capacity, when absolutized, is what can be called sacralization or sanctification: the power to fixate, beyond discussion, certain semiotic markers (but certainly not only for "semiotic" ends).

The role of power in religion has been discussed at length by Weber in the first two decades of this century, and more recently by anthropologists, sociologists, and historians of religion.[30] We hope that this and other theoretical discussions taking place in anthropology, sociology, political science, and literary theory should also take place in religious studies. There are several issues that require historical and theoretical consideration; those that come immediately to mind and that are related in many ways to the issues explored in this book include, beside the issue of power, the relationship between religion and ideology, the rhetorical aspects of religious structuration (the dialectics of structure and agent), and the political aspects of mystical movements and doctrines.

— 2 —

India, Sri Lanka and Religion

Ninian Smart

I am writing this (May 1987) when the communal tensions in Sri Lanka are taking the transparent form of civil war. It happens that around Meerut and in Delhi there is Hindu-Muslim rioting, but it has not developed into civil war. India is often disturbed by hartals, street violence, and mayhem, but it has held together since 1947 remarkably well. Since 1956 the ominous cracks in Sri Lankan society have widened in a slow descent into civil war, punctuated by a brief but bloody uprising, hastily suppressed, in 1971.

I wish in this essay to explore some of the religious and ideological factors that lie behind the contrast between the post-independence histories of the two countries. There is something paradoxical in the darker history of Sri Lanka, for Buddhism is a religion stressing peace, nonviolence, rationality and friendship. But because Buddhism is a cultural matrix for the majority of the Sinhalese, it has become interwoven with Sinhala nationalism, and in that way has become a contributory factor in the growth of civil strife. Moreover, this relationship to nationalism is not a new thing, and had both positive and negative roots growing long before the post-independence period. I want to sketch these factors before turning to the Indian scene.

Buddhism and the Ideology of Sri Lanka

There has been a trend in modern times to doctrinalize Buddhism—to cut out from it many of the mythic and ritual elements that in fact go to make up the religion on the ground. This Buddhist modernism[1] seeks to display itself as rational, scientific, spiritual, and ethical. Many of the actual features of Sinhala Buddhism are dismissed as popular accretions. This trend is intensified by anthropological distinctions between great and little traditions. Now there is no doubt that quite a lot of Sinhala intellectuals are and have been Buddhist

13

modernists, a notable example being the late K. N. Javatilleke (as in his *The Message of the Buddha*[2]), and so this is a fact which we have to be aware of in describing varieties of Buddhism, but it gives a misleading impression if it is taken as the model for the Buddhism of traditional Sri Lanka or of the modern masses. In fact, that Buddhism is a wider thing than anything you would find in the Pali canon. In particular the sacred narrative which the ordinary Buddhist takes as given goes beyond the stories found in the scriptures. They include the accounts of the Buddha's visits to Sri Lanka in the fifth-century *Mahavamsa*. Where he left his footprint, on Sumanakata, now popularly known as Adam's Peak, is, of course, a major place of Buddhist pilgrimage. The chronicles—the *Dipavamsa* of the fourth century, the aforementioned *Mahavamsa,* and the *Culavamsa* (thirteenth extended to the eighteenth century)—flesh out the idea of Sri Lanka as being a greatly favored and blessed isle, and the sacred carrier of Buddha's message, the *Dhammadipa*. This sense of the holy destiny of the Sinhalese is a conscious ingredient of actual Buddhism, and is even there beneath the rationalism of Buddhist modernism. So in the modern period, when nationalism has been deepened by the experiences of colonialism, there has been a revival of a kind of religiously suffused patriotism. Moreover, the chronicles often describe war between Sinhala and Tamils, and help therefore to underline possible tensions between the ethnic groups—tensions which were masked by the intervention of Europeans in the island's affairs and so called forth a more united front. For instance, in 1919 the Ceylon National Congress was formed out of Sinhala and Tamil political organizations. Modern times have also seen a revival of mainland Tamil nationalism, and though the two communities of Indian and Sri Lankan Tamils are historically separate except for imported Tamils working the tea and coffee plantations, their causes have become increasingly identified. It is wrong to be purist about Buddhism: its actual character in Sri Lanka has patriotic, even chauvinist, elements. For the ordinary Sri Lankan Buddhist the faith is entwined in the blessed legends of the homeland. And so we have emerging a modernized ideology of Sri Lanka as repository of the faith, its guardian and chief propagator. This notion was reinforced by the fair success that Buddhists had in their public debates and literary controversies with missionaries in the 1860s and 1870s.

But, one might ask, what faith? Obviously it was that of the Theravada. The fertility of foreign scholars—notably the Rhys-Davids—in creating and developing modern Pali studies helped to give Buddhist notables in Sri Lanka a sense of dignity and importance, as did also the support of the Theosophical Society with the visit of Colonel Olcott in 1880 to Ceylon, and the subsequent foundation of Western-type Buddhist organizations, such as the Young Men's Buddhist Association. The methods of Western mission and scholarship were harnessed to the revival of the ancient faith. The work of scholars reinforced the idea that the Theravada as found in the Pali canon is the early form of Buddhism. It is even now sometimes referred to as "early Buddhism." The Mahayana was seen as a later evolution and in some measure a perversion of the faith. So even Buddhist modernists could look on Theravadin countries and above all Sri Lanka as guardians of the pure and pristine faith. It might be that some mythic accretions had gathered around the Buddha's message, but if anyone wanted to know what the Buddha really said the Pali writings had to be the main source for finding out.

In this way both the traditional Buddhism of the chronicles and Buddhist modernism could combine in a sort of nationally focused Buddhism. It was an ideology which, however, did not have a very vivid expression in the movement toward independence, partly because of the relative smoothness of this development. Sri Lanka experienced a much stronger version of Sinhala nationalism after independence, when the glue supplied by a joint enemy had gone, and minority fears could be easily aroused.

Here linguistic nationalism had its part to play. The Sinhala language cannot, of course, simply be equated with Buddhism. Catholics and other groups who were Sinhalese without being Buddhists also used the language. Nevertheless, one could say as a nearly-perfect generalization that all Buddhists spoke Sinhala and all Hindus spoke Tamil. The very great mixing of Sinhala and Tamil families over the centuries mean that the chief markers of difference were not genetic, but linguistic and religious. Unfortunately, questions of language are vitally important in the modern State. There is the question of the language of the bureaucracy, the language of education, including higher education, and the language of national rhetoric. Naturally in 1956, during the election campaign which saw the victory of S. W. R. D. Bandaranaike and of his Sri Lankan Freedom Party, there was apprehension among Tamils, for the main slogan of that campaign was "Sinhala only." The Buddhist Sangha on that occasion played a notable part—another somewhat ominous sign. It was perhaps no coincidence that the failed coup d'etat of 1962 was staffed mainly by Catholic officers. There was a blending of linguistic and religious nationalisms at work in the Sri Lankan Freedom Party's rhetoric. Thus the United Front of Buddhist Monks, formed in 1956, joined with the

Linguistic Front (and also the Congress of Indigenous Medical Practitioners) during the election campaign which saw Bandaranaike gain power.

Some commentators (for instance P. A. Saram[3]) have seen the subsequent tensions between the two main ethnic groups as being essentially ethnic and linguistic in nature rather than religious. It is hard to distinguish the factors. After all, the S.L.F.P. incorporated Buddhist rites into State functions, promoted Buddhism in the media and education (the two main *pirivenas* or seminaries were upgraded into universities), and so on. The later change of the island's official name also had religious as well as other overtones.

Nationalism tends to go with modernization, and there were up-to-date ingredients in the ancient heritage of the Sinhala people. The vast new and effective irrigation schemes, promoted before the war by D. S. Senanayake (the first Prime Minister) when he was Minister of Agriculture, followed to a great degree the plans and lines of the old works of medieval kings, notably the great Parakrama Bahu. Buddhist metaphysics, with its emphasis on the fluidity and impermanence of events, corresponded to one aspect of modern cosmology, while its conception of multiple worlds chimed in with new discoveries about the vast number of galaxies stretched out in the universe. There was no contradiction, in the eyes of the educated Buddhist, between antiquity and modernity. It was a harmonious picture, therefore, which underpinned the ideology of Buddhist nationalism.

These, then, were the primary ingredients in what may be called the ideology of Sri Lanka. It was something which never lay far below the surface as Sinhalese identity became so important in post-independence Sri Lanka. Nor were the ideas I have outlined merely elements in an invigorating myth. They impinged directly on jobs, because of the new avenues opened up by Sinhalese-speaking higher education to various kinds of advancement—or so at least it was thought. As we shall see, there were inherent problems about the new arrangements in universities and high schools. The proud emphasis on the Sinhala language could not change the wider economic significance of the English language in the world. But the new ideology of Sri Lanka had promise, and it helped to fuel, eventually, the civil war that has now broken out. It had a noble and intellectually satisfying side to it, but viewed by the Tamils it also brought with it an air of menace.

Buddhism and the Question of Tolerance

There was a negative side to the emergence of modern Buddhism. In this it moved in a very different way from modern Hindu ideology, which consciously projected a theory of universal religious tolerance. Of this we shall write further on, when we come to delineate the Indian contrast in more detail. Both religions, however, were faced by similar challenges—Christian criticism, democracy, modern science and education, capitalism, and so on. But Buddhism had a different response. As we have noted, it was able to represent itself as scientific, and it had no great problem with modern cosmology. As for evolution, its face turned away from the major part of the problem, from the perspective of Christian evangelists. There was no problem of the timing or nature of creation, since for Buddhism there was no divine creation. Though Buddhism had benefited from the encouragement of Colonel Olcott, its destiny did not lie in any theosophical direction. In fact, it stressed its modernity by allying itself more with humanists and agnostics. It was this strand of modern thought in the West that appealed to the thinking Buddhist.

It possessed a strong spiritual side, but one which was not connected to theism. Nor did it have an Absolute, so that Sinhalese were not especially attracted to Hegel and Bradley (more vital for Indian philosophers of the modern period). Moreover, the manifestation of popular religion was not in Sri Lanka ineluctable, as it was in India. No Hindu apologist could easily shrug off the multitudinous gods and the swarming temples. It was simpler in Ceylon to make the division between pure Buddhism and the superstitions of the masses. The Buddhist who was educated in the West did not have to defend the shrines to Vishnu and Kataragama, nor the pilgrimages to Adam's Peak. If he did, he demythologized; saying that these things were vivid reminders of the message of the Buddha. He did not even here have to worry about the Hindu phenomena woven into the practice of Buddhism. These were mere accretions on the essence of Buddhism.

Because there was no God in Buddhism there was no immediate rivalry with the Christian or Hindu deities. By the same token there was no fusing them together. The Buddhist was not in a position to say that here were three manifestations of the same One. There was no transcendental unity of all religions. Those who believed in God or gods were being distracted from the main truth. They were like a jungle. The eightfold path passed round the jungle, and those who wandered in it were not making progress to ultimate liberation, to *nibbana*.

Those Westerners attracted to Buddhism were often attracted by just these features: they wanted a spiritual path but could not believe in God. They wanted to get away from the hammerings of evangelical piety and the authorities of scripture and pope. So there was encouragement for Sinhalese modernism. But all this left a gap in the edifice of Buddhism, which might prove terribly dangerous. The gap was this: by and large Buddhism in Sri Lanka had no clear theory of other religions.

There was no theory of what to do about Christianity, beyond the recognition that there were values in Christian ethics. More seriously there was no theory of the Hindu tradition. There was a tendency to include it as an inferior practice within the rituals of the temple. It was a material and somewhat superstitious adjunct to the merit-making properties of Buddhist piety. But it was not much thought about in its higher spiritual and philosophical forms. There was no Buddhist theory of the place of Saiva Siddhanta. There was little in the way of ratiocination about non-Buddhist yoga. There were discussions about the tolerant nature of Buddhism, and on Buddhism and the race question. But there was no evolution of a concrete Buddhist theory of religions. (Insofar as this is happening at all, it is due to Mahayana Buddists, e.g., Masao Abe, in the last few years.) There was even a reluctance, after the debates in the latter half of the nineteenth century, to enter into dispute with Christianity and Hinduism. The Sinhalese had a good enough social relationship with Tamils and Christians (overlapping classes) during the British period, especially among the Western-educated elite. Ceylon was a cosmopolitan and easygoing society, so it seemed, and in the mild struggle for independence deeper problems of toleration could be left on one side.

So Buddhism prospered during the twentieth Century, but it had no clear theory of how to deal with other world views. This absence of a theory was only one factor in the troubles still to come, but it was one of the conditions making for strife in due course. There was no clear rhetoric for politicians to use in appealing for national unity. No such rhetoric was used, for instance, at the World Fellowship of Buddhists congress which I attended in Sri Lanka in the summer of 1985. Both the President and the Prime Minister addressed the delegates, but said nothing about the troubles or about the need for interethnic harmony.

Incidentally, it is not easy in general for Buddhism to have the kind of theory of the ultimate unity of religions that I have postulated here. Perhaps there might be some Kantian idea that the divergent religious ultimates, from God to *nibbana,* are rooted in some noumenon. It might be argued that the different faiths are stages on the way to liberation. But it is much easier for a faith that looks to a God or Absolute to deal with the problem by postulating a transcendental unity. For Buddhism—at least Theravada Buddhism—such a transcendental unity of which the gods are manifestations just does not work. It is, moreover, only fairly recently that Theravadins have trod the route of ecumenical dialogue with Mahayanists and others. Conversely, unifying theories, such as those of Radhakrishnan, Vivekananda, Schuon, and Hick, typically break down in trying to deal with the Theravada (and Jainism).

The J.V.P. Alternative

The S.L.F.P. were successful in their reform of education. The universities and other organs of higher education were transformed from being English-speaking enclaves. After the 1956 victory there was a move to allow the teaching of undergraduates by the medium of Sinhala and Tamil. This had its effects on the high schools, for it gave rural high school graduates opportunities to attend the university. But the economy was not expanding enough to absorb a whole new generation of upwardly mobile young people. Especially high school dropouts came to realize that the "Sinhala only" policy was a mixed blessing. It was among such young people, nearly all Sinhala educated, that a new revolutionary movement took root. The ultimate effect was the rebellion which broke out in April 1971, causing wide havoc and concern. It was led by the J.V.P. and espoused a quasi-Marxist ideology.[4] It was a revolt against the conditions imposed not only by government but by the world economy upon Sri Lanka. It was a revolt against the realism of those who recognized Sri Lanka's place in the capitalist order of things. To this extent its collective world negation had a certain logic. For, like the theorizing of Khieu Sampan, the Khmer Rouge ideologue and leader, the J.V.P. program envisaged withdrawal from the world capitalist order. It suggested new modes of self-sufficiency of Sri Lanka, based on agriculture. So although it used Marxist language it was no strict deduction from Marx. Not surprisingly, the Soviet Union and China (as well as Britain, India, Pakistan, and other countries) helped the Sri Lankan government in suppressing the revolt. The J.V.P. ideology was maverick and as much anti-Soviet in principle as anti-capitalist.

The similarity between Kampuchean and Sri Lankan revolutionary ideologies is striking, and suggests a perhaps unrealized input of Buddhist eschatology. There is the idea that a nation can become pure and solitary (like a Buddhist hermit in search of liberation). It can gain its true freedom not by transforming the world but by transforming itself, and in ways that make it self-sufficient. Marxist analysis is not in itself important, save that it provides the framework for working out how it is that withdrawal from the wider world becomes feasible.

The J.V.P. uprising was a symptom of the early failure of the Sinhala-only program. The increased vigor of Sinhala education in rural areas especially and the easier access to higher education were not matched by a corresponding increase in suitable jobs. The promise of linguistic nationalism was not fulfilled. The civil service could not expand sufficiently to incorporate the new cohorts—while businesses would have much more use for English-educated young people than for those who knew only Sinhala. By an irony the new policy lessened the competitive power of the Sinhalese young over against their Tamil opposite numbers. The uprising was a violent and somewhat blind protest against this situation. It was not ideologically religious, though it got the support of some monks; it was mainly a spasm of linguistic nationalism. Its suppression helped to reinforce the Buddhist flavor of Sinhalese patriotism.

Buddhism and the Hindu Revival

Despite the fact that Olcott and the Theosophical Society played a meaningful part in the evolution of modern Buddhist institutions, and despite Theosophical connections with the revival of Hindu thought in the nineteenth and twentieth centuries, there was little interest among Ceylonese Buddhists in the phenomena of a resurgent Hinduism. It was as if the administrative division between the Crown Colony of Ceylon and the Indian Raj was reflected in the soul. The souls of India and Ceylon seemed to be very divergent in sentiment. The lack of feeling for the great Hindu tradition was deplored, for instance, by Ananda Coomaraswamy. But the sense of a separate identity was itself more largely due to Theravada Buddhism than to British administration. Although Ceylon was integrated in many modes to Indian civilization and to the life of South Asia, its island character had helped it to preserve an ancient form of Buddhism after that religion virtually had died out on the mainland. The fact that even the Mahayana heritage of Sri Lanka (very evident in the Anuradhapura period and extant in varying ways in contemporary Theravada, notably in the cult of images) was not recognized helped to cut the cultural bonds between Ceylon and India. The gentler ride to independence in Sri Lanka and the lack of a need to emulate Gandhi and the other exponents of a resurgent nationalism may also have contributed to the sense of isolation from the Hindu revival. In any case, Buddhism in

Sri Lanka pursued its own path of modernization. It dealt with the challenges of colonialism in a different manner.

We noted above some of the elements in the colonial impact earlier: evangelical criticism of Buddhist ideas and ethics; modern science and education; democracy; capitalism. With Christianity there also came humanism, and there were rumors—and more than rumors—of liberalism in Christianity (Bishop Colenso's writings, for instance, were a hit in Ceylon). Buddhism felt adequate to cope with these various new ideas and forces on its own. Thus Christian ethical criticism was rebuffed by noting the high ethics of the Buddhist tests: as moral systems the two religions were often seen as virtually equivalent. This was Buddhism's "theory of Christianity" in effect: Christianity was good for generating fine ethical attitudes, so it was good for Christians to live up to their faith; hence the less tolerant missionary response to Buddhism was a matter of some initial surprise. As for other criticism, Buddhism was nearer modern knowledge than the Old Testament (where, after all, was the Garden of Eden?). The subtlety of Buddhist thought made the entrance into modern education no great problem; and there were democratic and constitutional elements in the very foundation of the Sangha. Buddhism in the early days had appealed to the merchants of the Gangetic basin and could adapt to modern capitalism. Socialism, too, supplied a modern alternative, and Buddhist socialism was to make its appearance in the twentieth century. So in all these ways, Buddhism was able to make a good case for its adaptability to the modern age and could plausibly represent itself as more in consonance with science than as Christianity.

The relative homogeneity of the Sinhala people, and the lack of perception of the need for some federal ideology, meant that there was no great interest in the inclusiveness of the neo-Hindu vision of the unity of religions. Moreover, the treatment accorded to Buddhism by Radhakrishnan and other neo-Hindu exponents was not plausible, since it repeated that the Buddha really taught the existence of a Self—a proposition virtually all Buddhists took to be false. Theravada Buddhism is, after all, the main counterexample to most theories of religion, including the theroy that all religions point to the same reality.

Preliminary Conclusions on Buddhism

There have, then, been various reasons why Buddhism in Sri Lanka has not evolved a theory about other religions, beyond the view that they may supply ethical values but do not offer ultimate liberation. There was therefore no clear view of the genuine role of Hindus (or

Christians or Muslims) within a nation increasingly seen as essentially Buddhist. Moreover, religious and linguistic nationalism combined. Consequently, though Buddhism is in essence an eirenic religion, given to a great degree of tolerance and friendliness, it has, in becoming politicized anew, acquired a chauvinistic color.

There is also a factor important in the island nation which should not be overlooked: it is what I call "the majority-as-minority syndrome." It is seen in a number of places of conflict: the Protestants in Northern Ireland are a majority but regard themselves as a minority vis-à-vis the Catholics of the South and the Catholics of the North; in Cyprus the ethnic Greeks, though a majority, think of themselves as a minority vis-à-vis the mainland Turks and the Cypriot Turks. Similarly the Sinhala, though a majority in Sri Lanka, add in their minds the mainland Tamils to the Sri Lankan Tamils, and so are vastly outnumbered, as they see it. This "majority-as-minority syndrome" is a stubborn one, for it encourages the majority not to make concessions. Magnanimity is drowned in fear.

The Modern Hindu Ideology

The whole history of modern India was very different from that of Sri Lanka. Had the latter been included in the Raj, things would have not been thus; but also, as we have seen, the Sinhalese have a long consciousness of having a separate Buddhist polity—being the true holders and guardians of the *dhamma*, which had been corrupted and had indeed more or less died out under the weight of Vaishnavism, Shaivism, Tantra, and other modes of the Hindu tradition, together with the appearance of Islam in the subcontinent. There had long been at least dim awareness of Indian history as being different, then, from that of the Sinhalese. But India was hardly a unified culture. There had been something approaching a pan-Indian Mughal Empire, but it was not Hindu. In this mellennium there had been few times when such an empire was operative, and the various kingdoms of South and North had striven against one another, as had various forces within the ambit of Hinduism. Indeed there was not anything like a full self-consciousness either of India as a nation or of Hinduism as a separate religion. This does not detract from the latter's importance; nor should we, relying on older material, deny, as some historians of religion tend to do, that there is a religion known as Hinduism. It may be a rather new one, but it has ancient roots, and its formulation has acquired great influence, both inside India and outside.

This modern Hindu ideology involves the selective use of some major items available in the tradition. Its forms vary according to differing people expressing it, but its main exponents have been Vivekananda and Radhakrishnan, with Gandhi as a contributor to its political adaptation. It was something borne of the impact of the British, and it appealed to the rising new class—the British-educated Indian, and especially the Hindu. It had its appeal also to some Parsees, Christians, Muslims, and others, for it provided an ideological basis for the emergence of a pluralistic constitution framed after the country's independence.

The so-called Indian renaissance has manifested other world-views and values—the Brahmo Samaj of Ram Mohan Roy, the Arya Samaj of Dayananda Sarasvati, the poetry of Rabindranath Tagore, to name the best known—but it was the recasting of Advaita Vedanta by Vivekananda and Radhakrishnan which was to be the most influential. Gandhi was not a philosopher, and was more a practical than an ideological teacher; but in principle he had the same outlook, substituting the vague Truth for the concept of Brahman. In practice he was pluralistic in his religion, as was witnessed by the variegation of his disciples and followers. We shall return to the reasons for the viability of the new ideology, both in mobilizing Hindu sentiment and appealing to the rising English-educated elite.

The Nature of British Rule

The establishment of the Empire of India after the events of 1857 had considerable significance. It confirmed the permanence of British rule over the whole of the subcontinent from the borders of Nepal to Cape Kanyakumarin. It gathered the realms of India under a single monarch, and it paved the way for a unified education system, giving Indians the perceived benefits of a modern, Western type of education. It strengthened the position of the missionaries, both because of their involvement in education and because of the Christian assumptions of empire. It is true that for more than thirty years after 1858 the Government of India pursued a laissez-faire policy regarding Hindu customs (for once bitten, over the "Mutiny," it was twice shy). But the Empire itself took on an increasingly ideological character: the easier access via the Suez Canal encouraged British furloughs and the arrival of British women, both making of the rulers of India a more conventional and Christian-thinking elite.

The British were pluralistic in the sense that the way India was governed was not monolithic, for it was peppered with princely states.

The maharajahs and nizams were like firebreaks. Their territories prevented the too-easy spread of mutiny and revolt. But in many other respects there was unification of the subcontinent. The railway system bound far territories together. The need for English as the language of bureaucracy became a pan-Indian phenomenon. The new nexus of universities, already started in the last year of the East India Company (with the universities of Calcutta, Madras, and Bombay), created a new class with new pan-Indian ideas. In a sense it was the British who were the authors of Indian nationalism. For nationalism required the concept of India, and that was supplied both negatively and positively by the British: negatively through presenting the figure of the oppressor of all India, or at least the enemy to be struggled against if independence were ultimately to be achieved; and positively by binding together India by railways and language.

It was overwhelmingly this English-speaking elite that provided the Indian nationalists.[5] They were very largely the product of the new higher education system. They imbibed not just English literature but also Western philosophy. They came to know something of democracy and justice. But there were problems with English education, in that it was easy for some of those who were to lead India to get cut off from their Indian roots. It was this problem that Vivekananda, Radhakrishnan, and Gandhi resolved in differing ways.

Nationalism in Vivekananda, Radhakrishnan, and Gandhi

I am conscious that I have not listed these three figures in chronological order. But the first two are more intellectual, and their work can be considered side by side.

In being chief progenitor of the Ramakrishna Math and Mission, Vivekananda was consciously tying it to the soil of India, for Ramakrishna was not at all a member of the new elite. He was very much the traditional holy man. His homilies and parables could speak to anyone. He was the crazy, inspired saint who could speak directly from the sphere of the Transcendent. Moreover his style was unmistakably popular. Together, Ramakrishna and Vivekananda made a most powerful combination. For Vivekananda was an educated and cosmopolitan person. He was able to dramatize the new (and yet old) Hindu message of pluralism and the unity of differing paths and images. His success at the World Parliament of Religions in 1893 in Chicago was gratifying and important for the spread of his ideas in India itself. The psychology of conquered peoples is to crave recognition from the victors; this accolade Vivekananda earned in full measure in his

American and European travels. The glittering Western civilization which had come to exercise its superiority over India had recognized this son of India.

Vivekananda's genius was to reach back to one type of philosophy in the Indian tradition (actually one which, despite its success in the neo-Hindu context, scarcely represents the most dominant motif of the Indian religious tradition) because of its possibilities in the novel inter-religious milieu presented by the conflicts between Hinduism and missionary Christianity. The Advaitin philosophy had many advantages. First it made a distinction between the Ultimate as without qualities and as with qualities—or as non-personal and personal. This "doubledecker" theory of God and of Truth was useful if Vivekananda was going to be successful in his quest to show that the various Gods conceal a Unity behind. This way of conceiving the Ultimate was also useful in warding off the accusations of idolatry that were so often brought against Hinduism. Anyone who thinks his own idea of God exhausts the truth or has absolute superiority is an idolater. Vivekananda turned evangelical assaults back on the Christians. Christianity could be narrow. But the saintly Christian is one who realizes that his own doctrines and means of worship are limited. Again, the Advaitin philosophy had harmonies with Absolute Idealism, which was fashionable in the late nineteenth century in Britain and elsewhere.

This new version of Hinduism, expressed in English and reaching out to the whole globe, not only emphasized some old, comprehensive traits in the Indian tradition, but also could be the basis for an Indian nationalism that was not just Hindu. His doctrines could appeal too to the minorities, Muslims, Parsees, Christians and others. If all paths reach the same destination, then we have a formula for coming together politically in a plural manner. At the same time the organization which Vivekananda put in place presented for middle-class Indians a means of canalizing their social service and reflections about the Ultimate. Its forms were substantially influenced by European models. Like many other Third World reformers, Vivekananda put Western models of organization to work on behalf of resurgent traditions.

Vivekananda's emphasis on the inner, mystical quest not only was in line with the yoga traditions of India but also suggests a new humanism in which true happiness was to be found within the human being. As such it also sought to comprehend the philosophies of utilitarianism (from a deeper point of view) and scientific humanism. Though it was not a philosophy that had wide influence among European and American intellectuals it had sufficient appeal in the West to represent a religious challenge. It was something which in its modest

way has become rooted in Western forms of faith, presenting an
alternative to Christianity for those in the West who are worried by
exclusivism and the narrow outlook of some forms of Christianity.

In India its national meaning was not hard to perceive. Here was
an ideology which could reassert the dignity of India without being
negatively hostile to the culture of the British. It was something very
believable on a Hindu basis, and modernly expressed. It was a rallying
cry for the new India, rooted through Ramakrishna in the masses and
forward-looking through Vivekananda in the hopeful quest for a new
India rid of the accretions of the invader.

But in the last years of Vivekananda's life the philosophical and
religious heritage of India was only beginning to be revealed, through
European scholarship and Indian researches, to a wider public. It was
S. N. Dasgupta who was the most fertile historian of Indian philosophy;
but it was Radhakrishnan who had the greater popularizing ability. He
was able, in his *Indian Philosophy* and many other writings, to paint
a readily understandable picutre of Indian thought as being essentially
comprehensive and synthetic. He was able to flesh out something of
the neo-Hindu ideology in a philosophical way. His own career also
procalimed the respectability of the ideology—professor, vice-
chancellor (university president), Oxford don, Indian ambassador,
President of the Republic of India. He also saw the transition from the
era of servitude to the new age of independence.

The importance of the ideas of Vivekananda and Radhakrishnan
lay above all in the argument for relgious pluralism. This was absolutely
vital in India if it were to survive as a democracy. Even given that many
Muslims were located in Pakistan (and later Bangladesh), there is still
a substantial minority in India itself, which is the fourth largest Muslim
country in the world and not far behind Pakistan and Bangladesh. Not
only that, but other communities play an important role in the fabric
of modern society—Jains, Parsees, Sikhs, Christians, and others. So the
pluralistic ideology was important to underpin the Indian constitution.
Now, of course, there are other factors which help to support Indian
pluralism; but imagine what the situation would have been like if the
Congress Party and other nationalist movements had espoused a non-
pluralistic ideology. We can conceive the horrors of Hindu-inspired
jibad. As it is, there is enough revival of Hindu militancy to cause severe
disquiet. But much Hindu leadership is persuaded of the essential
correctness of the kind of pluralism expressed by Vivekananda and
Radhakrishnan. And by Gandhi.

Gandhi's importance lay not merely in his providing a theory of
nonviolence that was adapted to political ends; in taking on the

appearance of the traditional holy man he was also able to mobilize the masses. Though himself middle class, he reached outward to the poor of India. Additionally he was able, in blending Christian and other motifs into his message, to incarnate the pluralistic message of the new Hindu ideology. All these were important contributions to the theory of India as a secular State.

The Concepts of Secularism

It is unfortunate that two quite separate uses of the word "secular" are in use. In one sense secular means nonreligious. A theory of secularization is a theory about how people or societies become nonreligious—there is a fading of rituals, a dwindling of the sense of the sacred, a diminution in the plausibility of doctrines, and so forth. But in a second sense, secular means pluralistic. So a secular State is one without an established religion: all religions are tolerated. In this sense the United States and India are two of the most notable secular States in today's world. When a secular (nonreligious) ideology becomes in effect the State religion, as in Marxist countries, there is some confusion. Often Marxist countries are thought of vaguely as secular States when, in the relevant sense, they are nothing of the sort. Conversely, because India is so very religious, people find it a little hard to believe that it is essentially a secular State. The framers of the Indian constitution were, however, clear about it. The sense in which India is secular is pluralistic. (Actually, there are some traces of religious bias in the Indian constitution—for instance provision for cow-protection—but states are wise to try to get actions which are offensive to a sufficiently large number of citizens proscribed, save when there is some conflict in this with basic rights.)

Thoughts on Indian Pluralism

If we now reflect about the emergence of a pluralistic neo-Hindu ideology, we may note that part of its role was to establish a sense of Indian identity which, while based on Hindu ideas, was nevertheless open to all. Muslims were sufficiently suspicious of Hindu intentions—and alert to see the pluralism itself as essentially Hindu—to make the splitting of the continent into two (later three) major states as being inevitable. The ideology was both positive and negative. Negatively it was a protection against persecution and the outbreak of religious conflicts—it was not of course altogether successful, and how could it be? But positively it provided a sort of spiritual basis to Indian nationalism. For after all, Hinduism was born in India. It was the outgrowth of the peculiar Indian genius for assimilation and plural forms. It was, with Buddhism, the major former of Indian civilization. Its philosophies were a major world achievement. And so it was suitable that the newly-emerging unified India should reach back into the Hindu past to find its identity. It was predicated on a unity in fact imposed and achieved under British rule; but it was also built on that Sanskritic lore which Brahmin predominance had in times past brought to the subcontinent, overlaying the diversities of peoples, languages and cultures of India. So the new ideology joined older unity to modern unity, and helped in this way with promoting a sense of Indian identity that, though Hindu, could also be acceptable to other religious groups.

It now may be crumbling, and new conflicts arise in India. Linguistic separatism, Sikh devolution, tribal struggles—these and other problems beset the Indian government in the 1980s. But the ideology has served India well, and has encouraged a federal outlook. There is a marked contrast with the case of Ceylon.

We have explored some reasons why Buddhism in Sri Lanka did not create a theory for dealing with other religions. There is a further one which partly emerges from reflection about India. India, as we have seen, is a partly artificial country—that is, it does not have quite the "natural" unity which a single people speaking one language has. It is a creation of loose Sanskritization in the past and of modern British unification through the Raj and all that came to mean. In order to weld itself together it needed a "doctrine" of itself. Other countries in their search for independence merely had to create a literary and common language, and a myth of the nation's history; India had to do more, and the new Hindu ideology became a component in the general mystique of the new India. (It parallels the United States, created in a sense by a constitution and by the philosophy underlying that.)

But though Sri Lanka could glory in a myth, largely Sinhala in origin and spirit, it did not, or at least the Sinhalese did not, require a theory to bind them together. There were already sufficient bonds in language and history. So that was an added reason why a "new Buddhist ideology" parallel to the Indian "new Hindu ideology" was not born.

But the question of dialogue with other religions remains. There has been much conversation between Christianity and Buddhism in Sri Lanka, but as yet the Theravadins have not gone deeply into the question of a Buddhist view of religions. Beginnings have been made, for instance, in using Freudian theory to account for various forms of theism. But just as there was ambiguity in the Buddha's attitude to the *devas*, ambiguity remains in a new form today.

— 3 —

Indian Secularism and the Problem of the Sikhs

Lina Gupta

Casual reading of recent news on the Punjab crisis is likely to give one the impression that India, far from being a secular state, is a federation of battling religous groups, each of which is attempting to procure for itself privileges to retain its identity at the expense of certains rights of others.[1] According to *U.S. News,* 6 April 1987, "In the past fifteen months, more than six hundred persons have died in bloody clashes in the Punjab . . . . The strife has exacerbated animosity between Sikhs and the Hindu majority in other parts of the nation. It has deepened already serious communal divisions by spawning a rise in Hindu and Moslem fundamentalism."[2] A more serious reading will make one realize that secularism is an ideal which is yet to be achieved in India, and the Punjab crisis is an excellent example of why India must go through with her own sets of adjustments and solutions to realize her secularistic ideals.

Since the adoption of the Indian Constitution in 1950, there had been an increasing amount of dissatisfaction and uncertainty with one of the major pillars of Indian democracy, namely, its secular character. Undoubtedly, one of the most serious problems in India today is her communalism. As Donald Smith explains, "It is the tenacious loyalty to caste and community which tends to undermine the secular state at every turn."[3] The most crucial challenge to secularism in India comes from the Sikh community, which developed a strong sense of self awareness and which demands formal recognition of its separate identity. That is, Sikh communalism is fundamentally a question of religious, cultural, and political identity.

In spite of the increased number of riots and clashes, growth in Sikh fundamentalism and the separatist movement is not as sudden as it appears to be. Both have deep social and historical roots connected with the emergence of a distinct Sikh identity, community, and organization. Moreover, developments spanning more than a century created an environment that nurtured this process. As the title for this chapter indicates, I intend to deal with the Sikh problem as it relates to the secular notion of India, and will show how the Sikh problem is in a sense partly rooted in the peculiar nature of Indian secularism. The paper is divided in four sections. Section I deals with a general account of the emergency, growth and consolidation of identity consciousness in the Sikhs. Section II examines the notion of secularism in India. Section III explores the religous, cultural and political demands of the Sikhs. Section IV offers an analysis and a possible solution to the Sikh problem.

I

In order to understand the close relation between religion, politics, and the Sikh demand for a separate state, it is necessary that we take a closer look at the important aspects of their world view and their political history. Due to the limited scope of this paper, I will only present a brief background which relates to the subject matter. Guru Nanak, the first of the ten Gurus, was the founding father of the Sikh faith.[4] Nanak advocated a simple monotheism of one omnipotent, omniscient, and formless reality who reveals Himself through His own creation. The way to liberation, according to Nanak, is to meditate on God's creation. Following the teaching of Guru Nanak, the Sikh Gurus regard this world to be real and meaningful. Therefore, one need not be indifferent to the world as a place of suffering and a place from which one needs to be liberated. Given the idea of the world being real and not an illusion, the obvious consideration would be to lead a meaningful life in this very world which is the true revelation of God. The only possible way to lead a meaningful life, according to the Gurus, is through God-centered activities which will promote righteousness and justice.[5]

The second corollary of the world being real is that one should experience full participation in life. For the Sikh Gurus, religious, moral, and spiritual activity covers the totality of life of the individual as well as that of the society. That is, life is one whole and cannot be arbitrarily compartmentalized into religious, social, and political arenas. Most important of all, the Gurus teach that an individual is not detachable from society. As such, the religious and spiritual problems of an individual cannot be separated from the moral and spiritual problems of the society as a whole.[6]

On the basis of this unitary world view, the Sikh Gurus gave the Sikh movement a two-pronged direction. The first one has to do with changing the value patterns of the individual and of the society, and the second one has to do with changing the inequality and injustice in the social, religious, and political sphere. The Sikh Gurus realized that it was not enough to have just an ideal; the ideal must be realized in action. As Donald Smith says, "Sikhism underwent a remarkable transformation from a religious sect with ascetic and pacifist ideas into a militant theocracy."[7]

Continuing in the same tradition, the Sikh Khalsa Panth or Sikh Community was formed essentially as a political organization of baptized Sikhs by Guru Govind Singh.[8] The Sikh Khalsa Panth, however, was not formed as just another community pursuing the traditional approach to religion. It was established with the aim of a total transformation of both man and his society in terms of his struggle against the antisocial, antihuman institutions like the caste system and the inequality of status and sexes.

In the light of the historical and ideological outline of Sikhism, it is partially understandable why Sikhs have been so tenacious in expressing themselves in Indian political life. It is a difficult task to single out exactly which force or factor operating in history played the most important role in the Sikh movement. We can merely designate the dominant factors which helped the movement to progress. The dominating factors of the Sikh movement are to be found in the Sikh world view and in their sense of identity which grew out of that outlook.

It may appear as if the Sikhs today are a distinct and separate people, yet their leaders fear that their community will someday be dissolved into Hinduism and the Sikhs would encounter the same fate as Buddhism.[9] In fact, their fears are not totally unfounded. There are two facets to this problem. One involves the dwindling number of the Sikhs. To quote Kushwant Singh, "When the Khalsa was in the ascendant, large numbers of Hindus began to grow their hair and beards and pay lip service to the Sikh Gurus. After annexation, these time servers returned to the Hindu fold."[10] With these departed Hindus left some of the genuine Sikhs who by then had formed family ties with the Hindus. Beside the decline in numbers, some Sikh sects, such as Ram Rai, have disappeared altogether.

The second aspect of this problem involves keeping Sikh religious doctrines, rituals, and practices separate and distinct from those of the Hindus. Throughout history, we find a strong tendency for Sikhism to incorporate certain Hindu beliefs, practices, and religous rituals in their daily lives, as well as in their religious behavior. In fact, Sikhism has often been regarded as an offshoot of Hinduism. This is due to the fact that the Granth Sahib, the holy scripture of the Sikhs, is filled with Hindu legends, ideals and spirit, which sometimes are used in the teachings of the Sikh Gurus.[11] Moreover, for centuries a common personal law and shared social customs left Sikh and Hindu identities connected and overlapped. Intermarriages were quite common. It was not unusual for a British Census authority to encounter Hindus who wanted to be recorded as "Hindu Sikhs" and Sikhs who wanted to declare themselves as "Sikh Hindus." The Tenth Guru, Govind Singh, united the Sikhs to the Khalsa Panth (Sikh community) and shared a set of common forms and symbols which outwardly set them apart from the Hindus.[12]

Despite the outward symbols of differentiation which the Sikhs used, the social and psychological ties between them and the Hindus continued to exist. In the last two decades, a significant change in the nature of the Sikh community has taken place. It is felt, at least by older and more orthodox Sikhs, that the majority of Sikhs no longer regularly follow the Sikh religious traditions with the same intensity. A general sense of laxity in religious matters became evident among the younger generation of Sikhs. It was the growing fear that Sikhs might be absorbed into the Hindu social and religious system and thereby lose their distinct identity that moved the Sikhs into an institutionalized campaign for assertion of a separate Sikh identity.[13]

The process of assertion of a separate Sikh identity continued, and it received further support from the Gurdwar Reform Movement and from the eventual emergence of the Shiromani Gurdwara Prabhandhak Committee (SGPC) and the Shiromani Akali Dal. Whereas SGPC became the religious custodian, the Akali Dal emerged as the fighting arm of the SGPC, the political guardian of the Panth.[14]

For the Akali leader, if independent Sikh identity was to be retained, it has to be in a state in which they form a compact group, where the teaching of the Gurumukhi[15] and the Sikh religion is compulsory and where there is an atmosphere of respect for the traditions of their Khalsa. The objective of a separate Sikh state of Khalistan was officially adopted by the Akali Dal in March 1946. According to the executive committee of the Akali Dal:

> Whereas the Sikhs, being attached to the Punjab by intimate bonds of holy shrines, property, language, traditions, and history, claim it as their homeland and holy land and which the British took as a "trust" from the last Sikh ruler during his minority rule, and whereas

the entity of the Sikhs is being threatened on account of the persistent demand for Pakistan for the Muslims on the one hand and of danger of absorption by the Hindus on the other hand, Executive committee of the Shiromani Akali Dal demands, for the preservation and protection of the religous, cultural, and economic rights of the Sikh nation, the creation of a Sikh state.[16]

As the British left, an independent India adopted a secular Constitution, and the Sikh struggle for identity became more intense.

II

In India, there is at best an ambiguous dividing line between the demands of religion and citizenship. This is because many religions do not define themselves simply in terms of belief and the interior life, but in terms of practice, which sometimes involves ritual and social performances of duty otherwise prohibited by law. The Indian government has had only limited success in using the Constitution to clarify and settle these ambiguities, partly because the Constitution is itself ambiguous and partly because of the complex interdependence of religious and social obligations.

Although the idea of secularism is there, the Indian Constitution neither defines secularism nor uses the word "secular" anywhere except in the Article 25 clause 2 and in the Preamble of the Constitution. It should be noted, that the word "secular" has been added by way of the Forty-second Amendment which came into operation on 1 September 1976.[17] Before that date, there was no reference to India as a secular state. No explanation was given as to the significance of this addition and to the Preamble twenty-seven years after the formation of the original Constitution. From the time the Forty-second Amendment became operative, the word "secular" appeared only once in the Constitution in Article 25 (2a) which authorizes the state to make laws "regulating or restricting economic, financial, political or other secular activity which may be associated with religious practice." Here again, nothing much has been said in order to define or explain the usage of the word "secular." The Constitution makers probably took secularism as a practical and useful concept that would mold and adapt itself according to the changing needs of developing India. They did not, therefore, confine Indian secularism in a definition, but simply incorporated in the Constitution its basic outlines and principles.

If we read the Indian Constitution, we find that it aims to establish a secular state. That is, in essence, that the state will not make any discrimination on the grounds of religion or community, or against any person professing any form of religious faith. No particular religion in the state will be identified as a state religion, nor will it receive any state patronage, or preferential status.[18] Secularism, like democracy, has come to mean different things to different people. Wide usage and various interpretations do not provide the necessary clarity of meaning. By secularism one ordinarily understands: *(1)* a system of doctrines and practices that reject any form of religious faith and worship; *(2)* the belief that religion and ecclesiastical affairs should not enter into the functions of the state; *(3)* the belief that the state morals, education, etc. should be independent of religion.

According to the late Prime Minister of India, Indira Gandhi, the Hindi translation of secularism as "Dharma Nirapekshata," which literally means religious neutrality and nonalignment, is incorrect. Indian secularism, Mrs. Gandhi stated, is equal alignment with each religion.[19] Prime Minister Nehru, right after Independence Day in 1946, mentioned at a press conference that "so far as India is concerned we have very clearly stated both as government and otherwise that we cannot think of any state which might be called a communal or religious state. We can only think of a secular, noncommunal democratic state, in which every individual, to whatever religion he may belong, has equal rights and opportunities."[20]

The question whether India is a secular state has concerned many people. Attention is often being drawn to the discrepancies between the implication of the word "secular" which, as an English word, is known to have a meaning of separation between church and state or religious nonalignment appropriate to its Anglo-Saxon derivation, and the realities of post-independent Indian law and life with Dharma Nirapekshata, or equal alignment with all religions. Fundamentally, secularism in terms of separation invoves two principles: *(1)* the noninterference of the state and religious organizations in each other's affairs; *(2)* the absence of a legal connection between state and a particular religion. Secularism in terms of noninterference was not accepted by India for various reasons. India, however, subscribes to the second principle.[21]

In order to understand why it is not possible to have a secular India where the state is nonaligned to all religions, it is essential that we understand the complexity of the Indian situation. First, India is a multi-religious, multi-lingual country with a history of several hundred years of foreign domination. Second, the religious consciousness of the Indian population is pronounced in all areas of a person's life. That is, religion seeks to regulate all human activities, disregarding the difference between the secular and the sacred. Third, the lack of any ecclesiastical organizations in two of the major religions of the country, namely Hinduism and Islam, necessitates state interference in the religious matters for religious reforms.

It is important to note that, according to the Indian Constitution, one is allowed both freedom of conscience and the right to practice whatever beliefs that do not infringe on "public order, morality, and health." This becomes difficult to negotiate, as in the example of Hindu marriage customs and in particular bigamy, which would ensure the existence of a male heir and therefore the family's salvation. Since Hindu religion also recognizes the institution of adoption, the state was able to enact legislation prohibiting polygamy.[22] The Hindu caste system provides an even greater challenge to legal efforts to present equal social rights for all in the context of restrictive and inherently inequitable religious hierarchy. For example, in the case of *Taher Saifuddin vs. Tyebbhai Moosaji,* the Bombay High Court upheld the constitutionality of the act which deprived a religious community of the right to excommunicate a member of its congregation when such an act would deprive the member of his legal rights and privileges. The Court claimed that "religion" is a matter of man's faith and belief, and is sharply distinguished from religious practices.[23] Interestingly enough, the West allows much greater prerogatives for ecclesiastical authority, and the state would never interfere in matters of excommunication. In India a man's social and religious identity are inextricably combined, and the state must opt to defend the secular notion of law as being equally applicable to all citizens, regardless of caste or social standing. Therefore, the state ruled that the Harijans are required to have access to Hindu temples, in spite of prohibitions by the Hindu laws. This is stated in the Madras Temple Entry Authorization Act.[24]

In summary, the notion of secularism as included in the Constitution must remain an ambiguous term. The guarantees for religious freedom must coexist with the precedents and sanctions for state interference in religious matter. Secondly, while the Constitution articulates the principles of nondiscrimination by the State, India still operates its own version of "affirmative action" when it makes special provisions for its underprivileged castes. Finally, the idea of noninterference of state and religious organization in each other's domain is extremely problematic. It seems, then, that the more India struggles to become a modern state, the more religion is being subordinated to a minor role as in the Western Hemisphere.

For the first time in her history, India must create a secular "myth" of nationhood which unites the many diverging minority religions without destroying their pluralism. How then, can we understand the notion of a secular state? Is it possible, therefore, for the state to accept all religions impartially? Or must it separate itself from all religions? Finally, is the latter option even possible, given India's geographical, historical, and religious realities? Religious realities of the Sikhs challenge the entire notion of Indian secularism.

III

The Sikh movement has to be understood as all movements should be, not only in the light of its ideological background, but also in terms of various demands brought in throughout this struggle, a closer look at which reveals a gradual progression from religious to cultural concerns, leading finally to a demand for a separate Sikh nation. In the first phase, demands were primarily religious, evolving from a question of religious identity. In this phase, religious identity was seen as a question of internal reform of Hinduism from caste system, Brahmin domination, etc. Given that it was shaped in a particular historical circumstances, it was seen as a militant religion. It was militant in terms of the agenda for reform such as the caste system and not so much in the political sense.[25] Determined to keep their identity separate from the Hindus, Sikhs tenaciously maintained their outward symbols of orthodox Sikhism. Fear of absorption of the Sikhs within the Hindu community was compounded by the fact of the mismanagement and corruption of the Sikh *gurdwaras* by the *mahants* or the priests. Coming from the Sikh sects such as Udasis and Sahajadri who never adhered to the Sikh orthodox form of symbols, most of the priests inclined to include Hindu forms of ritual and images in the *gurdwaras* worship.[26] Sikh religious identity was threatened; and this time the threat in a sense came from the very center, the Sikh place of worship. As a result, conflict with the British government began in the form of demand over *gurdwara* control. In this phase Sikh struggle was as much a struggle against the British government as against the priests.[27] Struggle was as much for *gurdwara* control as it was for internal reform. Although there were some questions regarding cultural and political identity, this was primarily a religious struggle.

In the second phase, a gradual transition was seen from a narrow notion of religious identity to a much more cultural view of religious identity. Questions about religious reorganization of the state, its language, the capital of Punjab—all came into the fold of religous questions. Sikhs always regarded the Punjabi language and culture as critical to their survival, integrity, and development as a distinct religious community within India. As Punjabi Hindus regarded themselves more and more as part of the mainstream of Hindu culture, the task of protecting Punjab's secular interests became part of the Sikh struggle. Politics now become a much larger factor in the question of Sikh identity, yet it was still seen in cultural terms rather than in terms of nationalism. Demand at this phase was more of a demand for cultural separation, or at least in autonomous culture, and not for a separate state or nationality.

It is difficult to pinpoint exactly when the third phase of demand for a separate nation started. As the economic power of the Sikhs increased, it became translated into political power where politics was no longer seen in a cultural light. The question of religious nationalism for the Sikhs came into the picture. The 1973 Anandapur Sahib Resolution has shown such signs of Sikh national consciousness. One of the major objectives, according to this resolution, is "maintaining the feeling of a separate independent entity of the Sikh Panth and creation of an environment in which the 'National expression' of the Sikhs can be full and satisfactory."[28] In October 1981, the Akali Dal sponsored an agitation in support of demands submitted to the Indian government. Since then, there have been several rounds of talks between the Akali Dal leader, the Prime Minister, and the leaders of the opposition parties. Although this particular agitation gave voice to the accumulated frustration of the Sikhs in economic, religious, cultural, and political spheres, concern was primarily in the political sphere.

The issues of their discussion fall into three broad categories: *(1)* those which concern the Sikh community as a religious group, *(2)* those which relate to other states besides Punjab, and *(3)* general issues. Two major demands which concern the Sikhs' identity as a religious group are: *(1)* the granting of "holy city" status to Amritsar on the pattern of Hardwar, Kashi, and Kurukshetra; and *(2)* permission for Sikhs traveling by air to wear *kirpans* (swords) on domestic and international flights.[29] Under the second category, the resolution sought the immediate merger with Punjab of Punjabi-speaking Sikh populated areas in Haryana, Rajasthan, and Himachal Pradesh besides Chandigarh. One of the major demands in the third category of general issues deals with a demand for fundamental change in the center-state relations. According to this particular resolution, change will involve limiting the authority of central government to defense, foreign affairs, post and telecommunications, currency, and railways. The 1982 version of this resolution emphasized the formation of a single administrative unit where the interests of the Sikhs and Sikhism will be safeguarded.

One must realize, however, that not every Sikh accepts the Akali cause, nor do all the leaders of the Sikh community stand for Khalistan. On the issue of Sikh nationalism, division exists as much among the elite as among the ordinary Sikhs. Like most other communities in India, the Sikhs are internally segmented by clan and caste. How far the consciousness of a "national" as distinguished from a religious or cultural identity has extended beyond the Akali party and a small section of urban intelligencia is questionable. Moreover, how much the Sikh peasantry in the village actually understands and, if they do, whether they agree with the political demands of the Akali are questions to which no definite answers are available at the moment.

IV

Sikh demands have been directed by a strong desire to preserve themselves as a distinct community apart from the Hindus and seek a political base on which they will be secure as separate people. Given the ideological and historical background, the point of conflict seems to be that, for the Sikhs, the freedom of religion allowed by the Constitution is unsatisfactory and meaningless unless they can express it by social and political means.

The present Constitution of India, the Sikhs complain, has provisions which militate against not only the autonomy of the Sikhs but the very self-identity of this minority religion. Sikh demands, the Indian government declares, cut the very root of a secular state. Sikh extremists argue that if religion can be allowed in an Indian context to be the basis of deciding on issues of morality, education, and personal laws, why can it not also be allowed to settle political questions with regard to an autonomous Sikh state? That is, given the special nature of Indian secularism, why cannot Sikh demands be met by the Indian government? What sort of implication does the Sikh issue raise for a better understanding of Indian secularism?

In order to understand why the Sikh demands for a separate state have not been met by the State, it is necessary that we take a look at Article 26 of the Indian Constitution. It states: subject to public order, morality and health, every religious denomination, or any section thereof shall have the right (a) to establish and maintain religious institutions for religious and charitable purposes, (b) to manage its own affairs in matters of religion, (c) to own and acquire property, and (d) to administer such property in accordance with the law.[30]

Article 26 deals with a particular aspect of religious freedom, namely collective freedom. It outlines the religious rights of religious communities. The Constitution, however, does not start with the assumption that the religious communities should have absolute autonomy over all the affairs related to their denominations. According to this article, freedom of religion is guaranteed to religious communities as long as they are dealing exclusively with matters of religion. There must be a dividing line bewteen these matters and the other concerns of the denomination. Given the fact that the religions in India still have considerably more authority over all aspects of life of an individual, or a community, how is it possible to separate religious affairs from the other affairs of the denomination?

According to the Constitution what constitutes an affair of religion must first be ascertained with regard to the doctrine of the religion itself. Second, it needs to be determined whether the particular affair is an essential or nonessential part of the religion. Although religion and politics are closely related in Sikh history, the demand for a separate state is not considered essential to their doctrine, according to the Indian Constitution. Since the Sikh demand for a separate state is considered a nonessential part of their faith, it cannot receive any special consideraton within the constitutional guarantee of freedom of religion.

This particular conflict between the Sikhs and the government can be partially clarified in view of *(1)* the different ways the Indian Constitution and the Sikh fundamentalists define religion and politics, and *(2)* the ambiguities which exist in concept as well as use and function of the principle of secularism. Whereas politics and religion are more and more inter-defining in recent Sikh history, they are defined differently in the Indian Constitution. In the Sikh sturggle for identity, religious rights are being increasingly defined in terms of political rights and vice versa. The Indian Constitution, on the other hand, can neither allow a political definition of religious rights, nor recognize, on religious grounds, the existence of a separate nation within the federation of India. Religious rights as we find them in the Constitution can be explained in terms of legal rights, whereas politics is understood in the Constitution as dealing with center-state relations. The Sikh fundamentalists are obviously not willing to separate questions of religious identity from the question of a separate nation. Under these circumstances, the government is faced with the alternative of handling the question of religious nationalism within the framework of center-state relations.

In order to know what it means to separate religious from political issues, it is essential that one know what are the affairs of religion and what are the affairs of the state. Although constitutional articles grant different forms of rights to the individuals and to the communities, nowhere does one find a clear line of separation between religious affairs and the affairs of the state. Those misunderstandings which eventually lead to conflict seem to stem mainly from the lack of clarification with regard to the basic principle of secularism. On the one hand, the Indian government by its principle of secularism is engaged in a constant effort to disentagle religion from politics. On the other hand, there are constant state interferences in the matters of religion. These ambiguities with regard to the use and function of the principle of secularism somehow blurred the demarcaton line between the religious matters and the matters of the state. Consequently, in the absence of a strict separation between these areas, the principle of secularism is being exploited by the religious communities to their advantages.

The question of identity is a crucial one—psychologically and socially. Sikhism with all its protests and escalated demands already proves that this question cannot be pushed aside. Being secularistic, the state simply cannot dismiss the demands without considering the nature and background of a particular religion, especially in the case of the Sikhs, where the question of identity is tied to many factors such as religion, land, language, and culture. The Indian government recognizes the complexity of the problem. Given the Sikh situation, economic, cultural, social, or linguistic problems not identified and solved as such are bound to become political.

Up until now, the Indian Constitution allowed for religious expressions, but had never really given itself to tackling religious questions on a national basis. Constitutionally, religious freedom has much more to do with giving minority religion a space and rights against domination from the Hindu majority. However, that right was never conceived as a nationalistic threat. On the question of secularism, there is nothing in the Constitution that is specifically geared to approaching and solving questions with regard to the religious nationalism of the Sikhs.

Given the peculiar nature of Indian secularism, Sikh demands for a separate state create a special problem which doesn't have any parallel in the Western experience. The problem has escalated to the point that the question of Sikh identity has now become explosive. Granting the Sikhs an independent state within the same union is simply not possible without breaking up the union or destroying its fundamental nature—its secular character. Also, there is no clear precedent for creating a separate state that will in a sense allow for a sort of middle ground for both the Akalis and the central government. And time is simply running out. Since the bloody storming of the Golden Temple in Amritsar in the first week of June 1984, India is facing her gravest crisis of nationhood.

What sort of solution can be worked out? One possibility will be for the central government to find some moderate elements among the Sikhs who will accept the central distinction between politics and religion which is the very premise behind a secular government. These moderate elements have to be prepared to allow explicitly political questions to be kept separate from cultural and religious questions. Political questions will be handled in an entirely secular way according to center-state relations, and the religious questions will be tackled in terms of rights and legal guarantees, and not in terms of political power.

It is one thing to have a definite dividing line between politics and religion in theory, and it is quite another thing to come up with such a hard and fast line in practice. In the present time obviously such a separation between religious and political issues has not been accepted by the Sikhs. Even if the particular separation is accepted, there is a danger involved. Any sort of mishandling of political issues on the part of the state will immediately open up the ground for the religious fundamentalist to come in and protest the matter from the religious point of view.

The Sikh problem we have been studying offers us a microcosm of the conflicts which threaten the stability and authority of the central government. The Indian people, separated by linguistic, cultural, and religious differences, still place their primary allegiance to caste, region, religion, and language and find it impossible at this stage in their history to define and commit themselves to an abstract ideal of secularism. The history and religious background of the Sikhs makes assimilation even harder for them than for the rest of India. The question that remains is this—can the Indian Constitution, at this point in its history, use its policies of secularism and equal alignment to integrate the regional identities of its inhabitants and unite the people behind the ideal of unity that will permit coexistence within diversity possible?

What is partly delaying the solution is the fear that too much concession to one religious community will lead other communities to ask for the same. For example, if the Sikhs feel that tobacco selling in the area of a *gurdwar* is not acceptable, the Muslims are justified in opposing music near their mosques and Hindus could be insistent on banning animal killing. Even though there isn't such a problem at the moment with the other religious communities, such as the Buddhists, the Parsis, or the Jains, it may be a matter of time before the floodgates open and various other religious communities come up with demands of their own. Most important of all, the aftereffect of such concessions could lead to interdenominational conflicts within a particular religion as well. Therefore, careful consideration has to be given in settling the matters with the Sikhs, so that it does not instigate any other demands on the part of any other religious communities which will be threatening to the secular state.

Apart from a negotiated settlement with the Akalis, it is equally necessary that the *gurdwaras* be divested of its factional fights. As long as there are factional fights over the control of the *gurdwaras,* most political problems in respect of the Sikh politics in Punjab will continue to exist.

If some sort of political solution can ever be achieved, further clarification or understanding of the secular principle will have to be worked out. Recent years the Sikh crisis of recent years is forcing India to the conceptual clarification of its secular principle. The notion of secularism also has to be clearly defined with regard to its use and function within the changing reality of India. Also religions will not just be granted their rights but will also be positively allowed some form of expresson, such as festivals, etc. Whether any solution of such nature could ever be possible in practice is uncertain. Given the explosive mixture of religion and politics involved in the Sikh case, the resolution of the Sikh nationality question will in the ultimate analysis depend on whether a middle ground could be found where Sikh identity will be safeguarded in certain ways, and at the same time some sort of loose connection with the federation will be guaranteed.

— 4 —

The Problem of "Superstition" in the People's Republic of China

Stephan Feuchtwang

Indirectly this article will have to do with a vast field of practices covered by the term "popular religion." But I shall be directly concerned with politics, and the statements with which I am concerned[1] contain no such terms as "popular religion." They concern "superstition" and couple it with "religion."

Now, the word "religion" is already inadequate to the description of the Chinese practices to which it has been applied. I refer to the many-centered or centerless networks of cults, of festivals, and of ancestor worship. I also refer to the fact of belief in spiritual agency which can be petitioned and divined but does not necessarily have attached to it recognizable ethics, the fact of professional practitioners without the organization and sanctity associated with European clerical hierarchies, and the existence of ecstatic spirit possession without prophecy. All these and more dilemmas for the notion of religion are presented by Chinese popular religious practices. Some of the same dilemmas are now presented to the social sciences and policy of the Chinese government which has inherited, along with the term "religion" that of "superstition" to describe these practices.

It is only in the last century that Chinese, possibly with Japanese mediation, contained the words by which "religion" and "superstition" were translated. The modern European terms are themselves recent. "Religion" now has a universal and agnostic sense, whereas the medieval word referred to a state of being bound by an order or to an institution; and "superstition" is a rationalist and critical term arising from the Enlightenment commentary upon religion. "Religion" was itself born in a critical frame of reference, the critique of the fear of God or gods.[2] The basis of that critique was increasingly an idea of what brings about virtue and peace of mind in the body politic. To this was added an idea of scientific truth. "Superstition" was then the castigation of either error or of absurd claims for a discipline and view which were rationally and empirically known to be no more nor less than regulation and a sense of a world, necessary for the social peace of a people. "Religion" therefore stands somewhere between "superstition," and social, natural, and scientific truths, and for an experience of awe or fear.

The Chinese translation of "religion" is *zongjiao,* a neologism consisting of *zong,* which on its own is translatable as "ancestral" or "clan" or "principal aim," and *jiao,* which is translatable as "teaching" and has for long been the common term for the schools and strands of organized religions (in the medieval European sense). Together they amount to an approximate socio-political sense of "religion" as the principal beliefs of a people, or a heritage. "Superstition," on the other hand, was translated into Chinese by the neologism *mixin,* made up from *xin*—'belief'—and *mi,* which is "disorder." Such "disorder" had since the seventeenth century been the object of popular didactic stories and tracts. They showed the way to clear the confusion *(mi)* obscuring the primordial and true nature of heart and mind by means of new teachings, claiming to be the truth behind those of the main teachings in China.[3] The positive complement of *mi* was *zheng,* "true" in the sense of "correct." *Zheng* means also "orthodox" in a more distanced perspective in which proper sacrifices and rites are to be restored as a matter of good civil order and virtue by example and education, and its opposite is *xie,* "heterodox." *Mixin* picks up these connotations and combines them with the word "belief," which is significantly opposed to the more respected "teaching" *(jiao)* or "religion" *(zongjiao).*

What follows is the account of some recent, and Chinese, vicissitudes in the history of these terms. I shall give separate consideration, first to general policy and theoretical statements, then to the other reality of reports and campaigns. "Real life" as a *Beijing Review* article on the distinction between religion and superstition put it (21 December 1979), is where "the situation is complicated." The "situation" consists in difficulties of implementation, the conjuction of more than one policy, and statements in many different registers.

"Religion" and "Superstition" in Law, Policy and Theory—1962–1986

The question I wish to put is "why does 'superstition' recur as a target of policy?" This is not the same as asking whether traditional popular religions survive and in what form, for I shall indicate how "superstition" is not a steady referent; it is not just another name for what others call "popular religion." Superstition is a term which occurs in various combinations with other policy concerns and with various connotations.

"Religion" *(zongjiao)* in contemporary Chinese statements usually refers to the major religions of the world. "Superstition" *(mixin)*, on the other hand, is a derogatory reference to lists of activities which always, when they are given, include various kinds of fortune-telling, or "fatalism," spirit-possession, "witches," and "sorcerers," festivals, the worship of gods and placation of ghosts, and the building of small temples. Less often it refers explicitly to funerals, weddings, and ancestor worship which, when they are described among minority nationalities, are named "customs" *(fengsu)*. "Superstition," which is often combined with the epithet "feudal" *(fengjian)* and sometimes, though contentiously, "religious" superstition, indicates a range of activities eccentric but also refractory to policies of socialistic construction and patriotic political movement. It raises questions of constitutional freedom and of the independence, or at least the indeterminacy, of certain symbolic and ideological practices from the main objectives of socialist strategy.[4]

To begin to see the distribution of political weight in the use of the couple of terms "religion' and "superstition," we can start with current law. Both constitutional law of rights and articles of the criminal code can be involved. The Revised Constitution of 1982 contains in Article 36 the right not to be discriminated against on religious grounds or on grounds of just believing in a religion. But it also emphasizes the requirement that religion "not be subject to any foreign domination." There are associations of Islam, Catholicism, Protestantism, Buddhism, and Taoism registered with and tolerated by the State Religious Affairs Bureaus, which include either the word "patriotic" in their names or the condition of being independent from foreign domination in their constitutions. "Patriotic" also means support of the leadership of the Communist Party and support of the socialist system. The same Article 36 spells this out in a number of exclusions. Religion is excluded from state provision of health, public order, law, and education. Any religious activity which can be said to disrupt public order, impair health, or interfere in state education is illegal.

A comment in a newspaper from one of the minority nationalities' regions draws out one of the main political objectives behind these exclusions beyond the separation of church and state standard in liberal democracies. "It is absolutely necessary," the comment states, "to adhere to the principle of separating religion from political power, the judicature and education."[5] Any religious opposition to the unity of the PRC or challenge to the leadership of the Party is in this comment expressly deemed a "use" of religion to sabotage them. Revival of religiously sanctioned privileges, and whatever can be said to be attempts to "coerce" people into becoming believers is, as is the reverse attempt to coerce believers into atheism, "absolutely forbidden." Here the criminal code enters, to protect existing religious beliefs and minority customs from the attacks which had been waged upon them in the Cultural Revolutionary years of 1966–1976. Article 147 of the Code, promulgated in July 1978 (in force from the beginning of 1980), declares that a state functionary who unlawfully deprives a citizen of his legitimate freedom of religious belief or violates the customs of a minority nationality to a serious degree shall be sentenced to imprisonment for no more than two years, or be detained in other ways.

But compare this with Article 165 of the same Code: a witch *(wupo)* or sorcerer *(shenhan)* who uses superstition to spread rumors or fraudulently to acquire money or articles shall be sentenced to imprisonment for no more than two years, or be detained, or be put under public surveillance, or in serious cases imprisoned for two to seven years. Here the economic crimes of fraud, speculation, and exploitation are incurred; I shall return to the economic field from which "superstition" is to be excluded. But note first the separation of practitioners from believers in the word "use." Expositions of policy on religion and superstition use phrases such as "under the cover of," "in the guise of" and similar notions of masking, and thus fraud. Hegel's idea of superstition as a conspiracy against the people by priests and tyrants is repeated here.[6] The policy is to distinguish believers in superstition, where improvements in education and cultural life are appropriate, from the propagators and practitioners of superstition where re-education and, should that fail, the criminal law is appropriate.[7] Note too the dominant distinction between religious and superstitious belief. But how to make the distinction is problematic. It has been problematic enough to local cadres for an interview with the vice-governor of Fujian province to have included an attempt to clarify the issue:

> (Question) Recently, superstitious activities have reappeared in some areas in our province. The situation is particularly serious in certain localities. However, *some people are unable to distinguish between legitimate religious activities and superstitious activities. They think that banning the superstitious activities may constitute a violation of the Party's and the State's religious policies.* My question is: What are the differences between normal religious activities and superstitious activities? Are there different policies for them?

(Answer) This is a good question. Normal religious activities are fundamentally different from superstitious activities. The main differences are: First, normal religious activities must be patriotic and law-abiding, and they must support the communist leadership and the socialist system; second, they must have a legitimate organization which is recognized by government departments concerned and which accepts their leadership; third, religious activities must be carried out within the scope permitted by the law, they must not interfere with politics and education and they must not affect production and the social order.

But superstitious activities like witchcraft, sorcery, use of elixers, fortune-telling, astrological practices, invocation to avert calamities, rain-making, supplication for offspring, treating disease with exorcism, practice of physiognomy, practice of geomancy, building village temples and so forth do not have the special characteristics of modern religions and they violate the regulations stipulated by law. . . .

While freedom of religious beliefs and legitimate religious activities are protected by our country's Constitution, law and other regulations concerned, they have specifically stipulated that superstitious activities carried out under the cover of religion are not allowed. . . .

We will act according to the law to eliminate the superstitious organizations resolutely and stop their superstitious activities. *We will promptly and harshly punish those who carry out criminal activities under the cover of superstitious activities so as to put an end to this unhealthy tendency.*[8]

Note incidentally how in the vice-governor's explanation the law is restated with the inclusion of noninterference in production. What is remarkable, and typical, is the way the distinction between religion and superstition is made by institutional fact: the existence or non-existence of legitimate organization of belief and its attendant activities. In other, similar, attempts at clarification[9], legitimate specialized locations and protection of the believer's home extend the institutional criterion. "All the normal religious activities . . . should be managed by religious organizations and religious believers on their own."[10] We should also understand in the phrase "do not have the special characteristics of modern religions" both the backwardness of superstitious belief and, as expounded by more academic commentators in China, the "modern" religious characteristic of a worked out world view. It should be plain that "superstition" is the negative category of "religion". The policy being pursued is the institutionalization of religion, in a sphere linked to final consumption at the periphery of a central and secular public sphere. Policy is to make the question of religious belief one of personal choice for a citizen: religion is "only a problem of ideological understanding . . . and a private matter of individual citizens."[11] Where the noise of religion exceeds its constituted boundaries, there is "superstition".

Comparison with the Constitution in force before 1982 reveals a shift from previous policies. The current criminal code forbids cadre interference in religious beliefs. The previous Constitution included in its fundamental rights not only the symmetrical freedoms to believe and not to believe in religion, but also the asymmetrical inclusion of freedom to propagate atheism without freedom to propagate religion, whereas since 1982 freedom of propagation either way is omitted. This indicates a movement in deciding the lines and the best means of keeping the lines without which religion should be instituted. The movement has swung toward establishing rules and encouraging reliance on them instead of the uncertainty of mobilization politics which characterized most of the years from 1957 to 1976. But there is no question of abandoning the socialist aim of education to the point where all citizens know and trust in the powers of science and society to acomplish the ends for which some still pray and others still seek spiritual divination. This socialist aim is still pursued in campaigns and not just in schools, but with warnings against disruption and offense to the masses:

> After 1957, the "Leftist" mistakes in our religious work began to aggravate. . . . They wrecked the religious organizations and ranks of activists of the religious cricles that loved the country and supported socialism and even forcefully banned the normal religious life of the masses of religious believers and destroyed and closed down all places of religious activities. . . . Moreover, they treated the customs and habits of some minority nationalities as religious and superstitious and forcefully banned the customs and habits, thus impairing national unity. They used violence in solving religious problems. They provided extremely favorable conditions for a few counter-revolutionaries and evil-doers to carry out illegal and criminal activities and counter-revolutionary sabotage activities in a big way under the cover of carrying out religious activities [which had been driven underground].[12]

This editorial is a very clear statement of the problematic distinction between the three terms: "religion," "superstition" and "custom." And if we now turn to the shift in policy which the editorial marks, it should be possible to see some of the problems for socialist policy plaguing these distinctions.

In published reports there have been, since 1949, two main periods of concern with superstition: 1962 to 1966 and 1978 to the present.

This does not mean that in other years there were no recurrences of "superstition" and actions against them; the latter could certainly occur without reported discussion. That seems to have been the case for the first three years of the Cultural Revolution (1966–1969), when the intense activity by Red Guards and rusticated youths against revisionism and the Four Olds—old thinking, old culture, old customs, and old ways of life—combined attacks on tight trousers, carefully flattened hairstyles, pointed-toe shoes and anything foreign with destruction of images of gods and ancestor tablets, as well as their temples. But the years preceding these events, not those of the events themselves, contained a good deal of policy discussion, policy on religion included, in the course of a second Socialist Education Campaign in the countryside (the first had been in 1957).

Indeed there was some theoretical controversy. By theoretical I mean statements concerning abstract categories or great empirical generalizations. To introduce this controversy the theoretical scene must be set for now as well as for 1962–1966.

Present theoretical discussion is more elaborate than it was in 1962–1966, because it is included in an academic establishment (research institutes and their journals) which did not exist until 1966, when it was immediately dismantled. Institutions now exist for the study of religion, pursued in many different ways. But only one of these provides the theoretical guide to policy—the Marxist science of religion—and its concepts now are little changed from their appearance in earlier statements. The other kinds of study of religion guide only its materials. They include an encyclopedic description of the world's religions, the translation, or re-edition of scriptures and commentaries on them, the histories of religions—their roles in social movements, and the histories of ideologies (philosophies) which either opposed or extended religious ideologies—and, in the 1980s, empirical investigations, notably that of "the nature of religion in socialist conditions" conducted by the Shanghai Academy of Social Sciences.[13]

What is common to the Marxist theoretical formulae is their assumption of a historical origin. The origin of the idea of spiritual presence and agency is according to these formulae a reflection of ignorance and the oppresiveness of natural forces—ignorance of the explanation of dreams and the inability to plan or insure against vagaries in the natural provision of subsistence. Engels is cited as authority for what appear to be evolutionary conceptions of religion much like those of E. Tylor. According to them, religion evolves from animism and progresses to monotheism and thence to internalized ethics, with survivals of the rationality of earlier stages remaining as the irrationalities of the present. But the adoption of evolutionary conceptions via Engles converges with a path via Hegel. Thus the more philosophical statements combine the teleology of progress toward science with more dialectical statements. Religion is the imaginary product (or projection) in thought of the actual self-alienation of social productive capacity. In the history of self-alienation, class society adds to spontaneous theism a social systematization, just as it adds to natural oppressiveness the social oppression of class rule.

These formulations start from the assumption of a raw human material that is atheist. The assumption constitutes a denial of theories of psychological need for belief in something supernatural. Original atheism will—with control of natural forces, and the overthrow of exploitation of man by man in the eventual reduction of government to the administration of things—become a new atheism of materialist awareness. Theism, superstition, and religion are social and historical phenomena. Theism is the generic category, almost equivalent to idealism. While religion is distinguished by systematized and organized belief in spiritual presence and agency supporting one or another class rule, superstition is random, induced belief in the supernatural for purposes of exploitation. But these theories allow for very different policy inferences, as we shall see. Even class struggle can be bracketed off and statements made simply about the sufficiency for superstition of mere ignorance, insecurity, and endangered subsistence. These universal historical conceptions of religion can also entertain the survival on a mass scale of the ideological remnant of overthrown systems of exploitation—feudalism and capitalism—and even of society before class struggle. By the same token religion and superstition are conceived to be fertile beds for the growth of class revenge.

The socialism led by a Communist Party is atheist. The Party is both a theoretical and a political vanguard. Its atheism is part of a much larger conception of material interests and their corresponding ideas. Whatever the existing beliefs and differences of belief among them, the people's material interests are to be distinguished from their beliefs. For the material interests are common, and are united in the leadership of the Party and its government, historically tested in the overthrow of the people's oppressors and in the construction of socialist relations. The pursuit of their collective material interests by this leadership and the advancement of awareness and scientific knowledge describes a sphere in which any interference from religious and superstitious beliefs and practices is to be excluded, by punishment of their perpetrators and by education of those whom they gulled. What this sphere contains and what is tolerated as being on the other "personal" side of its boundary in which beliefs are free to be chosen can, however, vary within these conceptions.

At the present time, as before, making collections for the building of temples or ancestral halls is banned. But there have been reports of temple-building activities.[14] One article in *Southern Daily* by a certain Wu Ming reported on a business trip through rural communes. An old comrade of Wu Ming observed to him that the building of new temples was far more common now than it had been in the 1950s. Why had it been allowed? Because, he pointed out, some cadres condone temple-building, saying "the state has built large temples, so the peasants have built small ones."

Since 1976 there has been a shift in drawing the line between heritage and religion on the one hand and superstition on the other, a shift in legality so that what was superstition once is religion or heritage now. Unlike the years 1966–1976 and many of the years before, cultural relics and places of what is also called "scenic beauty," in addition to places sacred to centrally organized and state-recognized religion have been refurbished with state funds, and collections have been allowed where state funds were not provided.[15]

In theoretical statements the issue reflecting this shift of legality is whether all religion is superstition. A Party expert on religion, Ya Han-zhang, argued in 1964 and 1965 that the original or generic category of both religion and superstition is theism, and that it is spontaneous, an idea of spiritual agency born of the inability to explain things and not necessarily therefore an opiate of the masses. Moreover, religion, which is organized and systematized theism, though a product of class society, is not always an opiate either. Its effect on the masses has to be known according to historically specific political circumstances. This he took from a point made by Engles that religious movements in feudal and late feudal Europe were also by necessity also political and often progressive. Superstition, on the other hand, is said to be always harmful. Ya Han-zhang has recently restated these views, identifying religion by the presence of organization, systematic philosophy, doctrine, rites, and a leadership and in general as a way of viewing the world, whereas "feudal superstition is a means by which some people practice fraud" through beliefs and questions about particular difficulties and requests to grant reward or relief from particular suffering.[16]

In 1964 and 1965 this respect for religion was opposed and defeated in official discourse by a number of writers arguing that religion, all religion, is superstition, whether or not organized, and whether part of a coherent world view or not. Belief in spirits should be the subject of careful ideological persuasion and education, and whether part of a doctrinal organization or not the practitioners of religion should be subject to legal sanctions. The criterion of implementation was explicitly (and still is) one of political strategy: not to engender dissatisfaction and dampen the constructive activism of believers. But in the opposition to Ya there was no question but that all belief in spirits and mystic forces, whether in pre-class or in class society, is an opiate. Taboo and fatalism block understanding and restrict action. Where Ya had attacked as "bourgeois" the notion of religion as offering solace, fulfilling a psychological need, his opponents accused him in turn of idealism in founding religion on mere error whereas its basis is in social reality. That social reality is precisely the organized and sytematized acceptance of fate, which Ya and his supporters had admitted to be a misapplicaton of the motivation to change fate.

Ya's opponents were merely extending the teleology already prominent in Ya's own Marxist arguments. According to this teleology, the results of scientific experiment and the revolutionary achievements of struggles which eventually form the basis of socialist aims are read back into all histroy as its potentiality. Ya's opponents were simply insisting on strict adherence to the teleology and the stage of progress already reached in China. At the same time their greater insistence on class struggle arose not just on grounds of therory but from a different assessment of the political situation in which their theoretical statements counted as guidelines. They insisted on greater attention to ideological construction and its supplanting of "feudal" superstitions, religious and nonreligious, because they also stressed mass mobilization rather than diplomacy and regulation as the means of forming political alliances and creating socialist culture. The urgency of this insistence was based on an assessment of some economic policies and practices which are now officially encouraged and were then the subject of considerable official dispute and uncertainty.

The contentious economic policies and practices were those which encouraged individual interest before collective effort. They were held to be an encouragement to old class enemies and class relations, revived under the guise of religion and superstition; they could breed new bourgeois elements. I shall want to argue by a different kind of reasoning that these economic policies, in encouraging independent household production and marketing, are indeed likely to encourage feasting, ancestral memorialism, and accompanying ritual; but here I am concerned to show how the kind of reasoning shared by Ya and his opponents has registered shifts of line. The current theoretical explanations of religion and superstition retain the same double formulation: of new bad elements as well as revival of old under the guise of superstition. The new elements, however, are this time not the product of any economic relations. They are the elements of what is called "modern superstition," which is a product of "unhealthy trends" in political and state relations.

Modern superstition is the current term for denouncing the cult of personality and the political rituals associated with it: the rituals of seeking instruction in the morning and reporting in the evening to portraits of Mao when he was alive. As against this, and as always against superstition, is opposed the correct scientific attitude, now in the formulation made famous by Deng Xiao-ping and opposed once as empiricist: "seek truth from facts." Political conditions giving rise to both cult of personality and belief in a divine provider were most sharply described in *Renmin Ribao* (People's Daily) 14 August 1981 by a certain Ma Wen. He linked them to what had been named "feudal" in other publications, namely the cult of the emperor and the bureaucracy of dynastic China. As he put it, there are outstanding individuals capable of giving leadership; but the individual who becomes an object of eulogy and the attribution of genius is a symbol of an undemocratic distribution of power. So it follows that political reforms are necessary if the cult is to be eliminated. "It is imperative to reform the leadership system of the Party and the government and to change the system of concentrating all power in one individual." It is necessary to end the system of lifetime tenure for leading cadres and of their appointing their own successors. It is necessary to promote people's congresses. All these reforms have, in fact, been attempted since 1981, meeting with opposition from more centralist Marxist-Leninists.

A similar kind of reasoning but with other elaborations was given in *China Youth* (27 March 1982) as an explanatory guide to the treatment of religion newly emergent among youth, including some members of the Communist Youth League. Moving from the familiar distinction between a handful of criminals and the beliefs in religion which they exploit, and from the explanation of those beliefs as stemming from the lack of correct understanding of natural and social forces, the article comments on present conditions. It first concludes that religions are doctrines of necessary suffering. Where the masses suffer and are powerless to do anything about it, religious belief is likely to rise. It then goes on to point out that current conditions exist which are both oppressive and which lead to lack of understanding. They include, according to the author Xiao Hai, not only "various evils handed on from the old society and not completely eliminated yet," but also "the country's economic backwardness," the fact that "the level of education is not yet high" and "because various serious setbacks and mistakes have occurred in our work there are still unhealthy trends such as bureaucracy and making use of connections to one's own advantage." For these reasons "a portion of people still do not have a thorough understanding of the great significance and great prospects of socialism and communism and have not fostered the determination and confidence to join with the Party and other people in overcoming difficulties and eliminating evils." So "they turn to religion in order to give vent to their miseries and seek spiritual sustenance." "What is worthy of attention, " according to Xiao Hai, "is that there are those who believe in religion because of spiritual depression. Due to various social problems caused by the decade of civil disorder [the years of the cultural revolution] some young people have met with setbacks in continuing their study, in getting a job, in marriage, and so on."

It is apparent that the tasks of political reform, of increasing material livelihood and of rasising the level of education are accommodated within the standard analysis of religion. Whatever the direction and substance of reform, the explanation is after all similar.

In both the Socialist Education and the current anti-feudal statements on religion and superstition, the belief in spiritual agency and in fated destiny which underlies both is to be ended by patient education and reform of the conditions which give rise to them. The differences of line concern the means and the vigour with which to do so, but even more they concern the identification of the "handful of criminals" who make use of false beliefs. Should they include the professionals of organized religious doctrine and ritual (or liturgy)? Where is the line beyond which to discern interference? That line, or lines, are around an agreed number of spheres: economic production, social order, political unity, and the material interests of the people, including their health and education. But developments, reforms, and changes of policy in these spheres will of course affect the lines by which they are demarcated, and the developments, reforms, and policies may themselves be opposed and interferences.

So I will now consider these lines of demarcation in practice, and start with production.

Problems of Implementation

What "hindering production" would be alters with a change in economic policy. What might be said to have been the result of false or backward beliefs in one policy direction is good socialist policy in another. Encouragement of greater commercial and conractual initiatives by households was part of the corruption, individualism, and renascent capitalism which Socialist Education was aimed against. And in detail the encouragement of commodity production and commerce does create problems of demarcation now. Is the production of incense to be banned? Or, as an article in *Nongcun Gongzuo Tongxun* asks, "how shall we regard the sale of sacrificial items on the market?"[17] A "report on the censorship of feudal superstitious publications such as prints of door goods . . ." had addressed itself to this subject. It concluded there should be a ban on them, despite such bans having previously done great harm when applied more grossly, and despite their current ineffectuality. Domestic altar prints, incense, and spirit money are frequently observed to be quite openly for sale.

How do you distinguish between *(1)* beliefs, which cannot be banned and should not be subject to administrative orders, *(2)* activities which might be, and *(3)* the banned material products used in those activities? The approach of the article is to inquire what the different possible uses of the material products are and then decide which of the products should be banned. Incense and candles present an impossible problem because they have other uses also—as insect repellent and as lighting respectively. What is more, they are used in some permitted religious activities, taking place in sanctioned religious institutions. So they should be sold to the proper unit according to prescribed quantities. But when it comes to the manufacture and sale of paper spirit money and figures used in funerals and ancestor worship, no one shold deal in them. "If education fails to right the situation, the case should be treated as an economic offense." Meanwhile folk artists should be encouraged to produce themes for New Year prints to replace the old superstitious prints of door gods and stove gods.

It must be difficult to decide whether production of such items are contrary to current economic policy. Rather, the decision to restrict or ban production and sale would have to be on grounds of cultural policy. Yet superstition is to be treated as an economic offense. Thus a festival which lasted for several days in a Guangdong commune included a procession of a woman in a sedan chair wielding a long sword and styling herself great king and father (apparently a spirit medium in trance), followed by armed soldiers including members of the Party. It was denounced in *Nanfang Ribao* (Southern Daily), 5 May 1981, for its interference in production and education. Farmland crops had been trampled, school classes suspended, and the spectacle attracted and made idle thousands of onlookers.

The category "superstitious activities" concentrated on the peddling of goods and services. The services most often listed are those of horoscopy, geomancy, spirit-mediumship and all forms of telling fate and calculating taboos. One objection, as we have seen, is to their engendering fatalism and restricting activities. They are also denounced as fraud, as being used to exploit poeple gulled into believing them, an economic offense. This is at a time when production of commodities by households is encouraged, and their direction by planning agencies reduced to almost nothing. Problems of economic discrimination occur. In a Sichuan commune the activities of producing and selling incense and spirit money and providing various forms of divination and rituals for the passage of the dead had come to the attention of the Center of the Party in Beijing and been investigated by the provincial Party committee; it found that the "superstitions" had been allowed by local cadres as "side-line activities," the name for commerce and the production for sale of anything other than staple or planned goods.

Side-line activities as a whole had been part of the package of abuses, including corruption and feudal superstition, denounced during the Socialist Education campaign. The same newspaper *(Nanfang Ribao)* which reported the procession in 1981 had in November 1962 explained that less was being distributed even though more was being produced per worker, because of a number of misuses of collective revenues by cadres. The list of misuses starts with feasts, goes on with theatrical performances, and ends with increasing subsidies for side-line production. Another report in the same paper the next year, February 1963, describes failure to meet collective production quotas as being due to putting main-line production off in favor of such side activities as repairing houses, household side productions, going to fairs, and preparing for weddings. All except the last are now, since 1978, encouraged.

Extravagance is, as it was in the Socialist Education campaign and for centuries before, an evil denounced in government diatribes against feasting and theater. When it incurs debt and therefore a definite relationship of control over future resources and when it uses resources that could have been put into productive rather than final consumption, extravagance is plainly a matter of concern for economic policy. But when precisely material livelihood and incentives to increase production are to be raised, plainly the issue of what final, unproductive consumption is, is not so easy to settle. In any case feasts, which are occasions for special kinds of food better than the normal fare, and theater, which provides better than everyday leisure spectacle, are not in themselves "superstitious." Although feasting, theater and fairs may surround and certainly have involved the invocation of gods and the foundation of new temples and new cults, they are also occasions for the sealing of contracts, the making of new contracts, and for commerce in general. Where there is as here no clear institutional separation of beliefs in spiritual agency from activities in which other beliefs and practices are involved, there is bound to be leakage through lines attempting to demarcate religious belief.

Thus in the complex of wedding customs it is not easy to say which are affected by and which will themselves affect either economic or religious policy. The marriage law promotes free and symmetrical rights in the choice of partner; even so, continuation of established patterns of residence and the extent to which the households are encouraged to be economic agents tend to reinforce their status as permanent corporations determined by a line of patrilineal descent. When at the same time there is increased reliance on domestic arrangements for welfare fucntions, in the case of the very young and the elderly and in insurance through savings against mishap, all this enters into the choice of partner and the decisions which marriage involves. These include whether the couple lives with their parents after marriage and with whose parents. They also include ideas of compensation for the labor power lost by the household left behind in the person of the marriage partner, and of the gains to the household joined potentially in the children to come.[18] These ideas, and the payments or rather gifts exchanged in the course of engagement and wedding, are deplored as "mercenary marriages," a recurrent item in lists of feudal superstitions. There was a spate of articles and broadcasts deploring them around New Year between 23 and 26 January 1980, a traditional time for weddings and engagements. The wording of these denunciations describes mercenary marriages as the buying of brides for household servants or slaves. But the exchanges to which they refer in most cases take place in marriages of partners who to some extent chose each other. They may have chosen to marry with the help of an intermediary, in relation to their family households. But they were not "marriages" by which a family gained female bond-slaves. The fact that the couple may pay obeisance to the ancestors of the household and to heaven and earth at some point in the wedding, as was tradition, is never mentioned. The "superstition' 'is again an econonic offense, of extravagance and of bondage, missing the reality of the situations of most households and in particular missing the implications for female inequality which current economic policies can be shown to entail.[19]

"Superstition" occurs as part of a condemnation of clusters of activities. The ones so far considered are those economic offenses broadly definable as the squandering of economic resources, interfering with production, and profiteering and speculation. We can now see that changes in policy on pricing and commerce, just as changes in policy on final consumption and material incentive will change the definition of economic offense. The present policy of encouraging independent commercial activity increases the difficulty of policing the boundary across which interference occurs. Profiteering and speculation refer to unregulated commerce in commodities and services which are of course not necessarily religious—building materials for instance—as well as those which are ambiguously religious like almanacs in farmers' calendars, or the incense and candles we came across earlier.

These offenses have themselves formed elements in longer lists of what are called "illegal activities" and have been the subject of regulations and codes of conduct issued by local Communist parties since 1979. Thus in December 1979 and January 1980 separate reports, from Anhui province and from Guangdong, publicized provincial Party meetings calling for the elimination of "unhealthy trends" or "sinister trends" by the adoption of regulations. These trends are then named: theft, larceny, gambling, profiteering, wanton tree-felling (for fuel and for building), feudal superstitious activities, mercenary marriages, and, in Guangdong, the instigation to emigrate and engagement in armed fights between clans. In the northern province of Honan, the provincial government is reported to have sent a task force of 10,000 cadres to the festival for the cleaning of graves in 1986 in order to quell endemic fights over graves and grave sites.[20] Thus we have the merging of economic offenses with offenses against order. The regulations were issued by what were called law and Order Conferences. In June 1981, certain organs of the central State Council including the ministries of Public Security, Commerce, Health and Medical Administration issued draft regulations to rural medical cooperatives for quality control of medicines and to outlaw quacks and peddlers of unauthorized medicines. A member of Changsha City Bureau of Industry and Commerce had already been reported[21] as seeking to strengthen management of markets to prevent the selling of fake medicines, gambling, and fortune-telling.

Interference with the people's health, gambling, and various crimes are included with "superstition" in this spate of regulations; and other special regulations have been issued to control performances and publications, not only the printing of door gods but larger lists. This was part of a campaign of censorship which included works of fiction such as those by Li Jian. He had refused to criticize himself for writing stories such as that of the rape of a pregnant woman during the Cultural Revolution years, or of a cadre's mistaken action which led to an orgiastic mass drowning, the washed-up corpses locked in strange embraces.[22] This is "pornography" clearly written in a Chinese tradition of "strange tales" which includes stories of spirits, fox fairies, and plagues of ill-luck. As to performances, a circular issued jointly by the ministries of Culture and Public Security to local licensing authorities drew attention to spectacles of acrobatics and self-mutilation which were harmful to young performers' physical and mental health, and which exploited children.

To include the restriction of feudal superstitious activities and the elimination of their professional practitioners with the regulation of marketing, of medical facilities, and of popular performances and publications is effective recognition of a close association of belief in deities and ancestors, forms of divination and petition to deities, and certain forms of commerce, medicine and popular culture. And the inclusion is also effective recognition that superstitious activities will be encouraged along with the encouragement of commercial initiative to stimulate production by loosening central controls and administrative forms of economic organization. But the nature of that association is conceived in the two ways I have already mentioned: as a form of exploitation and as the false ideas and unhealthy attitudes of the gullible made vulnerable by poor and insecure material conditions. Improvement of those conditions, particularly through the spread of public health measures, the securing of social order, plus elimination of the practitioners of superstition should, in this conception, leave only a problem of persuasion. Active promotion of scientific knowledge is needed still, but only because of the inertia of already existing ideas. The widespread capacity of ideas to survive on their own after the removal of their historic bases in feudal or capitalist class relations is acknowledged and indeed is seen as a delicate matter on which to offend would be to alienate ordinary working people. The practical, discursive, or formal reality of these ideas is dispersed, on the one hand as ideas and on the other as their social and material bases. But the ideal ghost of a past material base cannot be entertained without its masking a "handful of bad men" who can use it as a cover to restore the past.

Such an account of superstitions links mere ideas with counter-revolution or at least sabotage of current campaigns. In relation to religious beliefs, what can be deemed illegal is named "feudal superstition" and subjected to ideological education. In active policy the substitution of old for new ideas through education is coupled with the harsher discipline of public security. In deciding on what is the necessity to extend campaigns against the mere holding of beliefs, the continued leakage of those "ideas" onto new bases is recognized, and the decision always involves the harsher disciplines of reeducation and punishment for illegalities, in which practitioners are picked out and tried.

Ideological and Cultural Campaigns

The educational propaganda on superstition concentrates on material effects and their causes. Negative and positive examples are publicized. The negative examples conform to a pattern where someone is described as being the victim of physical harm either by direct agency or indirectly by neglect; and the reason for neglect or actual harm is a belief usually put about by a practitioner of one or another kind of divination. The falsity of the belief is not so much refuted by scientific reasoning; rather, the harm condemns the belief. There are many stories in local radio and newspaper reports of spirit healers, female *(wu-po)* and male *(shen-han)*, bringing about injury or death. In 1982, there was a report of a case from Shanxi province of a woman who had drowned a three-year-old girl and made unsuccessful attempts to drown two other children in the lavatory because her own young son was ill. She had consulted her sister-in-law who was a self-professing medium *(shenpo)*. The medium told her that in order for her boy to live three or four others had to die. This story was headed "Feudal Superstition Harms People and Harms Oneself."[23]

An example of neglect was reported from Hebei, where parents had disregarded their daughter's mental disorder and engaged three exorcists who, in the course of burning paper money and putting up charms and calling upon the demon to go, knocked on the girl's head and she died.[24] Another, from Henan, tells of a sixty-three-year-old woman refusing medicine because she believed her alloted life span was over.[25]

Other stories do not involve spirit healers but illustrate the absurd and harmful actions of people acting on belief in geomancy or in horoscopy. One of a collection of such reports again concerns mental illness, this time of man who had killed his children in order to bury them on a site diagnosed to produce wealth in the descendants of whomever was buried there. He believed his children had thereby become immortals *(xian)*.[26] The lurid and sensational elements in these stories have something of the condemned "strange tales" about them, while at the same time their violent absurdity and the frequent allusion to clinical madness is obviously a condemnation of the practice as irrational and harmful. There are other stories of less lethal but equally absurd actions taken by those guided by geomancy to avoid misfortune (burial of a savings book in a recommended spot; gone when the spot was dug up again). Less absurd and more closely related to traditional practices are the letters published in *China Youth* no. 3 (1983), all of which tell of young couples whose marriages have been prevented or ended on the grounds that their horoscopes did not match.

Positive examples propagate recognition of the social agency of good or ill and the renewal of optimism where fatalism had prevailed. Thus one reports an old peasant during the ten years of turbulence and restriction on side-line production praying to gods of heaven and earth for better times. Now when he is active, productive, and better off his daughter teasingly askes whether he is going to give thanks to the gods of heaven and earth, and he answers correctly that he knows it was the decisions of the Sixth Plenum of the Eleventh Congress of the Party which had put things to rights.

These and the other reports on economic offenses are apparently meant to condemn, by association, beliefs and practices which do not always, or even often, have such harmful outcomes. I have already pointed out how diffused in other activities are those considered to be "superstitious." Now I want to add the point that the absurdity and harm of the various kinds of divination and spirit-mediumship mentioned are not usually obvious, nor are these practices exclusive of the use of proper medical facilities and correct economic practices. Moreover, as with the denunciations of economic offenses and of mercenary marriages, there is nothing exceptional or exceptionable to a liberal democrat in what is *explicitly* condemned in these reports. Fraud is one of the reasons for banning or restricting the activities of cult leaders in the United Kingdom. The physical harm to individuals and to crops condemned in China are banned in most countries. They, and the sale of brides into bondage through marriage, are deplorable on nonsocialist grounds. There is indeed nothing socialist in their condemnation. There is no argument about harm to socialist forms of organization in what these reports are meant to condemn by association. But without explicit argument, the socialism being promoted comes in attempts to improve the conditions which are thought to characterize and give rise to "superstition." More than that, there are attempts to construct cultural forms and facilities to replace them.

Mistakes in attacking religion during the turbulent years of 1957 to 1976 are now argued to have done severe damage to national unity.

The mass campaigns of those years are now said to have caused the fatalistic despair where people resort to spiritual explanations and comfort, as well as having merely driven religion underground. Yet the present reform period, no less than the Socialist Education movement and Cultural Revolution, contains concerted campaigns to replace the condemned ideas and practices. The differences between the earlier and the present campaigns is in their agents as well as where their stresses are placed. The stress on mass mobilization and class struggle by the earlier campaigns contrasts with the present campaigns' stress on regulation and the provision of cultural institutions and their spiritual address to individuals' attitudes.

The agents of the Socialist Education campaigns were educated youth sent to the countryside and teams of cadres hoping by emulation and by organizational mobilization to establish mass organizations of the poor and lower middle peasants. There had, before Socialist Education, been Combat Superstition teams, and one of the objects of the campaigns appears to have been to make good of their failures. They had been formed to refute fatalism and promote science; but now there were stories told of their members being haunted by the spirits they sought to deny. The Socialist Education campaigns promoted the replacement of ancestral genealogies by the writing of village and work-unit proletarian histories. These were histories of revolutionary achievements in struggles against class enemies and in feats of construction and production. One educated youth, reported as an example to be emulated, had painted in the places where ancestral figures had been, picutres of the misery of life before Liberation. The campaigns sought to replace eulogies of family honor at funerals with eulogies of socialist construction. Feats of canal construction and the terracing of mountain sides were described in heroic terms as struggles with heaven and earth (nature), with reverse geomantic notions of more passive adjustment expressed in the saying "heaven leads, earth influences." Educated youth formed theatrical troupes to put on plays and songs propagating the "socialist new things" and promoting collective as against individual enterprise.

The frequency of reports of superstition since 1978 and what they note have similar targets to those of the socialist education campaigns and so are witness to their failure. There is even a report of Party cadres who had during the Cultural Revolution acted against gods and superstitions, now repenting before the gods to make amends.[27] Observers are reported to note great interest in the performance of funerals, in feasting at weddings and funerals, in the compilation of ancestral genealogies, in the building of ancestral and village temples, and all the activities, products, and publications which I have already mentioned.[28] The cadre force for the current institutional and organized campaigns waged against them is largely the membership of local branches of the Party, and the campaigns themselves are often first addressed to Communist Youth and Party members. For instance there is an exemplary report of a rural branch of the Party in Jiangsu province whose members resolved not to accept invitations to meals in order to put an end to the practice of currying favor by feasts; they also resolved not to burn incense at festivals.[29] A *New China News* report of 24 March 1981 publicizes the 920 Party cadres and members of a Hunan country branch criticizing themselves for having engaged in gambling, illegal economic activities, and superstition. Army and Party members are reminded of the simple wedding and funeral ceremonies which have from before Liberation been promoted to avoid various kinds of waste (cremation to save burial ground, flowers instead of food in respect of the dead, only the immediate family to join in the wedding meal).

Cadres are generally involved because the campaigns make heavy use of local and ministry regulations to correct "unhealthy tendencies." In direct contrast with the socialist education campaigns in the countryside are, thus, the Rural Regulations and People's Agreements *(xiang gui min yue)*. An example of these goes as follows:

1. Encourage members to work hard in order to accumulate wealth. Speculation is strictly forbidden; crack down on profiteering.
2. Encourage proper cultural entertainment and activities. Gambling is strictly forbidden. Combat low entertainment (which hinders the development of a proper social climate).
3. Encourage improvement in prevailing habits and customs, hard work and thrift. Feudal superstition is strictly forbidden; combat elaborate feasting and wasteful, conspicuous consumption.
4. Encourage plantation/afforestation and combat indiscriminate felling of trees.
5. Encourage family planning; combat aimless reproduction.
6. Encourage disclosure of "bad people" and "bad events"; combat indulgence and protection of bad conduct.[30]

These regulations are part of a campaign to construct Socialist Spiritual Civilization *(shehuizhuyi qingshen wenhua)*. I have already commented on the lists of illegalities in which superstition appears in such regulations. Here I am concerned with the attempts to replace or displace them with new institutions and practices. In the case of the

socialist education campaigns, mass organizations were to be the
displacing institutions. Now it is village people's agreements. Thus in
the same month as the regulations in Hunan were held up as an example,
other reports came out on decisions to curb activities in the coming
festival of sweeping the graves (Qing Ming). In a Guangdong county
"some villages" were reported to have decided to return to "the masses"
the money and food contributed for the performance of rites in honor
of ancestors which includes not only paying respects at graves but also
the repair and building of ancestral temples.[31] A letter to Changsha radio
(18 March 1981) on how Qing Ming gives rise to clan disputes over graves
received the response that "grave-sweeping must be civilized and
healthy." Apart from simplification, it is not apparent what civilizing
the custom would be, except "returning" it to individual families and
playing down larger kinship loyalties. But Quing Ming, like New Year,
has long been the object of a policy of transforming old customs from
within, rather than attempting to eliminate them. In urban areas Qing
Ming transformed is a celebration of revolutionary martyrs, and now
has attached to it the historical myth of Qing Ming 1976's demonstration
against the Gang of Four and in memory of Zhou En-lai who had
recently died. In the countryside, the reports indicate attempts to rid
a custom of superstition, a difficult operation made more difficult by
the idea that, unlike minority nationalities, the Han Chinese traditional
ceremonies do not have religious aspects (the long editorial in *Hongqui*,
16 June 1982, on the Party's policy on religion invites this inference
from a discussion of religious problems being intertwined with
nationality problems).

But something like a religious aspect, in any case a moral aspect,
is recognized to be at stake in the thrust of the campaign for socialist
spiritual civilization. The campaign is not concerned with rituals but
with proprieties, and only through them with the organizational forms
in which they are promoted. The recreational and other institutions
which extend from the proprieties are expected to replace the rituals
of feasting and worship.

What are these properties of socialist spiritual life? In the same
spring of 1981 a central organ of the Party issued directives to members
to promote in themselves four beautifications and five stresses.[32] The
four beautifications are:

    of the mind—fine ideology, moral character, and integrity, up-
             holding the Party and the socialist system;
    of language—polite speech (and unsalacious writings);

of behavior—doing things useful for the people, working hard,
being concerned for others' welfare, observing
discipline, and safeguarding collective interests;
of the environment—personal hygiene, preserving and construct-
ing sanitation in houses and in public places.

The five stresses form part of these beautifications. They are the
promotion of good manners, hygiene, discipline, and morality. Examples
given to illustrte these are instances of acts of public service, such as
some Youth League members who had rescued a boy from a frozen pool,
others who had contributed a wild swan to a zoo, and some others who
had helped in catching hoodlums.

This setting of examples extends to more concrete constructions
directly addressed to superstitious activities. *Fortnightly Talks* describes
how gambling and feudal superstitious activities grow because of a lack
of proper, healthy recreational facilities. There should be a village
cultural center including theater, cinema, bookstore, library, gymnasium,
and tea garden, where clubs can emerge and a new socialist climate
and the popularization of scientific knowledge can be established.[33]

The cadres of the production team in Jiangsu, already mentioned,
reported a combination of facilities to be constructed in their program
for a civilized village *(wenming cun)*. Their goals are not just the
promotion of "socialist consciousness," which includes patriotism, love
for one's community, enthusiastic completion of contracts and
promotion of domestic side-line production, respect for the old and
love for the young, conformity to agreed rules and laws, and the practice
of family planning. They involve a program of repair and construction:
new housing in residential areas for those in scattered homes, road
building, bridge repair; a program of education, the opening of evening
courses in sciences and cultural knowledge, infants schools, nurseries,
and creches for peak periods of work; a program of welfare and hygiene,
including the opening of "hygiene rooms" *(weisheng shi)*; as well as
a provision of cultural facilities in the form of "cultural rooms" *(wenhua
shi)* where TV and radio are installed and films shown, and from which
games and sports are organized.

These encouragements to engage in collective life must be
understood in the light of the dismantling of much of the collective
organization of production and consequent reduction in the collective
accumulation of funds for social welfare. It is not only, as explicitly
stated, to fill the space of cultural recreation which the new wealth of
the households can afford and which has tended to be filled by gambling
and popular religious festivities. It is also a call on households to join

in collective provision of social welfare; and this would be a way of securing against uncertainties in health, child-care, and income at times in the domestic cycle when labor-power is short, or in unforeseeable contingencies which are the subject of "fortune-telling" and potential "spiritual depression." The "cultural rooms" and educational facilities should also be understood as attempts to include villages in the cultural life available in towns and joining them in national networks of communication and creation.

At the same time the campaign is a way of integrating the Party and Army more closely with the institutions of everyday life, this time without the mediation of mass organizations. The campaign to build "civilized villages" was formally promoted by the General Secretary of the Party, Hu Yaobang, at the Twelfth Party Congress (1982), as a way of renewing good relations not only between Party and people but also between army and people. Army personnel in Baoding village had helped improve environmental sanitation and cultural life. And Baodin was only one of fifty thousand "civilized villages" at the time.[34]

Whether the "needs" or pleasures involved in ceremony and other kinds of ostentation such as feasting will be re-disposed into new senses of tradition, locality, and social identity by these means cannot be said without closer observation. To prompt speculation, I offer these items from the press. One is a drawing of people gathered in the yard in front of an open temple. Inside, on the altar stands a television set where the figures of gods would have been. The drawing is captioned "Buddha Abdicated, Television Enthroned," and it comes in a report on the construction of spiritual civilization.[35] Another, stressing the importance of distinguishing religion and feudal superstition, points out the contribution which religious activities in welfare, study, physical exercise, and medicine can make to socialist spiritual civilization.[36] Lastly, such toleration seems to have brought one village to have been led by its ancestral hall committee instead of the statutory Villagers Representative Committee.[37]

Conclusions

I have been concerned with statements of policy on and reports of superstitions. These statements and reports are in the very nature of the term "superstition" agitational, part of campaigns against whatever the referent of "superstition' is. I have asked, "What makes superstition recur?"

In the statements and agitation, superstition is coupled with religion. It is also coupled, as "false" ideas or "criminal" material interests, with "true" ideas and socialist, or the people's, material interests. Religion is sincerely held belief about the world, whether scientifically proven (true) or not. It is a constitutional right in the People's Republic of China to have, as well as not to have, religious beliefs, but not to pursue superstitious activities. Superstitious activities are treated as irregular or as criminal activities. In the same way that, in general, the illegitimate is a function of the legitimate and the irregular an effect of regulation, "superstition" is bound to recur. I distinguish three ways to describe what is bound to recur.

1. A number of separations are being instituted, to which the positive contrasts with "superstition" refer. They number among them the institutions or religious beliefs as separated from the institutions of economic and political activity. Where that separation is incomplete, or where it cannot be made, or where there is an infringement of the boundary of instituted religions, "superstition" will appear.[38]

   Another separation being instituted and which I have not investigated is that of traditional Chinese sciences, or just therapeutic practices, which can be shown to be effective. They are separated from the cosmologies and rituals in which they have traditionally been expounded and presented. Incomplete abstraction into, for example, medical institutions, or instances of practices which have not been subject to authorized positive testing will also be the sites of recurrent "superstition."

2. The political agitation and use of the term "superstition" are themselves new institutions. They attach to their referents the emotive and political-cum-legal charges of horror and of conspiracy to exploit. They create a category of irregularity, which is most usually one of economic mischief or one with actual or potential physically harmful effects. But these are closely linked with a wider discourse of condemnation for endangering the political order.

   Some of the terms of popular religion otherwise castigated are themselves used in political agitation: the "ghosts and demons" of Cultural Revolution attacks are the enemies of socialism, the moving of heaven and earth in mobilization to modernize. The stories of superstition themselves, with the strangeness to fascinate as well as condemn, including the perennial negative term "witch," enter the vocabulary with newer terms for isolating condemned practices as conspiracies (e.g., "black hand"). They consign practices to a historical past ("feudal"), but confess by the same token a renewal of the relics due for elimination through reform.

3. Certain ethnic practices, namely the social organization and means of forming associations for market-type commerce, have been very closely bound with feasting and festivals. Households as units of production and the family as a unity of property and a bulwark of social security tend to encourage at least parts of popular religious ideas (such as those associated with ancestral line). These will be "social bases" for practices and beliefs condemned as non-socialist, even while they are encouraged in economic policies aiming to increase production and the standard of livelihood. Campaigns and regulations constantly try to bring about a separation of the personal beliefs of the people, in their own households, from the practitioners who profit from those beliefs. But, as Anagnost points out, there are also reported cases of social pressures from the same "personal" sources inducing spirit mediums to perform, without payment.[39] Furthermore, the results of personal connections among households, made through domestic arrangements, feasts, and festivals, constantly escape detection and provide rewards. They constitute an informal public morality beside the formally encouraged institutions of socialist spiritual civilization. The two will compete and interact for some time to come.

— 5 —

Islam and Political Power
in the USSR

Alexandre Bennigsen

Relations between the Islamic establishment and the political power in the Soviet Union are complex and difficult to analyze. Too many mistakes have been committed by Western experts and also voluntarily by the Soviets. They originate from the absence of clear definitions: What is Islam and what is political power in the USSR?

The Islamic community in the USSR has a unique character which differentiates it from most Muslim communities of the world. For more than seventy years it resisted the political and ideological onslaught of Marxism-Leninism. In spite of this experience and contrary to the opinion of some Soviet islamicists, Islam in the USSR has not lost its "essence." It remains to this day unaltered. It is not threatened by any heretical or schismatic centrifugal movements (comparable to the sectarian trends within the Christian Orthodox community), nor by shamanistic practices. Despite strong antireligious and anticlerical pressures, Soviet Muslims have preserved orthodox beliefs, rites and customs. But in order to survive as a religion and as way of life, Soviet Islam was obliged to develop some specific features, in particular a dual hierarchy represented by *(1) the official Islamic administration*, which has a legal existence. It is recognized by the Soviet State and alone is empowered to represent Soviet Islam in the world abroad. Since World War II, its leaders have shown an unshakable loyalty to the Soviet power. *(2) Unofficial Islam*, also called in Soviet political literature "parallel," "sufi," or "out-of-mosque" (*vnemechetnyi*) Islam is not recognized by the Soviet authorities and thus has no legal existence. As a rule its representatives are hostile to Soviet power.

Both trends, however, belong to the same realm of Muslim orthodoxy. There are no theological, legal, or spiritual differences between them. Contrary to what some Soviet and Western observers believe, "parallel" Islam is neither a schism nor a sectarian movement.

The only difference—but an important one—between the two, concerns their respective attitude toward political power, that is, the Communist Party and Soviet State and administration.

Political power in the USSR also has a dual character. Like the Byzantine imperial eagle, it is represented on one side by the Soviet State and administration, a secular establishment, antireligious but not necessarily anticlerical. It can at times cooperate with the official Islamic establishment and even be tolerant of religion. But according to Marxist theoreticians the "antiscientific essence of religion" will always remain profoundly inimical to "scientific communism," however loyal and submissive the Islamic hierarchy may be to the Soviet regime. Therefore, the other head—the more important of course, represented by the Communist Party—is not only secular, but officially atheistic, both antireligious and anticlerical. It is equally intolerant of and hostile to all religions including Islam, and it has no contacts with the ecclesiastical hierarchies. The two heads of Soviet power are represented at the highest and middle level by the same people. They do not have different religious policies. If and when differences occur between the two powers, they are not doctrinal or strategic, but only practical.

The situation of Islam in the Soviet Union must therefore be analyzed as a quadrilateral, more or less conflicting relationship between, on one side, the two heads of the political power, and on the other side the two Islamic establishments. In reality the situation is even more complicated because serious differences and sometimes even opposition concerning antireligious policy exist between the policymakers, generally Russians in Moscow, and the executives, often Muslims, who apply or refuse to apply this policy on the spot.

The Soviet State and Islam

The Soviet Union is a secular state where religion has become a personal matter. Article 124 of the 1936 Soviet Constitution is worded as follows:

> With the object of assuring freedom of conscience the Church (or mosque) in the USSR is separated from the State and the School. Freedom to practice religion as well as to conduct antireligious propaganda is guaranteed to all citizens.

Therefore, the Soviet State is not neutral. It favors atheism and expects religion to die sooner or later. No religious education is provided in school, and atheism is taught to children from the age of four. The freedom to practice religion is limited to the right to observe religious rites and ceremonies only within an official house of prayer. Thus, all religious activity outside the mosque is illegal. Preaching outside the mosque and conducting public religious ceremonies are criminal offenses. Religious associations have no legal existence and may be treated not only as illegal but as "conspiratorial bodies." In particular, sufi brotherhoods are outlawed.

Religion is not a criterion for national determination. In theory, all Soviet citizens, believers and unbelievers alike, enjoy the same personal civil rights and are bound by the same duties. Officially, there is no discrimination between different creeds. All religions are, theoretically, treated in the same way by Soviet law, with, however, an important exception: some sects which are suspected of being "anti-Soviet" have no legal existence, and may be treated as "criminal associations."

In practice, the treatment of Islam by the Soviet State has undergone several dramatic changes since the Revolution. During the first years of the Soviet regime, the ideological and administrative offensive against Islam (and all other religions) was conducted simultaneously by the Communist Party and the Soviet State. All traditional Islamic institutions were liquidated during the first ten years of the new regime. The *waqfs* (religious endowments), which before the Revolution guaranteed the economic power of Muslim cult officials, were confiscated between 1925 and 1930. Thereafter the Muslim establishment—the mosques and Muslim schools—were bereft of their means of support.

The abolition of the Muslim legal system, including the *Sharia* (Quranic) and the *'Adat* (customary) courts, and of the educational system, took place during the same period. In 1924, religious courts ceased to have competence in criminal cases. In 1927 recourse to Muslim and customary law was prohibited, first as a test in some Central Asian republics. After successful experience this ban was extended to the other Muslim republics. In 1928 the last religious schools (*madrasa* and *mektep*) were liquidated. From then on, religious instruction could be given to Muslim children only secretly and illegally in underground schools.

In 1928 the Communist Party and the Soviet administration launched a great anti-Islamic campaign which lasted until the outbreak of the Second World War. Practically all government institutions took an active part in the fight against Islam, especially the educational establishment, from the kindergarten to the university, and all Party organizations—the Komsomol, the trade unions, and, most important of all, a communist front organization, the "Union of Godless Zealots." During the anti-Islamic offensive most mosques were closed and converted to cinemas, clubs, garages, and other public uses, "at the demand of the toilers." Their number fell from 26,279 in 1912 (not counting the emirate of Bukhara and the khanate of Khiva) to 1,312 in 1942. Muslim clerics were persecuted as "parasites," "counter-revolutionaries" and, from 1935, as "spies in the pay of Germany and Japan." Their numbers were reduced from 45,339 in 1912 to probably fewer than 2,000 in 1942. At the same time Moscow officially prohibited two of the five basic rituals of Islam: the *hajj* or pilgrimage to Mecca and the payment of *zakat* (alms), and strongly attacked a third, the Ramadan fast.

During the war, the Soviet government was for obvious reasons obliged to modify its anti-Islamic strategy. An era of relative religious liberalism was introduced by Stalin in 1942 and lasted until his death in 1953. A concordat was signed with Abdurrahman Rasulaev, one of the few surviving Tatar *ulema*, which granted Soviet Muslims an official religious organization: the four Muslim Spiritual Directorates. However, during the twelve years of détente which followed, the attitude of the Communist Party toward Islam did not change, and antireligious propaganda was not abandoned, although its character was modified. It became (or claimed to become) more "scientific" than anticlerical. In particular all personal attacks against Muslim clerics ceased.

Khrushchev's era (1953–1964) was marked in all the Muslim republics by a new anti-Islamic campaign which was once again both antireligious and anticlerical though less vigorous than the onslaught of the 1930s. The leaders of the official Islamic hierarchy were seldom criticized and never attacked personally. The new offensive, conducted under the slogan "Back to Lenin" (that is, to the doctrinal purity of early Bolshevism), was the joint endeavor of the Communist Party and of the state administration. Its avowed aim was the complete destruction of Islam (and other religions as well) in one generation. The number of "working" mosques was dramatically reduced, from around 1,500 in 1953 to fewer than 500 in 1964, but the overall results of the campaign were disappointing. According to Soviet surveys published after the downfall of Khrushchev, far from eradicating the religious feelings of the Muslim population forever, it gave an impulse to the various conservative and radical religious trends and currents which form "parallel" Islam.

A change took place in the late 1960s. Once again, under Brezhnev, atheism assumed a "scientific" outlook. Direct attacks on official

Muslim clerics disappeared from the Soviet press. Relations between the official Islamic hierarchy and the Soviet government became not only "normal" but friendly. In the late 1960s, Moscow inaugurated what was sometimes called in the West "Brezhnev's Islamic strategy"—collaboration between the government and the leaders of the four Spiritual Muslim Directorates, represented by Ziauddin Babakhanov, the *mufti* of Tashkent and chairman of the Spiritual Directorate for Central Asia and Kazakhstan. Soviet *muftis* played the role of itinerant ambassadors abroad, especially in the conservative Muslim states otherwise closed to Soviet influence such as Saudi Arabia, Jordan, Kuwait, and Morocco, and were hosts to numerous international Islamic conferences in Soviet Central Asia. The aim of the "Islamic strategy" was, and still is, to project to the Muslim world abroad the image of the USSR as the "best friend of Islam," a country prepared to act in concert with other Muslim countries against their common enemies, the Americans, the Israelis, and the Chinese. In 1980, cooperation between the Soviet government and the *muftis* was further strengthened when Muslim leaders began to be integrated into various nonreligious political front organizations active in the Muslim world abroad, such as "Soviet Afro-Asian Solidarity," "Peace Partisans," and the numerous "Soviet Friendship and Cultural Relations Societies" in foreign countries. Around 1968, the Soviet Administration started a new campaign—which is still going on—against the so-called "illegal activities" of "parallel Islam," in particular the sufi brotherhoods. From 1968 onward, the Soviet authorities began to treat Islam as two different entities.

Cooperation is continuing today but, after 1985, Gorbachev's administration became either more suspicious of its partners or more doubtful about the general usefulness of the "Islamic strategy." Visits of Soviet *muftis* abroad have become less frequent and only a few foreign Mulsim delegations have been invited to visit Central Asia. Moreover, Soviet-Islamic partnership and cooperation did not modify the basic hostility of the Communist Party to all religions, including Islam; the anti-Islamic propaganda was never discarded even during the heyday of the "Islamic strategy" in the 1970s. After 1980, it became more violent in Central Asia especially, probably because of the effects the war in Afghanistan and the Islamic Revolution in Iran had on Soviet Muslims. Today there is a huge gap between Soviet claims of support for the Muslim world at large and the treatment of Soviet Muslims at home, but this dual and contradictory policy toward Islam is still possible and "paying" because the Muslim world abroad is ignorant of and generally indifferent toward the real conditions of Soviet Islam.

The Communist Party and Islam

The relations between Islam and the Soviet State are *political*; those between the Communist Party and Islam are *ideological*. Soviet theoreticians have repeatedly insisted that it is not possible to build communism and to create a new communist man without real equality between Russians and Muslims within the framework of the socialist system. This could not be envisaged until *all* had freed themselves from the psychological hangovers of the past. They have also stated that the adherence of believers to the judicial and moral code of Islam distinguishes them from the Russians by erecting unbreakable psychological barriers between them.

For this reason communist leaders have considered themselves totally committed by their doctrine to a ceaseless fight against all religions—"false ideologies in the service of exploiting classes"; Lenin personally was a fanatical adversary of all religions. Tactically the Soviet State could accept a temporary compromise with an ecclesiastical hierarchy, but from the beginning the Communist Party was rigidly, adamantly hostile to any compromise, even a short-lived one, with its clerical adversaries. Marxism-Leninism—a "scientic doctrine" as it is proclaimed time and again—and religious "non-scientific ideologies" are absolutely incompatible and irreconcilable; they cannot coexist peacefully. Therefore the Communist party cannot remain indifferent or neutral toward religion, and it cannot cooperate with religious hierarchy. It must fight it and defeat it. For the communist, religion cannot be "a private matter."

It is significant that the Communist Party draws no dialectical distinction between the official (loyal) Islam and the nonofficial (hostile) Islam. They are treated equally as ideological enemies, and several Soviet experts on Islam have pointed out that a liberal *mullah* pretending to be loyal and even submissive to the regime may in the long run be more dangerous than a religious fanatic.

The anti-Muslim propaganda of the Communist party is not directed against any specific form of Islam, official or "parallel." Its themes have not varied much since the Revolution. They may be divided into two main groups.

Certain arguments are directed against all religions. Islam is the "opium of the toiling masses, distracting them from the struggle against the native exploiters and the foreign colonialists and imperialists"; it inculcates in man the spirit of resignation and humility, thus "diverting him from revolutionary activity." "It has always played and is still playing a reactionary role, being an instrument for the spiritual oppression of the toilers." "It is a false anti-scientific creed" projecting the dream of paradise into an "imaginary other world." It is a "hangover from the pre-socialist past," a "medieval survival doomed to disappear." These arguments, already used before the Revolution by Russian and foreign Marxists, are still repeated in official antireligious publications and constitute the basis of atheistic education for everybody.

Other arguments are used specifically against Islam and can be divided into six main types:

1. Islam is not a "national religion" but a foreign one brought to Central Asia and the Caucasus by imperialist alien invaders, Arabs, Iranians, or Ottoman Turks.
2. In the past Islam has always had a strong anti-Russian character, "though this did not prevent its leaders from being entirely submissive to the reactionary Tsarist regime."
3. Islam is the most conservative and reactionary and the least "social" of all world religions. It sanctifies the authority of the elders and humiliates women. It inculcates in its followers fanaticism and intolerance.
4. Islam is xenophobic; it sets "believers" against "infidels" and is therefore a major obstacle to friendship between different peoples of the Soviet Union.
5. Islamic customs and rites are un-hygienic. Circumcision and fasting during the month of Ramadan are "primitive, barbaric, and unhealthy."
6. Islamic morals deeply-rooted in the popular consciousness of the masses and of the elites are opposed to communist morals.

The Party has never accepted any compromise between communism and Islam either public or private. It has always condemned attempts to establish an accommodation, even a temporary one, with Islam. Today the hostility of the Communist Party toward Islam is even greater than in the early years of the Soviet regime because Marxism has ceased to be a conquering revolutionary creed to which people adhered with enthusiasm, while Islam is undergoing an intellectual and spiritual revival and appears more dynamic than ever. A striking illustration of the Soviet dual approach to Islam was recently given in the *Komsomoletz Usbekistana*, the organ of the Central Committee of the Communist Youth Organization of Uzbekistan. This article reproduces a dialogue between a woman believer and an antireligious propagandist:

woman: "The Soviet authorities do not punish us for believing in Allah?"

propagandist: "True, you are not punished."

woman: "Does it mean that the Soviet State is not opposed to our religion?"

propagandist: "The answer is clear and brief. It is opposed because religion obscures our brain and makes us lose all contacts with reality."[1]

The inroads Islam is making today among indigenous communist cadres and among the intellectual elite have recently been denounced several times at the highest level, and by Mikhail Gorbachev himself, who, speaking in November 1986 in Tashkent, attacked "those communist and senior officials who pretend to defend our communist morals and ideals, but in fact help to promote backward views and themselves take part in religious [Islamic] ceremonies." In the 1920s it was the Muslims who joined the Communist Party; today it is the communists who are being "contaminated" by Islam.

Since 1986 in all the Central Asian republics, special meetings of the local Communist Parties have been devoted to the question of "ideological work," in particular to the urgent need to fight Islam. For instance, in Uzbekistan First Secretary Usmankhojaev reminded his listeners of "the necessity to strengthen atheist education and overcome harmful religious survivals. Over recent years this work has weakened."[2] Usmankhojaev went on to catalogue a whole list of phenomena still to be found in Uzbekistan, including the activities of non-registered and "parasitical" *mullahs*; the spread of religious cassettes and video films; the construction of mosques with state funds and building materials; the participation of communist and Komsomol members in religious rites; violation of laws by many religious activists, "and the fact that many officials turn a blind eye to all this."

The Official Islamic Establishment and Soviet Power

The Soviet government has one religious policy applied to all religions, whether they have a regular hierarchy, such as the various Christian churches and the Buddhists, or whether they are decentralized and have no ecclesiastical hierarchy, as in the case of Muslims and Jews. During the Second World War, Soviet Islam was endowed with an official administration. The Soviet government thus followed the tradition of Imperial Russia. The official Muslim administration was modeled on the old Central Spiritual Muslim Directorate for European Russia and Siberia created by Catherine II in 1783 in Orenburg.

Through this administration, Soviet authorities expect to control the spiritual and also the political life of believers. It is divided into four Muslim Spiritual Boards (*Musul'manskie Dukhovnye Upravleniya*): Tashkent for Central Asia and Kazakhstan; Ufa for European Russia and Siberia; Makhach-Qala for Northern Caucasus and Daghestan; and Baku for the Shia Community of the USSR and the Sunni Community of Transcaucasia.

The two first are Sunni of the Hanafi *madhab*, the third, Sunni of the Shaf'i *madhab*, and the last mixed Sunni, Hanafi and Shia (Twelvers). Each board is autonomous in administrative and legal matters. The chairmen (*muftis* on the Sunni Boards, a *Shaykh al-Islam* on the Shia board of Baku) and the executive staff are a homogeneous group. They are young, have received excellent professional training, and are often of outstanding intellectual ability. The official Islamic establishment is heir to the brilliant pre-Revolutionary modernist, liberal (*jadid*), reformist movement which endeavored, as early as the late nineteenth century, to reconcile Islam with science and progress in order to guarantee its survival in any political environment, including a socialist one. Official Islam is served by a group of fewer than 2,500 "registered" mullahs, professional clerics appointed and paid by the four Muslim Spiritual Boards. They control all the "working" mosques (450 at most), nearly all of them located in the cities, and the two religious education institutions (the *madrasas* of "Mir-i Arab" in Bukhara and "Ismail al-Bukhari" in Tashkent). The Tashkent Spiritual Board is the only one of the four boards to have a regular publishing activity. It produces a quarterly review, *Muslims of the Soviet East*, in six editions: Arabic, Uzbek (in Arabic script), English, French, Persian, and Dari, an excellent propaganda publication, unavailable to Soviet Muslims. The Tashkent Board has also published several editions of the Quran and two collections of *hadith*. Its other activities are modest: no *Sharia* courts are left, and there is no *waqf* to administer, and all social and economic activity is strictly forbidden. The intellectual and spiritual life of the "working mosques" is limited to prayers within the mosque and to the preaching of the *imam-khatibs*.

It is impossible to evaluate precisely the contribution of "official" Islam to the preservation of religion among the Muslims of the Soviet Union, but it is obvious that official Islam alone could not maintain religious feelings among the masses. Without the activity of "parallel"

Islam, religion in Central Asia and in the Caucasus would have relapsed into ignorance.

The official Islamic hierarchy seems to be totally loyal to the Soviet State, and during the last ten years loyalty has reached the limits of submissiveness. Its leaders are honored members of the Soviet *Nomenklatura*. They never protest against or even mention the violence of antireligious propaganda. They never allow themselves the slightest criticism of Marxism-Leninism. On the contrary, since the war they have constantly proclaimed the perfect happiness of Soviet Islam. They also help Soviet propaganda by attacking all those abroad who criticize the antireligious character of the Soviet regime. But their cooperation with the Soviet State—and not with the Communist Party—is that of "partners," not of simple "agents" or "instruments." They have taken advantage of the religious "détente" to create around the four Spiritual Boards a kind of "general staff" of intellectually well-trained Muslim *ulema*, some of them graduates of Al-Azhar University. By serving the regime as propagandists in the world at large and as "moderators" in Central Asia, the Soviet *muftis* are preserving the existence of a basic but necessary religious establishment without which popular "parallel" Islam might have relapsed into superstition and shamanism. Moreover, all the leaders of official Islam, even the most submissive, remain perfectly orthodox from the point of view of Islamic dogma. They have never tried (contrary to some Muslim thinkers abroad) to conciliate Marxism and Islam, and when they accept socialism it is as a technique of power or as a program of economic, social, or political management, never as a rival ideology.

Toward "parallel" Islam, the position of the official Muslim leaders is ambiguous because their maneuvering room is limited. By pushing their partnership with the Soviet power too far or by making their submission to the regime too obvious, they would antagonize an important proportion of believers and push them toward the underground sufi brotherhoods, provoking a rift which both trends— official and parallel—are anxious to avoid. For this reason they resist the continuous pressure of the Soviet authorities to oblige them to condemn "parallel" Islam as illegal and "un-Islamic." But, until today, only a few *fatwas* have been issued by the *muftis* condemning some marginal practices of sufism, such as the presence of women at *zikr* ceremonies or the pilgrimage to the so-called "holy places."

The attitude of the Soviet authorities toward official Islam is also ambiguous. In spite of its fundamental hostility toward all religions, the Communist Party does not seem to wish the complete disappearance of the Islamic hierarchy. This is owing not only to the usefulness of the *muftis* domestically and abroad, but also to the knowledge that total destruction of the official hierarchy, far from favoring the progress of atheism, would rather reinforce underground "parallel" Islam. For the time being it seems that, in this unusual partnership, each party believes that time is on its side and that it will be the final beneficiary. For the Soviet authorities Islam—a simple leftover of the pre-socialist era—is doomed to disappear sooner or later; for the Muslims, communism, a false creed (*kufr*), cannot compete with the eternal truth of Islam.

The position of official Islam remains ambiguous not only toward Soviet power but also toward the believers. This is owing to the fact that Soviet authorities treat the leaders of official Islam as authentic ecclesiastical authorities, which of course they are not. The four *muftis* are treated like the archbishops of the Russian Orthodox Church, and the *mufti* of Tashkent, Shamsuddin Babakhanov, is supposed to play the role of Patriarch Pimen. But since Islam is a religion without regular "clergy," when a *mufti* expresses his opinion on legal or political matters, he does so on his own behalf and does not commit the community of the believers who may or may not follow his lead.

"Parallel" Islam and Soviet Power

"Parallel," non-official, popular Islam is an informal establishment, more powerful and more deeply rooted among the pople than the official hierarchy, but it is difficult to describe. It includes all those whom Soviet sources call "the convinced" or "fanatical" believers and who represent, according to Soviet sources, around 10 percent of the Muslim population of the country. They refuse to accept the idea that religion has become a "private matter" and want to live in a world ruled by the precepts of Islam. They are hostile to communism (because of its atheistic character), to the Russian presence, and to Soviet rule. Soviet islamicists describe them as an "antisocial," "reactionary" force. Far from losing their dynamism, these "fanatics" have shown a greater aggressiveness in recent years, especially since the invasion of Afghanistan. As a typical example we may mention the case of a sufi *shaykh* arrested in August 1986 in the Tajik city of Kurgan-Tübe for organizing public prayers for the victory of the Afghan Mojahidin and calling for the creation of an "Islamic State" in Tajikistan.[3] Another typical explosion of "fanaticism" took place in the town of Garm in central Tajikistan where a group of "fanatical clerics" (*mullahs*) gathered copies of the republican newspaper *Tojikistoni Sovieti* (which had published antireligious material) and publicly set fire to them.[4]

The "fanantics" of "parallel" Islam represent a heterogeneous group: one can find among them conservative believers of the older generation who think that, in order to live their religion, they must drive the "infidel" invaders out and build a theocratic state sanctified by *Sharia* law, and also representatives of the younger generation. Soviet sources wrongly call the latter "Wahhabis." They are often Komsomol or even Communist Party members, technicians, engineers, blue- and white-collar workers, teachers, who have rediscovered Islam after becoming disillusioned with Marxism-Leninism. Their ideology may be compared to that of the Afghan fundamentalists of the *Jamiat-i Islami* (rather than to the Arab "Muslim Brothers"). They believe that Islam must become a dynamic *political* and not only spiritual force.

A third component of the non-official Islamic Establishment represented by the adepts of the sufi brotherhoods (*tariqa*). These are closed but not wholly secret societies, well structured and hierarchic, with an iron discipline based on the personal submission of the disciple to his master and together by absolute dedication to a religious ideal. In Russia and in the Soviet Union their historical role has been to oppose foreign "infidel" rule and to preserve the purity of Islam. Three main brotherhoods dominate "parallel" Islam: the *Naqshbandiya*, the most important, particularly strong in eastern Caucasus, Daghestan and all Central Asia; the *Qadiriya* ("Kunta Haji" in Soviet literature) in the Chechen-Ingush republic, and, since the war, in Southern Kazakhstan; and the *Yasawiya* in Kirghizia, in the Ferghana Valley and in Kazakhstan.

Sufi orders are outlawed and operate completely outside the control of Soviet authorities and of the official Muslim administration. It is as a result of their constant acitivity that Islam has survived as a religion and as a way of life. Where "official" Islam is inadequate or absent (especially in the rural area), it is supplemented or replaced by the sufi orders. The adepts of the *tariqa* perform the essential family rites (circumcision, marriage, burial) and run the numerous clandestine houses of prayer and religious schools. They also conduct a counter-propaganda against official atheism. Sufi brotherhoods are not small chapels but mass organizations, especially in North Caucasus. In 1975 a Soviet expert, V. G. Pivovarov, calculated that half of the believers in North Caucasus belonged to a sufi brotherhood, which corresponds to at least a quarter of a million adepts.[5]

For the last ten years and especially since the invasion of Afghanistan, Soviet antireligious propaganda has been directed mainly against sufi Islam, a fact which testifies to its hold on the population. Sufi *turuq* are accused of maintaining a high level of "obscurantism" among the population, and of being the focal point for spiritual and political opposition to Marxism and to Russian rule. Soviet authorities know that in Islam spiritual, national, and political notions are tightly interwoven. They know that the militant ideology of Sufism helps to maintain in the Islamic community the idea that "we" (Muslims) are different and therefore opposed to "them" (Russians), thus encouraging feelings of pan-Islamic solidarity with the Muslim world abroad, and first of all with the Afghans fighting the "Shuravi."

Although the leading figures of "parallel" Islam (the *shaykhs* of the sufi orders) are unconditionally hostile to the Soviet regime, they are remarkably tolerant towards representatives of "official" Islam. To our knowledge they have never attacked them publicly.

Conclusion

Such is in its broadest outlines the complicated and paradoxical relationship between the dual Soviet power and the two faces of Islam in the USSR. The real picture is even more complicated. It is necessary to take into account the specific character of each Muslim region. In some areas, for instance in Daghestan and in Central Caucasus where the sufi *turuq* completely dominate religious life, the "official" clerics are obliged to model themselves on the more conservative elements of "parallel" Islam. In territories of former nomadism, in particular in Turkmenistan, Kazakhstan and Kirghizia, popular sufi Islam is still deeply linked to the clan and tribal structure of native society. Elsewhere, in Uzbekistan and in Tajikistan for instance, where tribal structure disappeared long ago, the official Islamic establishment is stronger and exercises a greater influence on the population. We must also take into account that for the last ten years Muslims of the Soviet Union have been receiving a constant flow of oral (radio broadcasts and tapes) and written propaganda from abroad which reminds them that they belong to the *Dar al-Islam* rather than to the Soviet Union. We know that this propaganda finds a favorable response.

The main problem of the future may be formulated as follows: How long can the Soviets pursue their contradictory strategy toward Islam, cooperating with an obedient but weak official religious hierarchy while trying to destroy a powerful popular Islam? How long can they favor anti-imperialistic Islamic movements abroad when these are anti-American or anti-Israeli, while fighting similar movements when they are anti-Soviet? Such a strategy was possible as long as Central Asia was protected by a tight Iron Curtain. Is it still possible today in an era of radio broadcasts and tapes?

— 6 —

Islam, Secularism, and Ethnic Identity in the Sudan

M. W. Daly

In April 1985 the Sudan enjoyed a brief moment in the international spotlight when its ruler since 1969, Jaafar Muhammad Nimeiri, was overthrown by his generals after a week of popular demonstrations against the regime. By mid-1987 an elected civilian government had come to power, and the famine of 1984-1985 had given way to abundant harvests. But in the southern region of the country a civil war continued to rage, pitting the forces of the Sudan People's Liberation Movement against those of the government. At stake was the future of the Sudan, Africa's largest country and a much-discussed microcosm of the African and Afro-Arab worlds. The struggle involves competing nationalisms, religion, ideology, ethnicity and "tribalism," personal and political ambitions, an awakening class consciousness, and, indeed, opposing visions of history. How the conflict is resolved is important; that it is resolved in all its parts is essential if the Sudan is to enjoy more than a respite from the cycle of bloodshed.

The problem of identity is as acute in the Sudan as it is anywhere in the Afro-Arab world. The civil war that has been under way since 1983, no less than that which lasted from 1955 to 1972, has as one of its principal causes fundamentally opposing views of what it means or should mean to be a Sudanese. These form bases for historical visions that are incompatible. It is for this reason that settlement of the civil war is unlikely along lines similar to those followed in the Addis Ababa Agreement in 1972; much more is seen to be at stake than constitutional formulas and degrees of power-sharing. Resolution of the conflict may therefore involve a major change in the social and political structure of the Sudan, and may in turn influence national politics and nation-building elsewhere in the region.

It is still possible (although increasingly imprecise because of demographic changes) to consider the Northern Sudanese as essentially

Arabized, Arabic-speaking Muslims, and the Southern Sudanese as mainly African, non-Arabic-speaking non-Muslims. (Important exceptions include the Beja, the Fur, and the Nubians, among others.) The dominant riverain Northern Sudanese have in the past placed great importance on their Arab ancestry, however problematic that is, a phenomenon facilitated by the patriarchal nature of their society and the relative unimportance of color in determining ethnicity. The political and economic history of the modern period has resulted in the creation from among them of an elite that is open only on its own cultural and religious terms. Thus a Muslim Northerner can take a non-Muslim Southern wife, and their children, raised as Muslims, will be "Arabs" in the sense that their father is. Since Islam forbids the marriage of Muslim women and non-Muslim men, an equivalent process of assimilation to non-Arab identity cannot occur. It has therefore been postulated, not unconvincingly, that a natural process of assimilation will inevitably result in the emergence of a Sudanese "norm" closely approximating today's Northern Sudanese identity. Recent attempts by various interested individuals and groups to posit the existence of an "Afro-Arab" identity have remained the stuff of academic discussion rather than of personal or corporate identity: while a Northern riverain Sudanese might off-handedly recognize his "Afro-Arab" ancestry, no Dinka or Shilluk, Bari or Azande will or can. That the Sudan as a whole is *becoming* "Afro-Arab" is another matter, viewed with satisfaction or dismay, accepted as a process of history or condemned as cultural imperialism.

The absense of a convincing alternative to this norm in the Sudan as a whole and within both the North and the South contributes to its appearance of inevitability. It was in part a perception of Southerners' inability to withstand the cultural colossus of Islam that underpinned the "Southern Policy" of the British colonial regime in the 1930s and 1940s. Then it was felt that limiting if not barring altogether the influence of Arabic and Islam would give Southern peoples time to strengthen their own indigenous institutions and compete with the North. That this feeling was hardly supported by money and imagination ensured the failure of a policy which was in any case regressive, defeatist, and insufficiently grounded in an awareness of local history — the Nilotic peoples have, after all, "withstood" Islam for centuries. Thus the colonial period witnessed neither measures to force assimilation nor effective steps to forge a Southern "national" identity as an alternative to assimilation. A sense of separateness remained, however, unsupported by positive development but buttressed by constant reminders of the nineteenth-century slave trade and by the facts of cultural, linguistic, and religious differences.

The adoption of Islam in the Northern Sudan occurred over centuries. In the modern era the process was accelerated and partly controlled by vibrantly aggressive and competitive *sufi tariqas*, which provided an institutional nexus for their members in the social and economic as well as religious spheres. This important subject, extremely complex and little understood, has only recently attracted the attention of scholars. Certainly the spread of sufism, especially during the nineteenth-century Turco-Egyptian occupation, was a factor in the integration of the Northern Sudan and its continuing contact with the larger world beyond. Controversy has surrounded the fact that Islam had not then extended to what is now called the Southern Sudan. Geographic reasons, especially the barrier posed by the swamps of the upper Nile, are most usually adduced but are unconvincing alone; the apparent cultural imperviousness of Nilotic peoples like the Shilluk and Dinka is a sounder explanation, and one that has continuing relevance long after mere geographical obstacles have fallen.

The Mahdist revolution of 1881-1885 had complex motivations. Beyond the charismatic appeal of Muhammad Ahmad, the Mahdi, lay dissatisfaction with the Turco-Egyptian regime's taxation and attempts to suppress the slave trade, the disgruntlement of *sufis* at their supersession by official *ulama*, and resentment of foreign, Christian administrators (of whom General Gordon is only the most famous). Above all, the regime itself was decrepit, immobilized by incompetence and corruption in the Sudan and by revolution and foreign occupation in Egypt itself. The success of the revolution and of the theocratic states it spawned was and is nevertheless a powerful factor in the mythology of Sudanese nationalism; it was an era when the Sudan experienced a brief independence from foreign domination and experimented with an "Islamic State." In the Southern Sudan, however, the period was one of great insecurity and violence, as the old regime fell but the new one was unable to assert itself. Thus, what is recalled by some as a golden age of national independence is seen by others as a time of unrestricted Arab depredation against Africans; in such a context present-day "Islamic revivalism" is of course even more highly-charged than it might otherwise be.

The Anglo-Egyptian conquest of the Mahdist State in 1896-1898 imposed a regime which ironically had more institutional commitment to Islam than to Christianity. If anything, the early British administrators of the Condominium had an exaggerated fear of Muslim "fanaticism," viewing the Mahdia as only a particularly devastating outbreak of an endemic disease. They therefore took steps to conciliate Muslim orthodoxy and quietism and to suppress Mahdism and other apparently similarly dangerous cults. One such step was the prohibition of Christian missionary activity in the North, and its limitation, really banishment, to the non-Muslim South. There European Catholic and Protestant missionaries, most notably the Verona Fathers and the Church Missionary Society, established themselves largely with the sufferance of the government but without its material or even, in many cases, moral support. During the first generation education was left entirely to missionaries, and after that was still dominated by them. The result was the production of a small, educated Southern elite, largely Christian and speaking English as well as Arabic and their own native tongues.

The British "Southern Policy" was a focus of Sudanese nationalist opposition from the late 1930s onwards, as the newly politicized Northern elite viewed with suspicion any British attempts to foster paternalism. The possible political separation of the South and its amalgamation with British East African dependencies was seldom if ever discussed seriously, but the nationalists can hardly be blamed for having discerned this as an ultimate goal of British policy. Although "Southern Policy " was ostensibly reversed in 1947, and the British thereafter took steps to ensure the integration of the South in the Sudan, various episodes during the rush to independence a decade later engendered continuing suspicion of British intentions in the South. One may well understand the opposing views; British administrators, especially those with long personal experience in the South, viewed independence without constitutional "safeguards" for Southerners as a betrayal of trust and the handing-over of innocents to the clutches of dogmatic Muslim nationalists and venal petty traders. The Northern politicians, on their part, saw independence as vindicating their determination to maintain the Sudan's territorial integrity and as a removal of an artificial barrier to the progress of Islam. In other words, just as the British viewed "Southern Policy" as a failure, Northern politicians and others saw it as having successfully interposed a break in the long historical progress of Islamization, Arabization, and hence of Sudanization. It is not suprising that after independence the Khartoum government, dominated by the Northern elite, tried to allow and even to force the resumption of that process.

However one judges "Southern Policy," it is clear that it did not prepare the South for a separate political existence. The regime had remained Arabic-speaking. The South's land communications were not reoriented from the Nile and the Red Sea. Almost no real economic development, on the success of which the region's "independence" would have depended, was undertaken, and after an initial regularizing of chiefs' powers, little political advance was attempted. Thus the effect of "Southern Policy" was almost entirely negative. Whether or not it "saved" the region from Islam is debateable: the alleged goal of making the South less dependent on the North was unmatched by efforts to allow the South to become more dependent on itself. The result was the reinforcement of a cultural watershed: in the North, Sudanese political consciousness was fed by the springs of Arab nationalism as it was emerging in the Middle East; on the other side of the divide was an embryonic Southern identity deriving its strength from other sources.

It is entirely to the Northern Sudan, in fact, that we must look for the roots of Sudanese nationalism, the development of the movement in the 1930s, and its successful confrontation with foreign rule in the early 1950s. Although Northern politicians paid lip-service to the rights of Southerners and nourished fears of British intentions in the region, still Sudanese nationalism was conceptually dependent upon the shared political and social experience of the Muslim Arab North, and could be broadened only at the cost of its real psychological and historical content. Indeed, the symbols and myths around which Northern Sudanese could unite to demand an end to colonial rule were themselves seen by educated Southerners as reminders and harbingers of an "internal colonialism." The solution that has presented itself most obviously since (and even before) independence has been the assimilation of Southern peoples through Arabicization, exogamy, and Islamization. As one foreign observer has put it, "The issue of biological inter-mingling when coupled with cultural assimilation has to be regarded as an important dimension in the slow process of nation-building".[1] Will the upheavals of the last thirty years rekindle and accelerate a "process" which many Sudanese believe was artificially curtailed by British imperialism?

A difficulty lies in the strong association of Islam and Sudanese national politics and hence the dominant view of Sudanese national identity. Although the nationalist movement in its origins was secular, its leaders soon discovered that mass support could be won only by appealing to the leaders of popular Islam. These then took over the movement. Thus in the 1940s and 1950s Sudanese politics was dominated by the sectarian rivalry of the Mahdists under Sayyid Abd al-Rahman al-Mahdi and the Khatmiyya *tariqa* under Sayyid Ali al-Mirghani. The Mahdist political party, the Umma, promoted "the Sudan for the Sudanese," while its rivals, the unionists, campaigned for the

Unity of the Nile Valley or political union with Egypt. The unionists usually but not always or automatically had the support of the Khatmiyya. Occasional attempts to break the dynastic and sectarian mold of Sudanese politics failed. The extent to which prominent unionists, especially their leader, Ismail al-Azhari, used unionism only as a tactic to win Egyptian support, has been uncertain, but the fact remains that it was a unionist government under him that led the Sudan to independence in 1956.

The achievement of independence may have come too easily to sustain the momentum of Sudanese nationalism.[2] Although the last decade of the Condominium was punctuated by demonstrations and strikes, these were often formal and symbolic, not spontaneous expressions of popular fury. Relations between British officials and nationalist leaders usually remained polite; Sudanese politicians early distinguished between private views and public pronouncements. There were few sentences of imprisonment for prominent nationalists, there was no opposition-in-exile, and for martyrs the movement had to recall the officers of 1924 who, however, had certainly not died for Sudanese independence.[3] Furthermore, the dominance of sectarianism had prevented the emergence of ideologically-based parties: the Sudanese communist party, though relatively strong, could not compete; the Muslim Brothers went almost unnoticed even by government police. There was, therefore, no clear vision of what to do once independence was achieved, and no one party or personality strong enough to impose a program.

Although no tribe or sect dominated Sudanese politics after independence, the succession to power clearly passed to a certain group or class, the Muslim Arab elite of the Northern riverain region. Sectarian loyalty allowed them a broad electoral appeal, even (or especially) in undeveloped and impoverished areas like the west. But to the Southern Sudanese the Northern parties offered little. In exchange for its parliamentary support of independence in 1955 the South was promised consideration of a federal system for the Sudan, to preserve cultural identity and minority rights and to decentralize poliical power. After independence the idea was summarily rejected by the Northern parties. Similarly, Sudanization of the administration led to the virtual exclusion of Southerners from all but a few subordinate posts; this was bitterly resented by the tiny Southern educated elite and seen generally as proof of Northern intentions. An air of mistrust, to which sullen British administrators contributed as they prepared reluctantly to leave, exploded in mutiny in August 1955. Peace was not to be fully restored to the Sudan until 1972.

The policies pursued in the South by both parliamentary regimes (1956-1958, 1965-1969) and military governments (1958-1964, 1969-1985) were essentially similar. Although the period to 1972 was especially clouded by disaffection and then civil war in the South, the entire post-colonial experience has common elements: continuing underdevelopment of the South (and other peripheral regions); a concentration of political and economic power in the hands of the Northern metropolitan elite; the collaboration of traditional elements in the Southern leadership in exchange for posts, titles, and money; emphasis on the forging of national unity, but with a shallow base of slogans and occasional highly-publicized development projects; and a continuing die-hard separatist sentiment in the South, sometimes dormant, sometimes bursting to the surface. The first parliamentary regime and especally the military government of General Abboud (1958-1964) pursued policies clearly designed to speed a process of nation-building that were, however, the very subjects of Southern grievance: Arabicization of education, government-financed construction of mosques and other Muslim institutions, expulsion of foreign Christian missionaries, and so forth. Thus by insisting on a "Northern" view of the Sudanese future the government unwittingly strengthened an embryonic Southern identity, and further impositions from Khartoum served to emphasize the differences between the regions.

The political history of what became a civil war need not be detailed, but some general observations help in understanding subsequent developments. First, Khartoum governments, whether civilian or military, preferred a military solution to one which might allow a real sharing of political and economic power. Indeed, the central government made blatant efforts to spread Islam and the use of Arabic in the region, seemingly careless of public opinion and intent on "victory" rather than consent. Second, although avowedly separatist (a fact ironically stressed in the propaganda of both sides), the Southern movement in fact contained a spectrum of political views but was united in unwillingness to accept Northern domination; thus compromise was possible. Third, Southern-ness was an inadequate ideological base on which to unite the people or confront the regime: the absence of ideology led to a frequent recrudescence of ethnic chauvinism and personal political ambitions. Finally, although a number of Southern politicians, both in Khartoum and in exile, gained prominence, the leadership of the Anya Nya guerrilla forces remained separate until a military and political alliance was forged under their commander, Joseph Lagu. Thus the period witnessed no real change in attitude toward the South among Northern politicians, but did see the emergence, after years of internal division, of a united Southern political movement.

The continuing vitality of sectarianism in the Muslim North had been a major determinant of national politics even during the second parliamentary regime of 1964-1969. The absence of a strong secular political party meant that the two main rivals, the Umma and the unionists, tried to outbid each other for conservative Muslim support. Thus, for instance, they repeatedly agreed on the need for an "Islamic" consititution and fought endlessly over details lest one be enacted. The emergence of the Muslim Brothers, more radically conservative and permitted by electoral impotence the luxury of irresponsible rabble-rousing, kept pressure on the traditional parties. The Sudanese communist party was banned and its property confiscated in a shameless parliamentary maneuver. In May 1969 an open alliance between the Umma and Khatmiyya leaders was in the making when the now-discredited regime was overthrown in a military coup.

The young officers who took over, led by the thirty-nine-year-old Colonel Jaafar Nimeiri, viewed themselves as radicals bent on overthrowing the traditional Sudanese political and economic system. Enthusiastic and idealistic, they faced, however, the same dilemma as would any Sudanese government lacking automatic sectarian support. The Mahdists were openly hostile; in March 1970 the army invaded their stronghold on Aba Island and massacred its defenders. Their spiritual leader, the Imam al-Hadi al-Mahdi, was killed; the ex-prime minister and leader of the Umma, al-Sadiq al-Mahdi, went into exile. Following a coup attempt in July 1971 the communist party was suppressed and its leaders executed. Nimeiri therefore emerged triumphant over both right and left, but remained dangerously isolated without the backing of any major political grouping.

Nimeiri's regime initially seemed destined to treat the "Southern Problem" as its predecessors had. Highly-publicized declarations of principles were issued, as always more certain in their analysis of past failure than they were imaginative in prescribing solutions. The war in the South continued. It was only after he had eliminated the immediate threat from the Mahdists and the communists that Nimeiri discerned both the opportunity and the need to negotiate seriously with the Southern opposition. The Anya Nya leadership, on its part, recognized a chance for favorable terms. The result was the Addis Ababa Agreement of February 1972, subsequently enshrined in the constitution of the Sudan, by which the South was granted a measure of autonomy. Regional government institutions were established, the Anya Nya guerrilla army was disbanded and amalgamated into the national armed forces, and arrangements were made for accelerated social and economic development programs in the South. Peace brought the return, however, of personal, ethnic, and tribal differences in the South, and these were deftly manipulated by Nimeiri. Southern politicians largely failed to gain for the region the economic progress which their crucial support for Nimeiri should have produced. In the end, regional automony lost much of its meaning in the absence of economic and social progress.

This was recognized as well by young Southern intellectuals as by the power-brokers in Khartoum. Although small in number, the "class" of Southerners who had entered the modern sector through education and labor had had important formative experience during the years of civil war. Many had been educated outside the Sudan, in East Africa, Europe, and the United States. Some began to discern in the politics of the 1970s and early 1980s a "unity" of Northern and Southern interests destructive not only of their African identity but also of an emerging class-consciousness. This realization was reinforced by the cynical maneuvers of Southern politicians, by the failure of economic development plans, and finally by the subordination of important Southern concerns to so-called "national" policies. Thus Nimeiri's country-wide imposition of the *Sharia* in September 1983 marked the final step back to the failed policies of the early post-independence period. Predictably, the South rebelled.

How could Nimeiri have been so foolish as a jettison the Southern prop that had supported his personal position since 1972? The question was often asked, and the answer seems to lie in the fact that the attitudes of the Northern elite, which had only reluctantly accepted the Addis Ababa Agreement, had not really changed then or since. A 1976 coup attempt directed from exile by al-Sadiq al-Mahdi, leader of the old Umma Party, failed only after several days of bloody fighting in the streets of the capital. Although Nimeiri had held on, he could not fail to realize how tenuous his position had become, and how adamant was the opposition of the religious right. He therefore sought to placate and co-opt it in a number of ways. An elaborate "process" of National Reconciliation was undertaken, by which al-Sadiq returned to the Sudan in exchange for concessions. The regime thereafter increasingly took steps toward a more "Islamic" system, steps which culminated in the September Laws of 1983. While one previous government (Abboud's) had fallen as an indirect result of Southern disaffection, none had yet been directly overthrown by it; in other words, the more immediate threat to the regime seemed to come from the religious right, and the reversal of policy toward the South, which had never in any case been popular or convincingly embraced in Khartoum, was the cost of reducing that threat.

The period 1983-1985 witnessed a steady escalation of political and economic crisis in the Sudan. Drought and government cynicism and ineptness led to famine. The precarious economy was battered by falling world prices for the Sudan's commodities, a decline in their production, and mismanagement of their sale. Huge cost overruns in highly-publizied development projects were financed by foreign loans. On the verge of bankruptcy, the government was forced in 1985 to implement unpopular reforms as a price for international economic assistance. As the same time, the campaign to impose the *Sharia* had itself reached a level of shocking lawlessness. Fanatical judges presided over special summary courts, while floggings and amputations were inflicted upon the urban poor. Early in 1985 the seventy-six-year-old leader of the Muslim reformist Republican Brothers, Mahmud Muhammad Taha, was convicted of "heresy" and hanged. All the while, the regime was supported in these steps by the Muslim Brothers, who saw in Nimeiri's growing isolation the opportunity to impose their demands.

While in the Northern Sudan these events were viewed with disgust, in the South they fueled the fires of open rebellion. In 1983 a Sudan People's Liberation Movement was established, calling for the destruction of the regime and the building of a new economic and political order in the Sudan. Insistently anti-separatist, the SPLM and its military arm, the Sudan People's Liberation Army, were portrayed by the regime (and thus by many outside the Sudan) as yet another Southern separatist movement. Winning wide popular support in the South, the SPLM/SPLA soon overran most of the region, holding government forces to the major towns. Secret talks between its leaders and Northern opposition politicians reflected recognition of the movement's potential role in bringing down the regime, but no overt alliance was achieved. The drain on the country's treasury occasioned by the war, coupled with the humiliation of the poorly-equipped and demoralized national army, were major factors in creating the conditions that led to Nimeiri's overthrow.

At the end of March 1985 demonstrations and riots in the capital were followed by a general strike. Nimeiri's generals, acting before he could return from a visit to the United States, announced his overthrow, disbanded the Sudan Socialist Union and other institutions, and formed a Transitional Military Council. Their call to the SPLM to lay down its arms and enter into discussions was rejected as "Nimeirism without Nimeiri.'' Toward the end of April a transitional civilian cabinet was formed of representatives from the old parties and from professionals and labor organizations. Elections were promised within a year. The infamous September Laws, though unenforced, remained in effect.

Attempts during the brief transitional period to organize new political parties along ideological lines failed, and in elections in April 1986 the old parties returned to power. A coalition of the Umma, which had won the largest number of seats, the Democratic Unionists, and a few minor parties, was formed, with the National Islamic Front of the Muslim Brothers as the principal party of opposition. Al-Sadiq al-Mahdi became prime minister, and the functions of head of state were vested in a committee chaired by Ahmed al-Mirghani. The two leading posts in the new regime were thus occupied by leaders of the two great sectarian rivals, the Mahdists and the Khatmiyya. In other ways too traditional politics was restored: token Southern representation in the cabinet; elaborate temporizing over constitutional issues, especially the role of Islam; tediously unimaginative proposals for ending the civil war; inattention to basic economic problems; and so forth.

During the transitional period an Alliance of various parties, unions, and professional bodies had been established. Although attempts to translate the broad but shallow support of the ''modern forces'' into electoral power failed, the Alliance continued to be a focus of hope for political reform. Leading members engaged in discussions with the SPLM, and in March 1986 reached an agreement with the movement at Koka Dam in Ethiopia. This called for the implementation of certian reforms leading to a cease-fire and the convening of a constitutional conference. Among these reforms was abolition of the September Laws, which the new government itself had promised to withdraw but now sought only to ''amend.'' Amid evidence of growing SPLA strength and increasing government efforts at improving its military position, contacts continued outside the Sudan. But the Koka Dam agreement was widely seen as embodying irreducible conditions for real negotiations.

While it is therefore unclear how the political and military situations will develop, some conclusions may be reached about the meaning of the current struggle in the light of the Sudan's modern history.

It is important to realize that the current civil war has some of its roots not merely in regional differences, but in radically opposing views of what those differences really are and what significance they have. In its manifesto and subsequent pronouncements the SPLM/SPLA has stressed a commitment to the unity of the Sudan and explicitly condemned separatism. To many observers, Sudanese and others, this has seemed less than convincing because they have been unwilling to conceive of any issue short of separation as serious enough to engender and sustain a struggle of the magnitude of civil war. But the SPLM/SPLA's announced goal, the creation of a *national* movement that will sweep away the old elitist political and economic structure, receives little attention because it directly threatens the interests of those who have dominated national and international discussion of Sudanese affairs. The SPLM/SPLA's call for unity based on the interests of the vast majority of the people in opposing the current power structure centered at Khartoum is an alternative to the old sectarian, tribal, and linguistic bases of identity.

An example of how the debate has been channeled concerns the very definition of Sudanese identity. Is the Sudan Arab, African, or "Afro-Arab"? The extent to which Sudanese and others have answered "Arab" sometimes surprises onlookers, as does the ease with which the reply "Afro-Arab" has been adopted in intellectual circles in the Sudan and abroad. One scholar has quite rightly argued that the Northern Sudan may be the most representative microcosm of all of Africa—more "African" even than the "African" South — because its people are so clearly of mixed descent. But this reading of history has been too eagerly adopted by others to justify the inevitability of assimilation by calling it something else: "Afro-Arabism." This political version contends that the divisions between North and South are wholly or mainly the creation of imperialism, and that a uniquely Sudanese identity—"Afro-Arab"—can and will emerge.

Proponents of this line tend to ignore or dismiss the obvious contention that Afro-Arabness, as evidenced in the Northern Sudan today, involves a synthesis in which the "Arab" element — Arabic, Arab descent, and Islam — is clearly visible, and in which the "African" element—color and a degree of cultural heritage—is submerged. The experience of independence and long years of North-South conflict have, however, made the popular acceptance of such a device, let alone its internalization, much less likely in the South. Rather, opposition has fostered an alternate identity, and the ideology of the SPLM/SPLA threatens to relegate Afro-Arabism to the status of a slogan, fostered in Khartoum for obvious reasons but irrelevant to the outcome of the Sudan's national crisis.

This does not mean that the Sudan will emerge as a pluralistic society in which religion, mother tongue, and ethnicity are secondary to a new "Sudanese" identity. Acculturation is a result not simply of a central government's policy, but of myriad individual circumstances and decisions involving education, labor, social mobility, belief, and other factors. The SPLM/SPLA has had only limited success thus far in broadening its appeal among non-Southerners. The strength of a secular ideology both as a unifying force and in comparison with ethnicity has shown its failure in the North where, indeed, a growing influence of conservative Muslim groupings has been much-remarked. There may therefore be a hardening of positions under way, in which sectarianism reasserts itself, however briefly, in the North, and separatism is re-adopted, however reluctantly, in the South.

Promulgation of "Islamic" laws and continuing discussion of full implementation of the *Sharia* ensure the continuation of civil war. The *Sharia* is not simply a matter of draconian punishment for certain crimes, but in fact excludes non-Muslims from the full rights of citizenship expected in a modern state: it "does not conceive of the permanent residence of unbelievers within an Islamic state. At best, unbelievers may be allowed to stay under the terms of a special compact which extremely restricts their civil and political rights".[4] As long as Khartoum governments cannot commit themselves unequivocally to non-discrimination, a significant element of the population will remain disaffected.

Furthermore, the fate of the Addis Ababa Agreement ensures that leaders of Southern Sudanese opinion cannot enter into similar arrangements with Khartoum. To do so would invite the repudiation of their own people, who have fought and died for something more than "regional automony." The SPLM manifesto indicates the wariness learned from history: the interest of traditional Southern politicians, it says, "like that of the Northern elite, is self-enrichment." They

> will try to hi-jack the SPLA/SPLM by infiltrating its leadership and taking it over for their own advantage, or, failing to hi-jack the SPLA/SPLM they will try to organize their own political parties similar to those of the 1960s with likely assistance from international reactionaries. The Southern and Northern bourgeoisfied and bureaucratic elites will sometimes be in conflict with each other as they were during the 17 years war, and at times in collusion as they were in 1972 when they concluded the Addis Ababa Agreement. Both will always try to deceive the people by using the nationality and religious questions to further their own advantage and keep the Sudanese people . . . divided and weak.[5]

Thus any solution to the crisis must embody a radical transformation of national politics, not merely delegation or devolution of authority to local elites.

One may conclude by asking how the Sudanese perceive the past, present, and future of their difficulties. Do we witness in the Southern Sudan a futile resistance to assimilation similar to the resistance of African polities to European imperialism? Is such assimilation the ulterior motive of Khartoum governments in the South, in peace as well as in war? Is Islam, as some have suggested, the best hope for building national unity in the Sudan? These are questions that customarily arise from consideration of the "Southern Problem." But other questions are perhaps more pertinent. An awakening class consciousness, expemplified not only by the SPLM but by other political groupings, poses an uncertain threat to the Khartoum elite which has held power since independence. Can that consciousness sustain the pressure exerted by divisive appeals that traditional politics will devise? Can new political groupings, based upon shared interests other than religion, be formed? A definite negative is indicated with reference to the current parliamentary structure inherited from the British and periodically revived. Although the ruling parties and their leaders appear to have changed little, the country has changed despite them. While Muslim Sudanese have voted repeatedly for parties advocating an Islamic consititution, they have also openly supported the coups that drove those parties from power.

Confidently to assess the likelihood of a particular outcome is difficult. The movement is a coalition, and it will be surprising if with time the pressures of setbacks and indeed of success do not widen some areas of disagreement within it. What, for example, will the SPLM/SPLA do if and when it succeeds in bringing the entire South, including Juba, Wau, and other large towns, under its control, but cannot make inroads in the North? Will it then formally declare itself a government, thus in fact if not in law proclaiming separation? There are many arguments favoring or against such a course.

Another factor in assessing the likelihood of complete polarization is the strength of progressive sentiment in the North. The Alliance formed during the crisis that brought down Nimeiri has continued to play a leading role in the search for common ground on which to base a dialogue. Although it has no parliamentary voice, the Alliance has influence far beyond its numbers because it clearly represents the progressive educated elite whose interests none of the traditional political parties seems to represent. That elite has from time to time grown impatient and thrown its support to extra-parliamentary methods. Any government has therefore to take into account the views of the Alliance and, indeed, of other important but underrepresented forces like the trade unions. Still, there has been little indication that the third parliamentary regime has seen a pressing need to make early progress on the nationality question. The time may well have come (or have passed) when a Northern Sudanese political leader must take bold steps to preserve the unity of the state. The more the Northern Sudanese elite tries to impose its vision of Sudanese identity, the less chance it may have to succeed.

This element of compulsion is central to a practical consideration of the political significance of identity in the Sudanese context. In the past, compulsion has been but one of many factors in the Sudanization of the North: trade, religion, education, social mobility, language, and intermarriage have been among other, more powerful and important factors. It is undoubted that, over time, the assimilation of Southern Sudanese peoples into a dominant Sudanese identity could occur through such peaceful means. Violent resistance to such an evolution would be difficult to justify and in any case almost certainly hopeless. But the Sudan would not be the first case of a multi-ethnic state in which the stubborn assertiveness of a ruling minority is itself the main focus of unity among an oppressed majority. Decades of violence and cynical politics have produced just such an alternate process of national growth. A separate and now viable Southern Sudanese identity has to a large extent been the product of a dogmatic and arrogant insistence that it cannot exist.

— 7 —

Privatization of Woman's Role in the Islamic Republic of Iran

Shahin Gerami

The rise of fundamentalism in the Middle East is becoming a widespread reaction to modernization and Westernization policies of the post-World War I era. The 1979 Iranian Revolution and its aftermath continue to surprise Western scholars and defy the application of established models. The rise of Islamic fervor during the Iranian Revolution puzzled many Western social scientists. They watched in disbelief as thousands of Iranian women clad in black chadors poured into the streets to protest against the Westernized Shah and brought to power Ayatollah Khomeini. Women's participation in the anti-Shah movement was baffling for two reasons. First, the gains made on their behalf by the Shah's regime were greater than those of previous governments. Second, theologians were on record as opposing women's participation in public life and as advocating a domesticated life for women. Since the establishment of the Islamic Republic, its leaders have set out to organize society according to the mandate of Islam. The issue of woman's role and her proper place in society is at the heart of this reorganization. It is interesting to note the historical changes that have occurred in that role before and after the Iranian Revolution.

In the literature of the sex role, woman's role is defined in terms of traditional versus modern. "Traditional" refers to the "natural" functions of women, like housekeeping and feminine occupations: teaching, nursing, etc. "Modern" roles are participation in productive occupations outside the home and other positions historically held by men. In modern sex role ascription, housekeeping loses its significance as the "primary" and "natural" role of women. The traditional division of labor historically has been justified by physical differences between sexes and the perceived psychological distinctions due to biological factors. Historically, with industrialization, the growth of capitalism,

99

urbanization, and the advent of the nuclear family, sex role transformation has been from traditional to modern. This trend is more
observable in developed industrial countries than in less developed
countries. While traditional activities have remained the primary
responsibilities of women in many less developed countries, Islamic
societies have shown a higher resistance to publicization of woman's
role. In other words, the degree of seclusion and exclusion of women
from public life in Muslim societies exceeds those in countries with
similar socio-economic conditions. Even in Muslim Middle Eastern
societies that have experienced some changes in woman's role, there
is a trend toward reversing the process and returning woman completely
to her "natural" role. Nowhere is this trend stronger than in the Islamic
Republic of Iran in which the authorities have launched a campaign
of privatization of women's lives. This paper attempts to test this
hypothesis by looking at historical data and providing a comparative
analysis of pre- versus post-revolutionary Iran.

The Islamic Definition of Women's Role

The Islamic Republic of Iran is trying to establish a new social order
based on specifications of Islam in which the readjustment of sex roles
has occupied a central place. In its reorganizational efforts, the
government tries to redefine sex roles based on Islamic mandates and
to reallocate social responsibilities accordingly. Turning against the
modernization of the Shah's period, the government authorities define
woman's role according to the strict interpretation of *Sharia*, which
divides the world of Muslims into private and public spheres—private
refers to home and family, and public to business, politics, and war.
A woman's realm of activity is centered around the family, while men
function in the public sphere.

This division of labor is based on the biological differences between
the sexes and the mythical, though strongly believed, psychological
personalities associated with these biological distinctions. Social
obligations of men and women are based, as one theologian states, on
"the innate and fundamental differences that exist between men and
women."[1] According to most *Sharia* jurists, Allah created man and
woman differently and assigned each a social responsibility based on
his or her mental and physical strengths and capacities. These mental
and physical distinctions and their concomitant social responsibilities
can be summarized as follows:

1. Men are physically stronger than women, thus capable of heavier work required in the public sphere. Furthermore, menstruation, child bearing and nursing hinder woman's functioning outside the home. And because of her emotional nature and lack of rational judgment, a woman is best suited for homemaking and supporting her husband. But, if she seeks a profession outside the home, let her pursue "midwifery, gynecology, the surgical needs of women, sewing, teaching in girls' schools and nursing."[2]

2. Men enjoy higher mental strength which makes them suitable for rational judgments required in the decision-making tasks of the public sphere. Allah has preferred men "in the matter of mental ability, and good counsel, and in their power for the performance of duties. . . . Hence to men have been confined prophecy, religious leadership, . . . [and] the giving of evidence in the law-courts. . . . They also have the privilege of electing chiefs, have a large share of inheritance and discretion in the matter of divorce."[3] Men are also "the maintainers of women, because Allah has made some of them [men] to excel others and because they [men] spend out their property [on women]. The good women are therefore obedient. . . ." (Surah IV, Verse 34 of Koran).[4]

3. When it comes to sexual behavior "woman is more in control of her passion than man. Man's lust is primordial and aggressive and woman's passion is responsive and reactive."[5] In this mating game, woman uses her beauty and charm to lure man, and man's insatiable sexual appetite moves him to seek women. If left unchecked, the game and especially man's lust will be sources of his destruction and downfall. Maintaining order and guaranteeing the sanctity of the family calls for controlling man's sexual drive; and to do so requires restraining woman's seductive power. It is this perceived causal relationship that promotes *hejab*[6] and seclusion of woman.

4. Woman's delicate physique and mental weakness are compensated by her emotional strength. While her sensitivity and emotional tendencies make her unsuitable for rational work, they allow her to raise and rear children and tend to men's emotional and sexual needs.

A consequence of these physical and psychological differences is a sexually segregated society ordained by Allah and prescribed in the Koran and the *Sharia*. Although all of these principles suggest separate realms of activity for the sexes, the underlying assumption is that the intermixing of the sexes creates a sexually charged environment unconducive to productivity. Man has an insatiable sexual desire that is provoked by the sight or voice of a woman, distracting his energy from social productivity to sexual action. "Which man can do more work? He who is exposed constantly to arousing and exciting faces of made-up women in the street, bazaar, office or factory; or he who does not have such sights?"[7] Thus, the solution to prevent sexual awkwardness and guarantee maximum productivity is sexually segregated functions and space. This segregation is efficient, functional, and above all, divine.

The Islamic explanation of woman's role has swayed between biological and psychological determinism. The biological theory of sex role is based on the premise that woman's reproductive capacity dictates her social functions as mother and sex object. Thus a social order based on the "natural" division of labor has specialized the social function of woman, which in turn makes it easy and desirable to exclude her from the male world. This biological determinism of woman's role, however, is not originally an Islamic theory. There are historical indications that Muslim theologians adapted Greek philosophers' rationalization for woman's specialized function and her subservient social position.[8] Aristotle emphasized the importance of reproduction for society and believed it is the only reason for woman's existence. In reproduction man and woman both participate, but man provides the "Form" or the soul, and woman provides the matter. "The Form is better and more divine in its nature than the matter; it is better also that the superior one should be separated from the inferior one. That is why whenever possible and so far as possible the male is separated from female."[9] This idea is echoed by Majlisi, a seventeenth-century Shii theologian who by citing *hadiths* [10] from the Prophet reinforces woman's reproductive duty and seclusion as divine orders. In one *hadith* the Prophet supposedly recommended men to marry virgins because they produce numerous children and their breasts have more milk. In another *hadith* he supposedly declared that "barrenness is a curse of the God."[11] As for segregation, Mottahari cites a *hadith* from Zahar, the Prophet's daughter, who says "the best thing for a woman is never to see a strange man and never be seen by a strange man."[12] Mottahari also indicates that "a civic society should be segregated . . . when man and woman work side by side, they are distracted from their duties to the extent that these cooperations lead to copulation."[13]

About woman as a weaker and incomplete being, Aristotle states, "We should look on a female as being as it were a deformity, though one which occurs in the ordinary course of nature." [14] Majlisi quotes a *hadith* from the Prophet, who allegedly likens "woman to a crooked rib that if you try to straighten it, it will break."[15] The same idea has infiltrated Iranian culture, which calls woman *Zaifeh* (the weaker one).

The earlier Islamic theologians like Majlisi based their sex role ascription on the biological inferiority of woman and presented her as weak, wicked, immature, mentally inferior, and physically vulnerable. She is considered in all respects inferior to man and thus must remain under his control and subservient to all his needs and whims. In contrast modern theologians have relied more on psychological and social factors to justify their description of woman's role and place. While they are ambivalent about the biological explanation of sex role, they emphasize "natural" psychological differences between the sexes as the divine rationale for sex role specialization. In comparing woman's psyche to man's disposition, Mottahari states:

> Woman is more emotional and emotionally unstable . . . . Man is colder than woman. Unlike man, woman enjoys grooming, fashion and ornaments. She is more cautious, more religious, talkative . . . and cowardly than man. Woman's nurturing emotions manifest themselves in early childhood, and she possesses an unconscious devotion to her family. As far as abstract reasoning and analytical understanding are concerned, woman lags far behind man but in literature, painting and other sensual areas she is not less than a man. Man can keep secrets; and thus by keeping unpleasant secrets to himself, he suffers from a higher rate of disorders due to secrecy.[16]

Mottahari emphasizes the importance of the patriarchal family for Islamic society and indicates that the specialized function of woman is not only beneficial to the society, but also is beneficial to her as well. Procreation and family responsibilities are woman's unique contributions to society and thus the source of her fulfillment and self-worth.

The importance of the patriarchal family as the primary institution and the focus of woman's existence is also manifested in works of unconventional philosophers of Islam, like Shariati. He criticizes Islamic theologians of all types for their deterministic explanations of woman's social existence. Through a romanticized biography of the Prophet's daughter, Fatima, he offers a new role model that is very different from the traditional Muslim woman.[17] This new role model is not only a mother and a wife, but she is also a political actor. Shariati recognizes woman's de facto political power and insists on the political citizenship of woman in a civic society. But despite his departure from classical

Islamic explanations of woman's role, he falls prey to the patriarchal values that are prevalent in a capitalist society. Reacting to capitalist exploitation of woman's sexuality, he ignores the human woman. His role model is an educated, active woman who cherishes her family responsibilities as much as her civic duties. Unlike the emotionally unstable woman of classical theories, Shariati's role model is strong, stable, and determined. She is a political machine. This new role model, which was widely emulated and embraced by young women of pre-revolutionary Iran (and in fact is still imitated in post-revolutionary Iran) lacks human passion and sexual desires. From Majlisi's sensual woman, whose destructive passion he warns Muslims to control; to Mottahari's sexual woman, whose sexuality is constructive as long as it is contained within the framework of family; to Shariati's asexual, political person, woman's picture and personality changes and shifts. While each of these "ideal" role models contains some elements of the truth, none is a real person; and furthermore none is representative of the real Muslim woman.

While this sex role ascription based on physical differences is not unique to Islam, it is the durability and completeness of the segregation that distinguishes it from other religiously prescribed sex role models. Separate and distinct functions assigned to each sex are rationalized on the basis of physical and intellectual capacities attributed to each and sanctioned by the Koran and *Sharia*. A logical consequence of this division of labor is spatial segregation of sexes where women are excluded from the public life of society. An extension of spatial segregation is *hejab*, practiced by women to keep away the desiring eyes of men. The origin of *hejab* in Islam is said to lie in the Koran, Surah XXIV, verse 31, which states, "And say to the believing women that they cast down their looks and guard their private parts and do not display their ornaments except what appears thereof, and let them wear their head-coverings over their bosoms, and not display their ornaments except to their husbands or their fathers. . . ." In most Muslim societies and some non-Muslim countries, women veil to cover part of their bodies from certain groups of men. The veil used by women—Muslims and some non-Muslims—comes in different forms and conveys different degrees of sex segregation. The history of veiling in the Middle East transcends Islamic tradition and dates back to the Persian Empire where women of nobility practiced veiling. The Islamic rationalization refers to the sexual implication of social interaction between the sexes: men are sexually agressive and women are potentially distracting and destructive. To protect men's social conduct and mental composure women veil themselves.

Thus the Islamic mandate for social organization is a division of labor along sex lines, which embraces all aspects of Muslims' lives. Such an ordained social arrangement has been endured more in urban centers than in rural areas. The labor intensive agriculture of these societies prohibits exclusion of half the population from productive labor. In urban centers, particularly among the more affluent strata of society, sex segregation was possible and furthermore, a status symbol. Those who could, provided for every need of their women so as to keep them indoors, and had access to resources which were beyond the reach of ordinary citizens. Among lower and working class groups, despite their declared strong adherence to Islamic ideas, practical issues overrode attention to ideological principles. Working class women did not have the luxury of complete segregation, and this gave them more mobility.

In many Islamic societies of the Middle East, women's realm of activity and existence has remained in the private sector of home and family. For middle class women this privatization has been maintained through several mechanisms. To begin with, the urban life of commerce, government bureaucracy, and some industry was controlled and operated by men only. Until the early 1960s this exclusive labor market remained intact and functional. The indigenous male labor force was more than adequate for running these segments without any help from women or guest workers. Thus, as far as the economy was concerned, women's labor in the public sphere of urban centers was not necessary.

With the influx of oil revenue and beginning of industrialization, demand for skilled workers and professionals necessitated the introduction of a new crop of workers. For many Middle Eastern countries the choice was between guest workers and professionals from surrounding countries or the introduction of women into the labor market. Several factors contributed to the selection of guest workers.

1. The urgency of demand for labor made skilled guest laborers an easy solution. Even if women were to become part of the labor force, their lack of training and experience in public life made them less desirable laborers. To train and educate women as workers required time that these newly rich and suddenly industrializing countries did not have.

2. The cultural background that prohibited a mixed work force had left men (who were in charge) as well as women unready for a sudden change in their work environment. Social and economic institutions that were administered and operated by

men were not readily adaptable to a female labor force. Men in charge of decision-making in these institutions found themselves more at ease with male guest workers, even from another culture, than with their own womenfolk.

3. The last, but perhaps the most significant factor, is the Islamic *Sharia* that prohibits publicization of women and strongly condemns mixed work environments.

These three factors have contributed to the continuation of middle class woman's exclusion from the public sphere in many Muslim societies.

The Pahlavi Era: Publicization of the Middle Class Woman

In Iran, however, unlike some Arab countries, from the early stages of economic growth the entry of middle class women into the labor market was promoted and encouraged. During the Pahlavi dynasty (1921-1979) many aspects of the Islamic order of sex roles were eradicated in large urban areas. While the Pahlavis did not attack the traditional ideology behind sex segregation, they launched efforts on several fronts to change traditional sex role behaviors. They attacked the *hejab* as backward, promoted universal education, enfranchised women, and presented highly visible female members of the royal family as new role models in the public arena. As a consequence of these policies and major socio-economic changes, middle class women became educated, employed, and achieved some degree of financial independence.

Sex role modification did not change men's activities and behavior as much as it affected middle class women. These developments occurred in the context of major historical changes which transformed Iran from a feudal agricultural society to a semi-industrial, capitalist one. Rapid economic growth introduced social changes that affected some segments of the society more than others. These changes were more pronounced in urban than rural areas and affected the upper half of the population more than the lower. Among major trends were consolidation of the central government's authority, a trend toward urbanization, a shift of labor from agriculture to the secondary and service sectors, and relative secularization of the society. Concomitant with these changes, the status of women also changed. On the legal front, more secular laws gradually replaced some traditional regulations. A few of these changes came during Reza Shah's regime

(1921-1941), such as registration of marriage contracts over family affairs, raising the minimum age of marriage, and, especially, the Unveiling Act.

In 1936, by decree, the monarch outlawed veiling, the customary dress code for urban women that meant covering the entire body except the face, and in some cases even the face. The Unveiling Act ordered Iranian women to take off their veils and appear in public in European clothes and hats. Soldiers and police officers were ordered to tear off anything short of a hat on a woman's head. The law was relaxed in 1941 and many women returned to the *chador*.[18]

The major legal changes came during the regime of Mohammad Reza Shah with the passage of the Suffrage Act of 1963 and especially The Family Protection Law (FPL) of 1967. The FPL modified the previous Civil Code based on the Islamic *Sharia*. With twenty-three articles and one note this law raised the minimum age of marriage for women, restricted polygamy, and changed divorce law. Under the *Sharia* a man may take a second wife if he can financially support her. The FPL, however, required the first wife's consent. It also restricted a man's right to divorce his wife without her consent or knowledge. Under the new law both partners could apply for divorce on the grounds of incompatibility. In the past the Civil Code had automatically assigned the custody of the children—sons after the age of two and daughters after the age of seven—to the father. Under the FPL, however, if the couple could not agree on the custody of their children, the court would determine custody. In short FPL placed restrictions on the rights of a husband over his wife and children, giving women more rights. Of all the government actions, the Unveiling Act and FPL had the greatest effect on the status of women.

In the twentieth century Iranian women have also gained access to educational institutions for the first time. From 1910 to 1933 the number of girls' schools rose from 41 to 870 and their students increased from 2,167 to 50,000.[19] During the Shah's regime educational opportunities for women improved even more. The primary school enrollment ratio for all female students rose from 27.0 in 1960 to 80.0 in 1977; and the secondary school ratio for women increased from 7.0 to 32.0 during the same period.[20] The number of women in higher education also increased. In 1970 women constituted about 25 percent of students in higher education. By 1978 their number had risen to 38 percent and almost half of students abroad were female.[21] While the majority of female college students majored in arts and literature, the number of female students in science and engineering increased considerably. Women also participated in the labor force in greater numbers. Women constituted 11.3 percent of the total labor force in 1960 and 14.2 percent by 1979.[22] Several laws guaranteed equal pay for equal work, allowed two months paid maternity leave, allowed nursing mothers to feed their children every three hours, and required organizations with more than ten mothers with infants to establish a nursery. In 1975 abortion was legalized, and in the case of a low income family was paid for by the government.

The objective indicators of the changing position of woman during the last two decades of the Pahlavis are well documented. It is also more or less agreed upon that these changes affected only a small segment of the female population. However, what is disputed is the magnitude and social significance of these changes.

The controversy over the position of woman in pre- and post-revolutionary Iran has divided observers into two camps. On the one side are those who warn that applying Western feminist standards to the case of Iranian women is misleading, and they remind us that middle class urban women who benefited from these opportunities were a small minority. [23] Yet these changes were immaterial to the lives of working class and peasant women; and their lives remained unaffected by government policies. They also remind us that Iranian women lack the group consciousness and political organization necessary for promoting feminist causes, and as a result their participation in the revolution was not for a feminist agenda. On the other hand there are those who lament the disappearance of women's rights after the revolution and document the inferior position of women advocated by the Islamic regime. They remind us that mandatory veiling and removal of women from the public arena are attempts to isolate women and deprive them of their basic human rights.[24] The true picture lies somewhere between these two extremes. The fact is that during the past fifty years Iranian women gained rights and opportunities that were inconceivable at the beginning of this century. It is true that only a minority had access to the new opportunities and could take advantage of the new-found rights. But it is equally true that this was a growing group and the number of those who benefited from new economic opportunities was on the rise.

Two major points are lost in this discussion. One is that had these changes continued, they would have impacted a larger group of women in the future, and secondly, the stereotypes concerning women and their abilities would have been dispelled. As far as the first point is concerned, by focusing on the number of actual beneficiaries, one must not lose sight of a larger group of potential beneficiaries. The fact that the changes had impacted only a minority of women did not preclude improvements for others in the future. Women who themselves were not directly influenced by changing circumstances could hope for a different future for their daughters. Mothers foresaw that their daughters could hope for something other than early marriage and consecutive birthings. This is not to say that they dreamed of professional, independent, and career-oriented daughters. Rather they envisioned for their daughters marriage in the later teen years instead of the early teens, some degree of education, and a modern husband who would set up a separate household with fewer children. This was a promising future for daughters of mothers who were married off in their early teens to men whom they did not know and who had gone through several pregnancies and been subject to the demands of tyrannical in-laws.

This rising expectation, that being a child-bride and going through numerous pregnancies is not necessarily the "natural" order of life for women, was one of the major contributions of the social changes of the 1960s and 1970s as far as women were concerned. Another result was the acceptability of women in public life, which helped to improve their economic and legal status. The "normality" of women's presence in the work place further reinforced the changing definition of woman's role. Employment opportunities and the fact that women were allowed to take advantage of them removed many restrictions on women's lives. The acceptability of the working women also erased some of the social stigma attached to her husband, that is, his inability to provide for his family. The point is that publicization of women introduced significant attitudinal changes and modified many traditional values about woman's proper role and place. As a result, a majority of urban families considered some education for girls not only acceptable but necessary, and the widespread social stigma attached to working women as symbols of family dishonor was generally removed. This was the extent of publicization of woman's role in pre-revolutionary Iran. However, woman's role would encounter further changes, or rather revert to more traditional status with the onset of the Islamic Revolution.

The Islamic Republic: Privatization of the Middle Class Women

It is against this background that the revolutionary regime tries to reintroduce separate spheres of activities for the sexes and return women to their "natural" and private place of the household world. The authorities denounce the social and legal changes of the monarchy as decadent and claim these changes led the country to Westernization and away from Islamic principles. Immediately after the takeover, the new rulers launched a campaign for "privatization" of women's lives and roles by changing their positions economically, socially, and legally. These policies were pursued on three fronts: legal measures limiting women's civil and human rights, exclusion of women from the paid labor force, and finally the social isolation of women through mandatory veiling.

On the legal front, the 1979 Constitution of the Islamic Republic under the section "Women and the Constitution" states:

> The human resources of the society, which till now were in the service of foreign exploitation, will be restored to their original and humane features for the building of Islamic social structure. As part of this process, it is only natural that women, who were subjected to greater injustice under the despotic regime, will enjoy greater rights.
>
> The family is the cornerstone of the society and the central institution for the growth and development of the individual. Nurturing common agreement and ideological belief in the principle that the establishment of family is essential for the future growth of the individual is one of the main goals of the Islamic government. According to this view of the family, woman will no longer be regarded as mere object or instrument in the service of consumerism and exploitation, rather she is restored to the worthwhile and precious function of motherhood by raising committed individuals. Woman also becomes the fellow struggler of man in different areas of life. Given the weighty responsibilities that woman assumes, she is accorded great value and nobility in Islam.[25]

Thus, the new system sees the primary responsibility of women as raising children and being housewives. In this sense the Constitution confirms women's realm of activity as primarily in the private sphere. In another section, the Constitution states "the government must assure the rights of women in all respects in conformity with Islamic rules." Furthermore, the Constitution requires the government to set up special courts to protect and regulate family affairs. Establishing special courts to adjudicate family disputes guarantees complete control of religious courts over the family and, consequently, over women. The Constitution also mentions that the state should "grant the guardianship of children to their mothers whenever suitable in order to protect the interests of the children, in the absence of legal guardianship." In several sections the Constitution emphatically states that the affairs of the country should be managed according to Islamic principles. And since *Sharia* has specific mandates for sex roles, woman's place in the Islamic state is clearly in the private sphere. The Constitution does not prohibit women from outside activities specifically, and indeed it spells out government responsibilities in terms of ensuring women's rights. However, these rights are assured only as far as traditional roles are concerned, and the Constitution falls short of guaranteeing the working mother's rights.

Nowhere is the inferior position of women more clearly stated than in the new Retribution Bill. In it, for example, the blood money paid for a woman is half of the blood money paid for a man, and two women's testimony in criminal court is equivalent to one man's testimony, and at times women's testimony is altogether immaterial and unacceptable..

> *Article 5:* If a Muslim man kills a Muslim woman wilfully, he will be sentenced to retribution (*gisas*) but the woman's guardian (or family) must pay the murderer one half of a man's blood money before he receives retribution.
>
> *Article 33:a.* Testimony: The case of willful murder is proved only with the testimony of two righteous men. b) a case of manslaughter or unintentional murder of proved with testimonies of two righteous men or one righteous man and two righteous women. . . .
>
> *Article 91.* Testimony: Adultery is proved on the basis of testimonies of four righteous men, or three righteous men and two righteous women. . . .
>
> *Article 92.* Note B: Women's testimonies alone or in conjunction with a righteous man's testimony does not prove adultery, but those witnesses will receive *hadd* (flogging) for libel.[26]

To complete the redefinition of woman's role, the government has enacted a series of policies which embrace practical aspects of women's lives. For example, the *majles* declared all regulations contradictory to *Sharia* as heretical and illegal, thus rejecting the family Protection Law. As a consequence, polygamy is legalized without any restriction, divorce is a man's prerogative, child custody is a father's right, and so forth. Abortion is illegal again, and the minimum age of marriage for women is thirteen. In addition, various laws encourage women civil service employees to stay home: for example, a man with a working wife is refused non-monetary benefits and privileges like shopping in government stores, and women who have worked fifteen years can retire while enjoying full benefits. Another law, passed in 1983, makes women primarily part-time workers. According to this law, female civil service employees can work part-time with the approval of their bosses.[27] On the face of it, this law with its generous provisions for part-time workers seems very liberal, but it has serious implications for women's employment opportunities. Women who prefer to work full-time despite the benefits of this law will be singled out and ostracized. Part-time workers cannot be ambitious about promotion to managerial or sensitive powerful positions. The law makes female workers unessential and auxiliary workers in the government bureaucracy, which is the center of the power structure in the country. Furthermore, it places them at the bottom of this hierarchy forever. The law reinforces the traditional occupations of women and implies that other activities are secondary and non-essential for women. This may be the start of further removal of women from the work place and their exclusion from the power structure.

In addition to laws, office policies of different branches of the government impose limitations on women's role outside home. There are numerous examples of purges which affected women more than men. In the early stages of the revolution women were prohibited from appearing on national television and consequently many women announcers, singers, musicians, artists, and others lost their jobs at the national level. Since *Sharia* specifically prohibits women from judicial occupations, women judges were removed from their positions. Women were also easy targets of widespread purges after the revolution because the rigid definition of proper behavior yielded numerous excuses like smoking, talking to male colleagues, and improper dress to eliminate women from the civil service sector. A government-run women's magazine reports that professional, educated women cannot find employment in the civil services. "The only women that the Islamic Republic hires are women physicians in order to prevent women from having to go to male doctors." The same report indicates that the private sector also is reluctant to hire female workers. "As a result employment positions for women in Iranian society are extremely limited and this group of the population is actually home-bound."[28]

The ideal Islamic society is sex-segregated, and this goal creates numerous obstacles for women's activities outside the home. Physical and financial problems associated with spatial segregation of employees make women a burden and thus undesirable in the work place. To achieve complete segregation, the state experimented with separate office space, classrooms, and public facilities—with chaotic and unsatisfactory results. The easy solution is to remove women from the office and public life.

Concerning education, the regime is adamant about segregated schools and the Islamic content of education. This approach is a two-fold hindrance for women. On the one hand, segregated schools mean no male teachers in girls' schools; since in many areas of science and mathematics there is a shortage of female teachers, girls automatically will receive no or inadequate training in "male" dominated fields. Furthermore, the content of textbooks is changed to fit the traditional Islamic sex role description. The goal is to socialize children to their "natural" role for the future of the Islamic state. Thus children see veiled girls helping their mothers around the house and boys following their fathers in their male activities. The minister of education confirms this point by stating that "in our design of text books for the following years, we are taking account of the fact that boys and girls have different educational needs. Above a certain educational level, the subjects will therefore be altered to cater to these differences."[29]

In higher education a line is also drawn to designate proper professional and technical training for each sex. As a result, women are barred from majoring in areas that are contradictory to their "natural" female dispositions, such as certain branches of engineering, geology, agriculture, mining, and technical training like machine shop operation. Men are also prohibited from majoring in "female" areas such as gynecology and nursing. While the law school still admits a few female students, these will be placed in staff positions in the administrative branches of the ministry of justice and the district attorneys' offices.

These legal measures and policies have had a two-fold result. By establishing the *Sharia* as the basis of social organization, woman's role and rights outside the home are severely restricted. The new regime emphasizes the importance of the family as the primary institution of Islamic society and thus requires a full-time member, who has limited rights and obligations outside of this domain, to be at the service of the family. To achieve this end, the Islamic system limits woman's rights as a full participant in society.The social expectation and legal inducement is for her to marry early, bear children, and remain at the service of the household for the rest of her life.

The second result, and a very essential one, has to do with the elimination of women from the paid labor force. Since the establishment of the Republic there have been systematic efforts to exclude

women from economic production in urban areas. While the
restrictions on village women or those who produce at home for the
economic market (like carpet weaving) are limited, outside work is
perceived as un-Islamic and counterproductive for women. And as the
opportunities for employment decline, so does woman's financial
independence, consequently reducing her social and individual
autonomy.

The final chapter in the exclusion of women from the public
sphere is the imposition of veiling. The authorities of the Republic have
shown an obsession with the women's dress code since the early stages
of the revolution. In March 1979, two weeks after his return, the
Ayatollah declared the veil as a symbol of committed women who are
different from the lackeys of *Tachot* (the despotic monarch). Women's
demonstrations against the regime's policies, though well-attended,
were ineffective in stopping the privatization process that started with
the new regime. The authorities retreated a few steps. However, they
changed their strategy, and due to a dearth of organized opposition
they suppressed spontaneous demonstrations and gradually installed
hejab as the only alternative for women. In June of 1980 Ayatollah
Khomeini issued a decree for "administrative revolution," denouncing
the opponents of veiling as supporters of imperialism and counter-
revolutionaries. As part of this revolution, women were required to
wear Islamic *hejab* to their offices. In July the government started
reinforcing compulsory veiling and dismissing those who refused to
comply.[30] Since then *hejab* has been mandatory for all women nine
years of age and older. In practice girls have to wear *hejab* even at
a younger age in order to attend school, get a passport, receive
government-issued insurance cards, etc. So in fact the entire female
popoulation—except during infancy—is subject to compulsory veiling.

The rationalization for veiling has two components. One is to
safeguard social order from the disruptive forces of sexual desires of
men and women. "In order to prevent the spread of prostitution and
sexual immorality we must take preventive measures. And the best
preventive technique is limiting contact between men and women."
To achieve the latter, the President of the Republic believes, women
must veil and the best *hejab* is the *chador*.[31]

Another aspect of this rationalization, a by-product of the first,
is the revolutionary obligation of women to safeguard the revolution
from imperialist forces. According to state rhetoric, colonizers and
imperialists use women to infiltrate society, destroy its moral fabric,
promote consumerism, and spread immorality. As a result society
becomes weak and they dominate it and exploit its resources. Fashion

and makeup are imperialist tools to enslave the women of a country and through the women break resistance. Most slogans promoting *hejab* in Iran contain ideas such as "sister, your *hejab* is a damning blow against imperialism." Ms. Rahnavard, the editor of a women's magazine, echoes this idea by stating that "we can look at the issue of veiling and unveiling from the strategy of cultural colonization. We will then see this strategy uses women as a cultural base for Westernization. And from her base (colonizers) not only destroy national and religious stands, but values like clean love, honestey, chivalry and sacrifice are also forgotten and destroyed."[32]

In the years preceding the revolution there was a trend toward Islamic values and rejection of the Westernizing policies of the Pahlavis. Young, educated women in urban centers responded to a biased picture of the Western woman as presented by Hollywood and returned to traditional, "wholesome" values of Islam. Philosophers like Ali Shariati played an important role in the revitalization of Islam among the youth of the cities. A symbol of this dedication was modest clothing for both sexes, which for women was the *Islamic hejab*. The *Islamic hejab,* which found some support among middle-class college students before the revolution, is different from the *chador*, which is a loose cloth covering all of the body and held by both hands. An *Islamic hejab* usually consists of a large scarf, covering all of a woman's hair, a long and loose robe of mostly dark colors, and loose trousers. During the anti-Shah demonstrations the *Islamic hejab* and traditional *chador* became the universal dress code for all women participants. For many of these women, wearing the *hejab* was a sign of solidarity, not a commitment to veiling. For young women, especially college students, wearing the *Islamic hejab* was a political statement and a sign of rebellion against the establishment, not absolute submission to male domination. The present regime is making the same mistake only in reverse. Young women of the 1970s were donning the *hejab* to declare their opposition and challenge the establishment that belittled *hejab* and Islam. The young women of the 1980s are resisting veiling to challenge the establishment that refuses them a minimum of individual freedom. However, this time the choice is illegal and the violators are punished—given up to seventy-five lashes. This resistance that the regime has labeled "bad *hejabi*" involves an actual and perceived minor violation of strict dress and behavior codes.

The opponents of the bad *hejabi,* under the leadership of President Khamenehi, are mostly *Hezab Allahs* who oppose any behavior or outfit that deviates from their perception of true Islamic conduct. While all women must have the *hejab,* its form and color are not explicitly defined or agreed upon. Most government offices have a regulation *hejab* code, consisting of a tightly wrapped large scarf, a long and loose robe and trousers, all of dark colors. No makeup, perfume or cologne is allowed. Shoes must have low heels and be of dark color. The same code applies to teachers and students. This is the minimum acceptable dress code for workers and clients of the state. The *hejab* preferred by government officials, however, is the black *chador*. Outside government offices there are more varieties and colors and at times ingenious attempts at observance of fashion in the *Islamic hejab*. There are implicit standards of modesty for men too. Colorful clothing, short-sleeve shirts, and unconventional haircuts are indications of bad *hejabi* among men and unacceptable in government offices. The same is true for ties and colognes.

Regarding specific definition of bad *hejabi* there is no clear agreement, but it goes beyond dress and appearance: fostering Western values, watching videos, buying Western clothes or selling them are some examples of bad *hejabi*. For the President, a crusader against bad *hejabi*, this is considered a cultural disease and extends beyond veiling. In a Friday prayers' speech he explained that there is a conspiracy to destroy the moral fabric of society through the spread of bad *hejabi*. He warned government officials to deal with "bad *hejabi* as a serious and dangerous phenomenon" designed to disrupt society. He believes that the Western powers have created "studios (workshops) in the world to produce videos and tapes. They use psychologists, sociologists and intellectuals who are experts in [the areas] of prostitution and corruption to produce the most disgusting tapes and videos and smuggle them into the country . . . and distribute them among Muslim families . . . [and] spread and diffuse their cultural values among the youth." He continues, "We believe, we must seriously deal with this phenomenon, this the most rotten gift and the bitter and harmful fruit of the Western culture, and we will fight against it."[33]

The campaign against bad *hejabi* not only targets consumers of bad *hejabi* items, but also producers and distributors of these goods. Stores that sell "Western and undesirable clothes" or musical tapes and videos are frequently fined and closed.[34] The *Hezab Allah* is in the forefront of the campaign against bad *hejabi* and in many of their demonstrations attack individuals or establishments suspected of bad *hejabi*. To organize and regulate these activities the governor of Tehran with the approval of the Ministry of Interior has set up a special office called "amer-b-marouf-v-nahi az monker" (The Office of Public Morality). This office has squads of men and women roaming the streets on the lookout for violators of Islamic behavior. Among the offenders that they control are women wearing makeup or clothes that are against the strict definition of the *Islamic hejab,* young men wearing fashionable clothing, and eating in public during the month of Ramadan, etc. However, their main targets are women. If they notice a woman wearing makeup they take her to their vehicle, lecture and admonish her for her Western imperialistic behavior and then offer her cotton balls to remove her makeup. If she is considered to be uncooperative, she is taken to the headquarters where she will be processed and punished.

The overwhelming obsession of government authorities with the dangers of contact between the sexes and its ensuing sexual corruption has led to an uneasy social arrangement. The social interaction between the sexes involves various techniques of avoidance underlined by sexual overtones. During interviews with college students at the Tehran and National Universities, female students stated that they do not talk to male classmates for fear of stigmatization and perhaps reprimands from the authorities. In personal contacts man and woman avoid looking at each other's face; when talking to the opposite sex women look to the ground and men look at a distant point. This social segregation comes complete with the avoidance of physical contact, social stigmatization of violators, and official punishment.

Conclusion

The authorities of the Republic are trying to set new standards of propriety for women's behavior and for the kinds of punishment imposed on those who do not abide by the norms set for them. The essence of these policies is the reorganization of society along the distinct though sometimes overlapping spheres of life. The immediate impact of these policies is mainly felt by women in urban areas. It is the urban woman's life, social conduct, and aspirations that the government desires to control. The Shah's policies of modernization and secularization targeted urban centers and the impact of these policies was mainly felt by the middle class. So it was middle class women who benefited most from expanding educational and occupational opportunities and gained some degree of financial independence.

An important, though unnoticed, result of publicization of women was their modest access to the power structure. Upper class women initiated and pushed for improvement in the social and legal status of women. The Islamization policies of the present regime which have forced women from the paid labor market have also blocked their modest access to social and political power. Government employment constitutes the majority of job opportunities available in the country, and most middle class women find employment in the civil services. The state bureaucracy is the center of the power structure, and women have access to this power structure through direct and indirect avenues. In the civil services, they have, through clerical and staff positions, access to decision-makers. But as they move up in the bureaucracy women have an opportunity to participate directly in policy-making. By removal from the paid labor market and their gradual dismissal from government offices women have lost access to a valuable source of power. Some observers see women's participation in demonstrations, Friday prayers, and their recent activities on behalf of the war effort as indications of their power. In fact, what these activities show is that the religious devotion of women is effectively used by government authorities to promote their own goals. These women lack a genuine organization and an independent social agenda dealing with the special needs and problems of women under the Islamic Republic. Their public appearance and their collective actions are mostly orchestrated by the state.

The state propaganda claims that publicization of women was a major source of corruption in pre-revolutionary Iran and proclaims that women's presence in public life symbolizes the depth of the immorality of the Shah's period and thus must be reversed. Official rhetoric stresses that equality of women must be achieved in a separate sphere of life; women should relinquish competition with men in the public sphere and return to the private sphere of home, family, and service to men and children—just as men are required to relegate service in the private sphere. The definition of these separate spheres of life and drawing clear boundaries with as little overlap as possible has proven to be problematic. Yet the future structure of Iran depends on the interpretation of the religious codes and their application to a modern society. Women as a significant component of society can assume responsibilities far beyond their traditional roles. To isolate this group indefinitely might have serious consequences for economic growth and development of the country, unforeseen by the authorities of the Islamic Republic.

— 8 —

Jewish Religion(s) and Jewish State: The Case of Conservative and Reform Judaism in Israel

William M. Batkay

An intriguing phenomenon of contemporary public life in Israel is the absence of full freedom of religion for members of non-Orthodox Jewish denominations. That is, freedom of private worship for the non-Orthodox Jewish majority is respected and protected, while public worship as well as freedom of conscience has been and continues to be restricted both formally by law, and informally by precedent, custom, and hostility from the government-supported Orthodox establishment. The state of Israel directly and indirectly denies Conservative and Reform rabbinic functionaries full legal and symbolic recognition and religious legitimacy.[1] Yet American Reform and Conservative Jews have been willing, even eager, to identify their Jewishness to a significant extent with the state of Israel, that is, they have adopted the ideology of Jewish nationalism despite the apparent rejection of their movements by the very object of their nationalism, Israel. Equally noteworthy has been the inability of the majority of non-Orthodox Jews in Israel to consider seriously any organized, institutionalized religious alternative to a widely ridiculed Orthodox establishment that continues to enjoy a state-supported monopoly over all public Jewish religious expression there.[2]

The purpose of this article is three-fold: to examine the current situation of non-Orthodox Jewish movements within Israel; to explore why the conflict between Orthodox and non-Orthodox Jewish denominations in Israel has been so muted for so long; and to suggest the likely future of non-Orthodox denominations in Israel.

Conservative and Reform Challenges to Orthodox Control

While actual and perceived Orthodox control over public Jewish religious expression in Israel has never gone unchallenged, in recent years the intensity of the conflict between Orthodox and secular Jews has reached critical proportions, threatening to erupt into what some fear will be a full-scale *Kulturkampf* or even civil war.[3] Virtually unnoticed by the non-Jewish media, and generally underplayed even in the American Jewish press, the non-Orthodox branches of Judaism have in the last two decades slowly begun to mount their own challenges to Orthodox dominance of public religious life in Israel. Conservative leaders have generally favored "quiet diplomacy," while the reform leadership has taken the opposing view and has not refrained from confrontation with the authorities when its demands have gone unmet. But since at least the late 1970s both movements have been increasingly impatient with non-recognition in Israel.[4]

These challenges are remarkable in two ways. First, they developed relatively late in the life of the state. Second, they are seen to have been ineffectual in weakening the institutional and cultural dominance of the Israeli Orthodox establishment.[5] Before attempting to assess the significance of these points, we must review precisely the nature of the Conservative and Reform challenges.

Most obvious, perhaps, has been the growth of the non-Orthodox presence on the organizational level. The number of congregations identified as Conservative or Reform has grown significantly, if slowly, during the past two decades. Although both movements established themselves in Palestine in the 1930s, by 1963 there were still only six non-Orthodox congregations in Israel, two Conservative and four Reform; ten years later the number had grown to twenty-two, of which seven were Reform. By the 1980s, of some six thousand synagogues in Israel, at least forty were affiliated with the two non-Orthodox movements. Indeed, some Conservative sources have claimed upwards of forty Israeli congregations as affiliated with the Conservative movement alone.[6]

At the same time, modest efforts have been made to establish a non-Orthodox religious beachhead in the kibbutz movement. The Reform movement, for example, has administered the successful Kibbutz Yahel in the Negev since 1976; a second, smaller Reform kibbutz, Har Halutz, was established in Galilee in 1985. Meanwhile, the Conservative movement has founded its own settlement in Galilee, Kibbutz Hanaton.[7]

Moveover, both Conservative and Reform movements have expended considerable effort and money to establish a visible institutional "presence" in Israel. In 1958 the Conservative movement built Neve Schechter, a student center in Jerusalem, to accommodate American students studying in Israel. Later, both movements broadened their programs of rabbinical training for American students to include a year in Israel, and the Reform movement inaugurated a rabbinic-studies program for native Israelis; the first Israeli-born Reform rabbi was ordained in 1980.[8] The Reform movement has gone so far as to transfer the headquarters of the World Union of Progressive Judaism, its international branch, to Jerusalem, setting up offices, publications, and a visitors center. The Conservatives have created a specialized research facility, the Schocken Institute for Jewish Research, which parallels the Biblical Archaeology Center of the Reform Hebrew Union College-Jewish Institute of Religion. Finally, since 1960 the Reform movement has been affiliated with the Leo Baeck Educational Center on Mt. Carmel, a major object of favorable public attention and a source of training for Israeli scholars with a reform perspective.[9]

Another component of the non-Orthodox religious challenge has been legal actions, particularly by members of the Reform movement. In a landmark case involving the refusal of local municipalities to lease public space to reform congregations for services, Reform Jews sued in the secular courts and eventually won an Israeli Supreme Court ruling against such obstructionism. Most recently, a woman converted in the United States by a reform rabbi successfully sued to compel the Ministry of the Interior to register her as a Jew, thus winning implicit legal recognition of the legitimacy at least of those Reform conversions performed outside Israel.[10]

The Conservatives have been more circumspect in their approach to "legal" roadblocks. Even they, however, have occasionally threatened to bring suit over such issues and have apparently only been dissuaded by political pressure from the highest authorities in the state.[11]

In the political arena, the American Conservative and Reform movements belatedly recognized that their failure to affiliate with international Zionist organizations only hindered their advancement and recognition in Israel. Accordingly, a degree of reconciliation has occurred in recent years. For the Reform movement, this meant abandonment of its ideological hostility to Zionism; for Conservatives it necessitated a shift from merely passive or simply financial support for Zionism to something more positive and active. As a consequence, the conservatives have created MERCAZ, the Movement to Reaffirm Conservative Zionism, in an effort to institutionalize their Zionist stance. On the Reform side, ARZA, the Association of Reform Zionists in America, was established for similar purposes.[12]

As American Reform and Conservative leaderships have begun to stress Zionism, they have also promoted their views more forcefully in the press, denouncing lack of freedom in Israel for their denominations. Spokesmen for the two movements have also become considerably less restrained in their public comments on particularly egregious Orthodox maneuvers. In a recent episode, leading Conservative and Reform rabbis in the United States strongly condemned the decision of the Minister of the Interior to indicate on the official registry of new immigrants whether they are converts to Judaism, an action that would have subjected Conservative and Reform converts to even closer scrutiny by Israeli rabbinic authorities and public officials.[13]

Finally, official Conservative and Reform bodies and representatives have attempted to play a more active role in practical politics. They have exchanged promises of electoral equality, and they have sought to influence legislation bearing their status and rights. But perhaps the clearest indication of this activism has been their repeated intervention to secure defeat of proposed amendments to the Law of Return, the so-called "Who Is a Jew" law, which would have denied legal recognition to Conservative and Reform conversions performed abroad.[14]

These developments have resulted from deliberate and conscious efforts by non-Orthodox religious movements to broaden their presence in Israel and present themselves as an alternative to both Orthodoxy and secularism. Although it is difficult to gauge the political impact of this growth, the terms of religious debate in Israel have certainly been altered, however subtly, by the establishment and expansion of institutions whose very existence on Israeli soil challenges the Orthodox claim to exclusive legitimacy.

Late Efforts and Limited Success

Despite recent stirrings and consequent gains, an observer of Conservative and Reform Judaism in Israel is struck by the long willingness of these movements to accept inferior status there. The situation appears odd for two reasons: first, the numercial, financial, and organizational dominance of Reform and Conservative Jews in the United States and the apparent indispensability of their support for Israel; second, the longstanding commitment to Zionism and Israel on the part of the Conservative movement and the more recent, but even more enthusiastic, commitment of the American Reform movement.[15] For this reason, and because of Israeli pretensions to Western social and political democracy and the close similarity of many Israeli social institutions to American models, it might be expected that the American pattern of Jewish religious pluralism would have been replicated in Israel. That this has not occurred requires explanation.

Structure and History

Among explanations for the failure of Reform and Conservative Judaism to establish more than a toe-hold on the Israeli scene is the absolutely and relatively small number of Conservative and Reform Jews in Israel. Although both movements boast a growing number of congregations and adherents, both are still virtually invisible in Israeli public life. In other words, as the Israeli scholar Shlomo Avineri has said, if Israelis do not go to synagogue, it is still primarily to an Orthodox one that they do not go![16]

This simple fact derives from the small number of immigrants to Israel from North America and Western Europe, where adherents to the Conservative and Reform movements have been most numerous. Statistics on immigration are imprecise, partly because American immigrants are frequently classified together with Canadians, and partly because many Americans who immigrate to Israel do so as "potential immigrants" and leave after a year of two.[17] Clearly, whatever the psychological disposition of these newcomers, they do not contribute much to the potential strength of the non-Orthodox movements in Israel.

North American immigration was negligible under the *Yishuv*, the pre-independence Jewish community in Palestine, and from the founding of the state in 1948 until 1975 American immigration averaged only 1,300 per year, compared to several thousand per year from Europe.[18] Further weakening the position of non-Orthodox movements is the fact that most of their members are in North America, England, and South Africa, the very areas that have provided such a small proportion of immigrants. Furthermore, most Israeli Conservative and Reform congregations have been led by older rabbis who immigrated to Israel after retiring from active congregational service in the United States; it is not surprising that these men have shown little interest in agitating on behalf of their movements' legal status.[19]

By contrast, since the 1967 war the largest number of North American immigrants have been Orthodox.[20] Such immigrants, increasingly both self-confident and self-righteous, further isolate conservative and Reform groups and strengthen the organizational links between Israeli and American Orthodoxy.

This Orthodox preponderance among North American immigrants indicates a second feature in the historical record of Conservative and Reform Judaism: the failure to emphasize *aliyah*, actual immigration to Israel. While Solomon Schechter, then-chancellor of the Jewish Theological Seminary in New York and thus leader of the nascent Conservative movement in the United States, wholeheartedly and publicly embraced Zionism as early as 1906, the Conservative commitment to Zionism tended to remain ideological and financial.[21] The hoary definition of Zionism as the process by which one Jew sends a second Jew to Israel on a third Jew's money may have been coined with traditional Conservative Zionism in mind. Reform Judaism, on the other hand, rejected Zionism outright until after the Holocaust and the creation of the state of Israel.

As a consequence of their indifference or hostility to *aliyah*, Conservative and Reform Judaism was, for all practical purposes, conspicuous by its absence from Palestine during the crucial period of the *Yishuv*. When religiously based political organizations, like Agudat Israel and the forerunners of Mafdal, the National Religious Party, struck deals with and derived significant patronage benefits from the political leaders of the *Yishuv*, Conservative and Reform organizations were invisible. When pre-state patterns of interaction became integrated into the political rules of the Jewish state, Conservative and Reform movements were therefore excluded from the arena.[22]

Closely related to this exclusion was—and remains—the failure of conservative and Reform leaders fully to understand and exploit those opportunities for parliamentary, electoral, and coalition politics, and the patronage at the heart of Orthodox political and organizational success in Israel. Whether this failure derived mainly from practical political inexperience or an ideological perspective that simply ignored the political dimension is unclear; the negative results of the failure are not.[23]

Conservative and Reform success in Israel has also been limited by Israel's resistance to American-style religious pluralism. Following a recent altercation between Orthodox and Reform Jews in Jerusalem, for example, the Minister of Religious Affairs, Zevulun Hammer, reiterated support for "complete freedom and protection of private worship"; at the same time, he opposed "importing problems" generated by the kind of religious pluralism found in the United States and elsewhere. Whatever its theoretical desirability, therefore, this pluralism has been perceived as a luxury Israel can ill afford. In its first decades that state had more pressing problems than the denominational sensitivities of Conservative and Reform rabbinic functionaries, particularly if these disrupted long-established patterns of political influence and reward, thereby threatening government stability.[24]

Another problem has been suggested by the Reconstructionist Rabbi Jack Cohen, a longtime Hillel director in Jerusalem, who has argued that non-Orthodox movements have made little headway on the Israeli scene simply because they lack relevance to the spiritual needs of Israelis. Dissatisfied as Israelis may be with the ossified Orthodox establishment, the American model of the synagogue— shorter services held in the "vernacular" language, with organs and choirs, and rabbis who are spiritual "leaders" of their congregations— offers little to non-Orthodox Israelis. For Cohen and others the stagnation of the Reform and Conservative movements in Israel stems as much from their own historical development outside Israel as from peculiar political patterns within the state.[25]

Finally, difficulties have arisen from relations between Israel and the Diaspora. Given the small number of American immigrants to Israel and the weakness of Conservative and Reform movements there, the leadership of the majority movements in America might have brought pressure to bear to change the legal position of their co-denominationists in the Jewish state. Action was the more to be anticipated because of the central importance of Israel in the American Jewish *Weltanschauung* during the past two decades. The dependence of Israel for material and political support on Diaspora Jewry, especially in the United States, would seem to put the latter in a strong position to exercise considerable influence over Israel.[26]

Such limited efforts as were attempted, however, largely failed to force Israeli religious and secular authorities to legitimize the Israeli copies of American Reformism and Conservatism. This failure may support Liebman's view that, for all the affinities between American Conservative and Reform Jews and Israel, Diaspora influence in general is regarded as illegitimate in the Israeli political mentality. It is likely too that American Conservative and Reform movements simply lack effective channels for influencing Israeli domestic politics: regular continuous structures of influence such as the Orthodox possess through their connection with such powerful Israeli political institutions as the National Religious Party. Either way, the result is the same: Diaspora influence on Israeli policies is slight.[27]

Society and Culture

Structural and historical variables, however, fail to explain completely the fate of Conservative and Reform Judaism in Israel. Social and cultural factors impinge as well. The Israeli Orthodox establishment benefits from a peculiar set of values and perceptions that appears either to make non-Orthodox religious alternatives in Israel effectively invisible or renders them unsuitable or otherwise inaccessible, when their existence is perceived at all. Orthodoxy appears to embody what in another context has been called the "dilemma of the one alternative."[28] Among the values that support the Orthodox establishment and militate against non-Orthodox religious movements, two predominate: "unity" and "authenticity."

Unity in this context means the "unity of the Jewish people," a term innocuous in its usual ritual incantation on public occasions, but charged with hidden meaning when applied to specific political situations. The phrase is employed typically to defend the past or prospective denial to non-Orthodox movements of some religious concession—for example, the right legally to perform marriages in Israel, or to have those converted by non-Orthodox rabbis officially registered as Jews. The justification for the denial is usually the safeguarding of the "unity of the Jewish people," which would presumably be jeopardized by extending legal recognition to ritual acts performed by non-Orthodox rabbis.[29]

Orthodox authorities profess concern for the marriageability of Jews with other Jews, that is, for the halachic (traditional legal) boundaries of the endogamous marriage pool. By refusing to legitimize the ritual acts of non-Orthodox religious authorities, the Orthodox rabbinate insures that *it* retains the power of approving the choice of marriage partners for Jews. From the perspective of the Orthodox leadership in Israel, the goal is to protect Jewish peoplehood; from the viewpoint of non-Orthodox movements, however, the main objective of the Orthodox leaders is the consolidation of their own power.[30]

Of equal interest is how Conservative and Reform leaders as well as ordinary lay people have been socialized to accept the paramount value of unity on Orthodox terms, particularly when it is buttressed by references to the centrality of Israel in the unity of the Jewish people. Thus, when Conservative or Reform claims challenge the "gate-keeping" function of Orthodox authorities, the latter frequently turn for support to Israeli political authorities, who in turn invoke the shibboleth of "unity"; more often than not, non-Orthodox leaders blink first, yielding to the entreaties of the politicians to defer their claims "for the sake of unity."[31]

Deference to the idealized value of "unity," however, does not fully explain the refusal of non-Orthodox religious movements to defend more forthrightly the integrity of their versions of Judaism. Rather, the political ground under the Conservative and Reform movements is shaky because of what one American rabbi recently called a lack of "self-esteem," that is, a failure to believe in their own "authenticity." Put simply, many Conservative and Reform Jews in America appear to believe that Orthodoxy represents "real" Judaism and that Orthodox Jews are therefore "more Jewish" than they are. Among Conservatives, this attitude was influenced by the neo-Orthodox proclivities of many early leaders and spokesmen of the Conservative movement, especially those associated with the Jewish Theological Seminary in New York.[32]

Numerous methodologically rigorous surveys have been conducted within the American Jewish community in recent years, but few have been intended precisely to discover the underlying "ideological" adherence to Orthodox, Conservative, or Reform positions on a range of Jewish issues.[33] Yet there is indirect evidence that such adherence and identification are weak. Rabbi Stephen Lerner, a prominent Conservative scholar at the Jewish Theological Seminary, has argued that "Conservative Jews are those who belong to Conservative synagogues; they don't believe in Conservative Judaism. . . ." Rabbi Marc Tannenbaum, the noted American Jewish spokesman, believes that most financial contributions to American Orthodox *yeshivot* (day schools) come from Conservative and other non-Orthodox Jews; moreover, leaders of the non-Zionist Agudat Yisrael have stressed the importance of Conservative and Reform financial support for ultra-Orthodox (*haredi*) groups in Israel.[34]

Many members of Conservative congregations in the United States grew up in Orthodox households and appear to retain attitudinal and emotional links to Orthodoxy, even in the absence of overt organizational ties, a fact that may also account for their support of Orthodox organizations. Reform leaders have been less wary of confronting and challenging Orthodox statements and actions in the public realm, but the Reform laity occasionally behave in a manner as "emotionally" Orthodox as their Conservative brethren: according to an American Reform leader, much of the funding for the Lubavitcher Habad movement comes from Reform Jews.[35]

Israelis too appear to regard Orthodoxy as the embodiment of authentic traditional Judaism, even though surveys confirm that the majority of Israelis consider themselves non-Orthodox. It is the Orthodox who set the tone and constitute the "benchmark," as it were, for non-Orthodox Jews, whatever the degree of personal religious observance. Indeed, even among the aggressively secular, the Orthodox religious presence in public and communal life is tolerated if not embraced as a necessary component of the specifically *Jewish* character of the Israeli state. Consequently, at the state level, as opposed to the level of individual observance, neo-Orthodox Jewish tradition has been increasingly incorporated explicitly into public ritual as part of the emerging Israeli civil religion.[36]

Other ideological values also weaken the Conservative and Reform response to their near-exclusion from the Israeli religious scene and contribute to the apathy of the American laity toward the issue of legitimacy. Particularly in the post-1976 period, American Jews have been hero-worshippers of Israel and Israelis. The stunning victory over the Arabs, the reconquest of Jerusalem and the reestablishment of a Jewish presence in the Old City (especially at the Wailing Wall), and the territorial expansion of the state into the West Bank (the biblical region of Judaea and Samaria), all fostered an uncritical admiration of the Jewish state. The setback in the 1973 war turned admiration into a defensive and loving solicitude, an orientation even less likely to encourage concern over religious prejudice in Israel.[37]

An equally recent phenomenon is the devotion of American Jews to the centrality of Israel to the Jewish people, a cardinal tenet of what has been termed the Jewish-American civil religion. For American Jews, in other words, Israel's importance lies in its very *existence*, not in its specific *behavior*. While not completely uncritical, particularly of such foreign policy controversies as the war in Lebanon, American Jews are largely ignorant of and unconcerned with empirical social and political realities in Israel, particularly religious ones.[38]

Lay Conservative and Reform Jews—and a substantial number of their leaders—have historically regarded themselves as Jews first and as members of specific Jewish denominations second. In other words, what we may term the "stratification of commitment" of Conservative and Reform Jews has generally led to the subordination of denominational concerns to the perceived requirements of Jewish peoplehood as embodied in the state of Israel, even when this benefits primarily Orthodox institutions.[39] Thus the intensified dissatisfaction of American Reform and Conservative Jews with the prejudice against their movements in Israel may denote the belated maturity of these movements as full-scale denominations within Judaism. As such, their interests are no longer necessarily coextensive with nor exclusively mediated by the interests of the "Jewish people" and of Israel.[40]

Finally, from the Israeli perspective, virtually all scholarly investigation of the Jewish religion in Israel reveals most Israelis' unfamiliarity with religious Judaism other than its Orthodox recension, a cramped outlook characteristic of the founding generation of Zionist pioneers. As a result, the religio-political universe perceived by the majority of Israelis, including the most aggressively secular, embraces varieties of Orthodoxy and super-Orthodoxy, but virtually excludes non-Orthodox religious Judaism.[41]

Thus the legal and organizational constraints on the Conservative and Reform movements in Israel cannot be ascribed exclusively or even primarily to an Orthodox monopoly. Rather, organizational, historical, and socio-cultural circumstances have complicated the efforts of non-Orthodox denominations to move from the margins to the mainstream of Israeli religious life. Complication, however, need not imply failure, and it is possible to look at the record of Conservative and Reform Judaism in Israel in a more positive light.

Achievements

The record of the Conservative and Reform movements in Israel must be viewed in the light of their generally non-confrontational, accommodationist approach. This feature of the movements' activity may actually have conformed well with Israeli political style. Knesset debates may occasionally be raucous affairs, and controversial government policies such as the invasion of Lebanon occasion sometimes violent public protest. But the day-to-day fabric of public life is woven primarily from bargaining and compromise, usually on the basis of group preferences that are both understood and generally accepted by the attentive public.[42]

The non-Orthodox movements have achieved some measure of symbolic recognition and acceptance in Israel by their willingness to operate by these rules of accommodation. The issue of premises for construction of houses of worship, administrative offices, seminary and related facilities, for example, has long been settled, over Orthodox protests and disgruntlement. State dignitaries have been willing to attend non-Orthodox ceremonial functions, and the Labor Alignment has from time to time made public promises to ensure recognition of non-Orthodox movements in Judaism.[43] The Reform and Conservative movements receive frequently sympathetic coverage in the public non-

Orthodox press. Nor can one overlook their rather dramatic success in repeatedly forestalling further amendments to the Law of Return, thus formally preserving the legitimacy of at least their non-Israeli rabbinic functionaries.

Both movements have been the beneficiaries of significant practical concessions, primarily informal but in some cases judicial. Especially noteworthy in this context are the legal and political victories that secured Reform access to local public buildings as places of worship and procured land in Jerusalem for the national reform organization's building expansion. Not to be overlooked also is the fact that in the early to mid-1970s, a number of Conservative rabbis were informally authorized by the then-chief rabbis of Jerusalem to perform marriages in the city's central synagogue (a privilege apparently now withdrawn.)[44]

Finally, some Conservative and Reform congregations have received funds, however inadequate, from the state treasury, and a number of religious schools with an essentially Conservative curriculum are now part of the national school system on the same basis as Orthodox ones. In short, the record of the two movements in Israel has been a positive one, especially in light of the necessity of funding institutional operations, rabbis' salaries, and the like almost entirely from private donations and subventions from their American branches.

Conclusions

Our analysis suggests four major conclusions about the future of Conservative and Reform Judaism in Israel. First, existing patterns of Israeli politics and government will continue to be determinative. Non-Orthodox Jewish denominations are viewed similarly to a long line of small and politically inconsequential interest groups, divorced from any institutional relationship with a party or bureaucratic agency. Accordingly, they are likely to continue to be given the same kind of short shrift accorded such groups. A proposal to overcome this disability through the creation of a kind of Conservative counterpart to the Orthodox National Religious Party has apparently fallen on deaf ears, whatever its inherent merits.[46]

Secondly, Jewish religious pluralism in a permanent legal sense, as opposed to ad hoc behavior, will probably continue to be a concern of only a small minority in Israel. Religious pluralism of the American variety is generally without historical precedent anywhere in the Middle East and at wide variance with the current pattern of practice there.

Of course, an unforeseen decrease in the number and intensity of domestic and foreign policy issues confronting the Israeli state could occur. Such a change might provide an opening for a determined and politically skilled Reform and Conservative leadership to place religious pluralism on the political agenda. Even then, the periodic calls from American Conservative and Reform rabbis for the "disestablishment" of Orthodoxy, or the separation of religion from state on the American pattern, would likley continue to meet with incomprehension if not derision.[47]

Thirdly, further advances by the Conservative and Reform movements in Israel would virtually require the development of a more robust demographic base. It is difficult to see why Israeli society would dislocate itself for the sake of only a small number of devotees of non-Orthodox religious paths. At the same time, the two movements are unlikely to attract more adherents unless they can demonstrate some ideological relevance to the major issues confronting Israeli society. So far, their chief interest seems to have been in jockeying for a more preferred position vis-á-vis the Orthodox establishment.[48]

Finally the fate of the Conservative and Reform movements in Israel will largely depend on broad social developments, including the increasing salience of the role of religion in the public life of the state.[49] Of particular relevance will be the course of the much-feared *Kulturkampf* between religious and secular Israelis. Also significant will be the future course of the incipient rifts among Orthodox factions themselves. Lastly, the integration of the Conservative and Reform movements into the Israeli religious universe may depend on the degree of integration of the less rigid, more flexibly religious Sephardic Jewish majority into an Israeli society dominated thus far by extremes of belief and non-belief.

At present, neither movement is accepted as fully legitimate in Israel. The ritual acts of their Israeli rabbis are not accepted as legally binding, and regular attempts continue to be made to de-legitimize their rabbis who are practicing in America; their religious and educational institutions in Israel operate with virtually no state support; such minor symbolic recognition as is forthcoming—for instance, the issuing of a series of postage stamps honoring the Conservative, Orthodox, and Reform institutions of higher education in America—is hotly contested by the Orthodox establishment at every turn; the Reform movement in particular has been regularly vilified in Orthodox pronouncements as a "danger to Judaism and the State" and an interpretation that "misrepresents Judaism"; and individual Conservative and Reform Jews are subject to arbitrary harassment by state organs as well as by the official rabbinate.[50]

Still, there are encouraging signs. One is the implicit recognition of the legitimacy of Non-Orthodox approaches to Judaism in Israel that was embodied in an accord between the ultra-Orthodox local Chief Rabbi Eliahu Abergil and the Reform Rabbi Levi Weiman-Kellman, following a potentially violent incident of conflict in the Jerusalem suburb of Baka in 1986. Another is the recent establishment in Jerusalem of the first fully autonomous rabbinical seminary in Israel, under the auspices of the Israeli Conservative movement. A third is the indication of a growing political awareness signaled by the opening in Jerusalem in 1986 of a Reform Action Center, headed by an Israeli attorney, to monitor and counter any future assaults on the Law of Return.[51]

Finally, the Conservative Jewish Theological Seminary of America held a week-long centennial celebration in Israel in 1986. President Chaim Herzog hosted a ceremonial dinner on this occasion in the Knesset. A special conference and convocation featured prominent Israeli scholars and educators, and several leading political and cultural figures received honorary doctorates.[52]

These may be unimpressive developments in the eyes of those who demand instant full legal recognition and equality with the Orthodox rabbinate in Israel. But considering their late start, the unfavorable socio-political climate in Israel, and the indifferent attitude of the bulk of their American laity, the non-Orthodox movements have made surprising advances on the Israeli religio-political front. There is reason to think that further advances are possible, even likely.

— 9 —

American Foreign Policy through Benediction: The Case of Russell Conwell

Warren L. Vinz

And now oh God! wilt thou save Mexico! Wilt thou use the United States of America as thine agent to save those millions of people to civilization and to thee. We ask it in Jesus' name. Amen.[1]

Such was the benediction intoned by the Reverend Russell Conwell, minister of Temple Baptist Church, Philadelphia, following a stem-winding sermon oration on a Sunday morning in late 1919 imploring the congregation to support mission efforts to send teachers, build schools, and invite Mexican teachers to the United States for training in order to "change the nature of the Mexican people through education and good deeds."[2]

Conwell is not normally remembered for servons and benedictions of this sort. He is known as the cleric who delivered his famous lecture, "Acres of Diamonds" over 6,000 times across the land. Conwell, the builder of a great institutional church providing a total program of day care for children of the proletariat, educational programs for people wanting to earn a better living; Conwell, the founder of Temple University and three hospitals; Conwell, the exponent of the gospel of wealth declaring that material fortunes are a trust from God to be used for the benefit of humankind or, more crudely if realistically put, declaring that the wealth of the entrepreneur trickles down to the masses through established institutions: these are the things for which the Temple Baptist minister is normally remembered.

But Conwell was much more than all of this. He was a clergyman who produced a couple of sermons each week, spoke to civic groups in Philadelphia and around the country, a political activist, world

133

traveler, writer of thirty books including biographies of the Presidents, confidant to senators and representatives, and educator to his flock on issues of national and international importance in an age of burgeoning industry, big-time military power, and domestic and international political and economic hardball.

He was also a reflection of his times in the sense of sharing the ambivalence which America enters the modern industrial world as described by Henry Marx's *The End of American Innocence*—an age in which America enters with a guilty conscience for leaving the arcadian existence of the clean living agrarian life to that of the sinister, corrupt, big time of modernity. And yet the guilty conscience is salved by an optimism that America with its newly acquired power emerges on the world scene in the nick-of-time to begin the process of democratizing and Christianizing America and the world. The text of Esther seems appropriate for America and the times: "Who knows but what you have been raised for such an hour as this."[3] Henry May again: "Together, most social conservatives and most social reformists perceived their century as a (trumphant) march forward of American society and American religion."[4]

So on balance Conwell, reflecting the times with its uncertanties yet exuding optimism, was especially outspoken, if sometimes peripatetic, on America's role in foreign affairs.

In keeping with this observation of Conwellian vacillation, this paper attempts to demonstrate that Conwell displayed a nationalism in the center of two extremes: on the one hand, at his most bellicose, he was not a rabid advocate of expansionism and empire; on the other hand, at his most nationally repentant, he was not a pietistic preacher condemning any sort of intervention in world affairs.

On the one hand hear his nearly unbridled huffing and puffing for the nation state, then muted by prophetic warnings and criticisms of American pride and greed for empire. On special holidays—Memorial Day, Flag Day, Fourth of July, Labor Day, and Thanksgiving—the sanctuary was decorated festooned with draped flags, the worship service ringing with patriotic songs by the congregation and choirs, veterans organizations invited and sitting in a body. To rally the people to the Cuban cause the Young Men's Congress, one of several Temple patriotic organizations, called on Congress to "recognize Cuban rights to belligerency as soon as it may be done according to international law."[5] Organizing a pro-Cuban rally as early as October 1895 to influence the government, with Conwell the featured speaker, the Young Men's Congress arranged an audience for the Temple minister that included the governor of Pennsylvania and the mayor of Philadelphia. The

Temple guard, another of the Temple's patriotic organizations, performed rifle and machete drills to the thrill of the crowd.

On the other hand, as though the hyper-rallies of the day should have no lasting impact on the media and the people, the Temple minister warned of dangerous pride and newspapers' boasting of national power. Acquiring the Philippines so easily we have lost our balance of judgment, he declared Boasting to be the greatest naval power in the world, we have forgotten the poor and afflicted Cubans, "acting more like Bonaparte."[6] Moreover, in our greed we must not take territory. "Shall we govern the Cubans, the Philippines or Puerto Rico, tell them they can't have privileges we have? Or shall we look on our history and remember that God has prospered us when we have adhered to Chrisitian principles? Never must money be a consideration in determining our policy toward the Philippines and a stepping stone to dominate China,"[7] he said.

In perhaps his sharpest criticism of American foreign policy ever, Conwell excoriated the Government for its passage of the Platt Amendment. "Cuba must obey or starve," he thundered. "Is that freedom?"[8] Accusing the United States of pretending brotherhood to liberate the island, he saw the intention of American policy as to dominate the island. Still fuming, he remarked: "I have never been so disturbed or indignant over anything the nation ever did as I have been over this wickedness and foolishness concerning the Cuban tariff."[9] As for Puerto Rico, Conwell was adamant that this small island not be dominated by the Screaming Eagle either. Rather, America's providential role should be to help them and then withdraw.

In a mode emphasizing America's humble yet influential beginnings, Conwell on numerous occasions reminded his audiences that the United States had more influence in the world during the years before its big armies and navies. With a navy of only five vessels and a meager army of 18,000 men, the United States was alleged to be more powerful in world affairs than ever since, "unless it be just at the present time [1919]",[10] he conceded, the inconsistency of his argument hardly registering. His romantic perception of the American past oozed throughout the Temple on a Sunday morning as he described the presence of only six million Americans scattered in the woods in 1800 and in back of them "the great enemy, the North American Indian."[11] In spite of being at such a disadvantage this grubby and newly independent nation forged a Constitution with democratic ideas emerging— people willing to die for the principle that "all men are created equal— no high, no low, rich or poor, every religion tolerted, working together as brethren",[12] while in contrast there was Spain—how different its aristocracy, titled nobility, hierarchy of the church, its decadent and superstitious religion, and its expulsion of Jews. And while the Spanish were rotting silently the United States was winning the moral battle. "Little United States, six million people quietly chopping wood, hewing timber, engaged in their own occupations, singing gladly the joy of liberty. Those men unshaven, those men in skins of animals, those men meeting the forest at its very edge and fighting the wild beasts and the more wild Indian."[13] Those American patriots, intent on building their utopian republic, minding their own business, were alleged by the Temple minister to know nothing of the rest of the world. Yet in their simple and pure way of life they were winning the battle for the mind around the world, aware of neither the battle nor the winning. Furthermore, the witness of two Christian American businessmen in Chile around 1800 Conwell perceived as leaven leading to Chilean overthrowal of Spanish rule, and disavowal of the Church of Spain, and the Inquisition. Venezuela, Haiti, and Mexico follwed suit. They all copied the American Constitution, with Mexico "taking only eight hours to draft a constitution" because of such pilfering. Such defections occured from Spain, which had a powerful army and navy, while the United States, whose influence was pervasive, had no military.[14]

Stretching to absurd limits the theme of America's humility and power without the use of any military was Conwell's perception of how the United States got Panama. Once again, not American military power, but her moral leadership in the Western hempisphere allegedly induced Panamanian loyalty. In what would be considered sickening patronization in some quarters today, Conwell cited "Little Panama" with only 31,000 square miles, two-thirds the size of Pennsylvania, with 221,000 people or nine people to every square mile. "One would think that President Roosevelt would need a small pen with which to sign the treaty with such a nation as that and require a microscope with which to read the treaty."[15] How could all of this happen?— such a small country coming over on its own to the United States, Conwell rhetorically asked. Why was Panama in such a hurry to get United States recognition? "I do not believe they are in such a hurry simply for the ten million of dollars. I cannot feel that, because Panama fifty years ago adopted the American Constitution and determined then to imitate us in the common schools."[16] Incredible naivete concerning Panamanian motives and American "success" by the Temple minister! America's power was moral, and it was the greatest and most successful power on earth—not needing armies and navies to achieve it.

Shifting to a mode emphasizing America's military power and influence, Conwell displayed great pride in American military might.

For rhetorical purposes America may have been more influential in the days before her armies and navies, but Conwell knew better, and on most occasions praised the American military as indispensable to freedom for the American people and essential for the liberation of oppressed peoples everywhere. In one of his great sermons on the meaning of the flag, Conwell declared that the flag not only represents the great wisdom of the American people—a people with greater intelligence than any other nation in the world; it not only represents an educational system for all citizens, religious progress and equality, but it represents *power* as well. Go anywhere in the world and if arrested by the police of a foreign country—Turkey, for example—and a Pasha arrests you, "immediately a mighty Navy is at your command and within five days you could have the forces of this government to your aid to demand your freedom because that flag now represents power, power!"[17]

What a stark contrast to his words proclaiming the United States to have been most powerful and influential when least powerful militarily. But more than mere starkness of contrast is the deeper significance to be attached to the inconsistency. The United States had it both ways. It was influential in the world without military might—a pure and simple characteristic that seems to be the reason for becoming a world power in the first place—with armies and navies developing later and having the added task of making the world safe for democracy. The Weberian model explaining the relationship of the Protestant work ethic and capitalism is useful. Even as hard work and saving one's earnings leads to accumulation of capital which can then be invested in some business enterprise resulting in even greater wealth, so America was humble, hardworking, not needing armies and navies, which resulted in prosperity that was invested in armies and navies to defend, protect, and spread great Christian moral principles. In both, the success was not only a sign of God's favor, but a divine mandate of moral responsibility to the world.

In this light it is understandable that Conwell was haunted by the fear that America would misuse her newly acquired power, and Americans would become vainglorious brags gloating over their elevated position in the world. His concern, mixed with unabashed pride in American power, was consistent with an era seeking to get focused in the face of dizzying change—a people told on the one hand that their real power and influence in the world was moral, but invited on the other hand to take an inordinate satisfaction in watching the Spanish navy (symbol of an arrogant wealthy, powerful, and decadent society) gurgle helplessly to the bottom.

But if a substantive portion of Conwell's message was peripatetic, a greater portion was resoundingly unequivocal. America's superior morality as an example to be emulated by the world was one unmistakable theme. When the *Titanic* went down the alleged cry was to get the women and children off to safety in life boats: great Christian heroism, said Conwell. Moreover, in the Temple minister's mind such male bravery would never occur in Turkey or China or in any of the "heathen" countries of the world. "On the contrary, they throw their children into destruction. They kill their children and the women are the last thought of, and always sacrificed for the safety of the men. But Christianity changes this."[18]

In Conwell's vision America not only cared for its women and children, it was magnanimous in victory toward its defeated enemies. Indeed, the human way the Americans allegedly treated the vanquished Spaniards was more important than the victory itself. Americans were people who treat defeated enemies like honorable men, giving them the utmost comfort " better than you and I enjoy," Providing them food and the privilege of communicating with their families.[19] Some prisoners were even invited as dinner guests. Moreover, Americans in victory did not exact reparations or demand that Spain pay for the war. Rather the American government said "to this ignorant and benighted nation, 'If you will make these people [Cubans] free for whom we are unselfishly contending, we will take upon ourselves our great debt and all its hardships and pay it ourselves.' "[20]

This perception of American moral superiority was extended to the American admirals and generals. Commodore Schley, after the victory at Santiago said, "Three cheers for the men behind the guns," "A peculiar American sentiment," says Conwell, while Europe's generals by contrast say, "Three cheers for the King or Officers." This simple illustration was cited to demonstrate that in a Christian democracy, as America was perceived to be, even in the military the same honor was given to the commoner as to the generals and admirals. Indeed, to Conwell, the average American foot soldier displayed superior intelligence and moral fiber to any soldier in the world. Consisting of college graduates, educators, business leaders, and most of all Christians, "these men—foot soldiers—privates have the intellectual power to so control themselves as to adjust themselves at once to all the needs of war." Such superior background made them magnificent soldiers, contrasted to "the ignorant dummy in all other armies who simply obeys the commands of his superior."[21]

Moral superiority and purity of motives were attributed to Theodore Roosevelt and his open door policy toward China. Roosevelt allegedly engineered this policy because he was concerned over the ignorance of the Chinese and their seclusion from the world with no chance for exposure to Christian civilization. Even his Panama policy was graced with halo and wings. Quoting Roosevelt to prove the assertion, the Panama Canal "shall be for all the nations of the world. America is not doing this for ourselves; it is a work for all mankind and consequently a work for God."[22]

In a moving sermon titled "The Saviour at the Panama Canal," Conwell spoke of the Christian influence of America on the world in creating the canal—an engineering feat greater than the pyramids, Karnak, Baalbec, Babylon, or medieval cathedrals. Said he, "We have done the greatest thing in the history of the world in building that Canal."[23]

But more than the material witness was the Christian witness in the construction of the Canal. In Conwell's mind labor was treated as the Bible teaches it should be, with some 50,000 workmen being given more in wages than requested,[24] and hence there were no labor troubles in the project. Additionally, workmen were allowed to earn even more through overtime. "Who would have thought that in working for the government a man would ask for more working hours?"[25] Such employee-employer harmony was perceived as unique and directly attributable to Christian flexibility. The Temple minister exulted that the Christian employer "does not, like Shylock, demand the exact pound of flesh to the closest items; he does not like some men, with mathematical exactness come down to the fifteen millionth of an inch, but always allows a space for adjustment." Therefore the construction of the Panama Canal "holds up its banner to the sunlight and proclaims to the nations of the earth the greatest accomplishment of any age of the world."[26]

More dramatic still was Christ's healing work in Panama. Whereas the French were driven out of the canal zone by disease and serpents, "the Christian government of the United States went down . . . where there lurked in the swamps the most poisonous of serpents; where malaria lurked in every breath, and fevers were scarcely ever escaped by the healthiest men, and . . . changed it into the healthiest place on the face of the entire earth."[27] Under the banner of Christian civilization the swamps were cleansed.

Moreover, with the construction of the Canal came Christian education to Panama. Panamanian children were perceived as having a better opportunity for education than any other children on earth. Schools were operated on the American model. Entertainment furnished by Christian America was uplifting and wholesome, movies "high and elevating," music and musicians "of the finest," plays in theaters "uplifting and pure." "Oh it is a blessed, ideal, Christian state," says Conwell. "It is the ideal city they have there; the ideal village; the ideal land, and the reason it was possible to bring it about was because it was under the paternal Government of the United States; a government that loves God and loves mankind."[28]

America's superior morality was demonstrated further through the integrity displayed by the Presidents. "Not one president," declared Conwell triumphantly, "was ever elected to that office because he could play a good game of cards."[29] Rather Washington was known for his purity, Adams his honor, Jefferson his love of humanity, Madison his purity, Monroe and Lincoln their honesty; Pierce was known for his morals, Harrison his bravery, and Jackson his love and respect for pure womanhood. Such good choices for President made by the enlightened American electorate was also seen as evidence of God's direction for His Chosen.

Convinced of American moral superiority, Conwell was equally convinced of the moral inferiority of foreign lands. His harsh words and patronizing attitude toward Mexico represented his position toward much of the world, Western and Eastern. Mexico's moral, social, political, economic, and religious depravity was to be expected since they had no experience in democracy, no school system like the American system, and no privilege to worship God freely. Mexicans lacked "the intelligence, and the patriotism, and the generosity, and the Christian knowledge of the people of this country,"[30] So it was unfair of Americans to judge negatively the Mexican government. While Mexico copied the American constitution it was too much to expect that it would work for them since they "are larely savage people, uncultured, and they have not the intelligence to follow that Constitution even though they copied it."[31] Consisting of twenty-seven different states and fourteen different languages, evidence of hopeless political and cultural division, Mexico most of all was "yet an adulterous country, given over almost completely to the worship of wood and stone, as though it were in the interior of India or the farthest islands of the sea."[32]

Conwell's world view was scarcely more optimistic as revealed in a major sermon on the League of Nations titled "An Unfair Partnership."[33] "Shall the United States join the League of Nations?" Conwell rhetorically asked. To help the congregation decide on its own "without being told how to vote" the Temple minister loaded the decision-making deck with an illustration that not only revealed the Temple minister's adamant position concerning the League, but laid bare his conviction of the moral depravity of the world. The setting for the illustration was the story of an Englishman in Victoria, Australia, needing $7,500 to buy mining machinery to mine gold. The five investors who invested in this enterprise were the usual stereotypes associated with ethnic and racial backgrounds. The Negro, invested $1,000 and his labor, the "Chinaman" $2,000, the Irishman $1,500, the Egyptian $1,500, and the Jew $500. All had different talents to contribute to the enterprise. The Negro was athletic, having little education, the Jew had contacts to sell the product, the Englishman was skillful in the wise purchase of goods "and desired, of course, as is natural to Englishmen, to conduct the whole affair and get the profits out of the whole business."[34] But according to the original agreement all were to share equally in the profits. The man who invested $2,000 would get the same as the man who invested $500. The result of the arrangement is predictable: the Jew realized that if he owned the whole enterprise he could make all the money by selling to people he knows personally. The Englishman was skillful and knew he was more valuable than any of the rest, and hence should have a greater salary than the others. The Negro contended he should have an advancement beyond the Irishman, and so on, leading to a disintegration of the enterprise.

That, said Conwell, is the structure of the League of Nations. Smaller nations having as few as two million people have the same vote as any nation, except for Britain which having five great empires combined in one, would have five votes. American shipping interests would be at the mercy of the British, and the large, wealthy, and well-educated United States would be an equal partner with "one of the South American states or with Mexico or with Japan or some of the smaller states of Europe in our voting power."[35] But more serious than the mere voting discrepancy would be the moral and religious discrepancy. Basing his position on St. Paul's warning, "Be not unequally yoked together with unbelievers,"[36] Conwell in turn warned that Americans must not be unequally yoked with Moslems. Moreover, all Christians believe they should live the Great Commission,[37] meaning that all Christians must insist that all nations become Christian. "That is our duty! . . . Then shall we join a League of Nations and go into a partnership with Turkey with all their extreme ferocities; with all their dredfully extreme doctrines?"[38] Extending the condemnation, he asserted that the German Christian religion was inferior, that Jews, if they ever got political power in the United States, would impose their religion on everybody else, and the "Chinaman's" worship of Buddha was obviously blatant paganism. Therefore, "If this nation is to be Christian we will build a Christian navy . . . and we will have a Christian army . . . that shall ever set its face against the infidels and against the heathen, and never, never permit them to weaken us.''[39] The conscience tingling a bit, Conwell acknowledged how unkind this proposition seems at first, but quickly recovered to reminisce about his travels in those Eastern lands where they have "deep and severe . . . prejudices." Hence the great barrier to the League was not so much a difference in skill, or capital, but religion, precluding any contract with nations having different religions since such arrangements implied in the Temple minister's mind approval of those religions, (a logic no different than that which is inconsistently displayed by the American government toward communist governments unworthy of diplomatic recognition). In a parting shot in his sermon Conwell asked, "Shall we encourage the Buddhists, the Moslems, giving them equal chance with the rest of the world and let them get great sums of money so that they can build their mosques and armies to conquer the world? No—never. Christ is the only king and he should be recognized by every nation on earth.''[40]

In light of America's moral superiority, contrasted to the rest of the world's moral depravity, the obvious solution to the discrepancy, given adherance to the imperative of the Great Commission, was to democratize and Christianize the world. American responsibility to the world made up the bulk of Conwell's sermon themes on foreign policy. Like Israel, America is a chosen people not to bask in luxury, power, and greed, but to serve mankind, spread the good news of the gospel, preferably through education, medicine, and technology, but through the military if necessary.

America's responsiblity to the world included an obligation to defend people who suffer at the hands of oppression anywhere in the world. As such the United States should have entered World War I upon the German invasion of Belgium, or with the sinking of the *Lusitania*. Turkey should have been "wiped off the face of the earth as a political power . . . or exterminated for massacring tens of thousands of Armenian Christians by the Kurds, drowning more than 3,200 in a day in 1894.''[41] Such treatment, reasoned Conwell, was appropriate since one could not expect anything else from an infidel Sultan.[42] The best solution for the Turks, were it ever possible, would be to give them schools and a new religion.

Another responsibility laid on America's shoulders by God was to preserve the peace of the world. This issue was a preoccupation of Conwell's, and it seems inconsistent when considering the extreme solution he advocated concerning the Turks. However, coming from Conwell's perspective, it is not hard to see how he resolved such a conflict. It was his conviction that war is sometimes needed to bring peace. Indeed war is inevitable even as the surgeon's knife must draw blood to effect a cure. Since backward countries do not know any better than their pagan ways, it may be necessary for the United States to initially compel them through force of arms or other kinds of pressure to change their ways, wean them from their pagan past, and set them toward a Western future, ultimately releasing them for self-determiantion within democratic and Christian parameters. Only then would peace on earth be possible.

Conwell also felt that American responsibility to the world included an educational mission. He was always quick to follow up a call for military action with a call for pedagogical action. As necessary and as successful as World War I was in accomplishing the goals for which it was fought, more than armies was needed. Democracy can not come with laws or armies, he said. Rather democracy comes through education, and education of a particular sort. The Germans, for example, were educated in technology, music, and philosophy, having their schools and universities. "But they are still the most ignorant people of the world in politics unless it be the Russians, and their religion is vastly inferior to religions in America."[43] And obviously peace was impossible with Mexico or Turkey or any uneducated or uneducable nation. Therefore, the only way that America could conquer the world for Christ was to establish educational institutions around the world and send missionaries—an army of missionaries—teachers for the "preservation of democracy of the world." We must go to China and help the ignorant and "Americanize them."[44]

Curiously, for Conwell an excellent means to spread Christian education to the world was seen through a bill in Congress to subsidize private enterprise for the purchase of surplus ships from World War I. Such purchases by private enterprise could be profitably used to promote trade and spread the gospel of Jesus Christ. Conversion of sailors was also seen as essential so that they would truly represent the American nation.

The particular sort of educational message to be taught to the world was that a Christian democracy, which America had, is the best form of government. Moreover, a Christian democracy is a theocracy of the holy whereby the majority will is the will of God. This form of government is the wave of the future. Indeed, God is establishing this form on earth. Even as churches are turning to a congregational form of government so enlightened, educated people are insisting on a congregational form of government for their nation states. Conwell could not have said it more clearly: "The voice of the people is finally the voice of God.''[45] The only true democracy is a theocracy,'' and ''the American democracy stands for that ideal. . . .''[46] Conversely, a rule by majority of non-Christians was logically impossible within Conwell's scheme.

Conwell not only dramatized America's responsibility to the world in grandiose terms, he also exhorted concerning American responsibilites to specific problem areas of the world. Mexico, for example, was a major frustration of his. ''Poor Mexico is a disgrace,'' he said in 1913. ''It would be well for Mexico. . . if we had a protectorate over it long enough to compel them to recognize the great Christian brotherhood of man, enough to accept the rule of the majority, which is, after all, the rule of God. . . .''[47] After the World War his frustration was still virulent. If the Mexicans were doing right ''their present condition would not exist,''[48] he fumed. But since they were not doing right, the Untied States had the right and duty to intervene and straighten them out. Intervention was also seen as protection from foreign exploitation in their weakened, depraved condition. However, justification for intervention always carried with it a warning against American exploitation. Said he, we must go to Mexico ''with the same altruistic spirit with which we went to Cuba,''[49] after the Spanish American War and with the same spirit allegedly manifest in the Great War. Indeed, it appeared that the time was ripe as never before to send the gospel to the ''heathen in Mexico.''

Conwell's central focus toward Puerto Rico and the Philippines was to insist ultimately on Christian home rule. ''The only thing the American nation can do'', he said, ''is to let every people govern themselves by a principle of Christian home rule.''[50] Concerning the Philippines specifically, he warned that Americans must not take them or make money on them. Rather, ''We can only generously say, 'now you are free, make the best of it yourselves. You may have the same liberties we have, and the same education we have, and the same freedom of religion we enjoy.' ''[51] With vintage ''White Man's Burden,'' however, Conwell wasn't ready to throw the Philippines to the wolves of international greed or the cannibalism of tribal political factionalism. ''Shall we abandon them now like cowards and sneak away from the poor people we have encouraged to seek their liberty?''[52] Never. How long the United States should remain in the Philippines for their own good was never explicitly spelled out by the Temple minister, but his conviction that America should never consider ownership or control of the Philippines for commercial or profit motives was consistent. And Conwell was certain that Americans as Christians subscribed to these high and noble motives, making America the first nation in "the pages of history willing to do that. . . ."[53]

The Cuban question was another matter for Conwell. Whether it was because Cuba was seen as potentially less adept as self-government, or because of its proximity to the United States mainland, Conwell seemed to advocate ultimate statehood for the island. "Do we let an ignorant people flounder with local quarrels and allow them to select officials who are unfit for positions, thereby wrecking their newly discovered liberty?" he asked "Or shall we accept them as a state in our government?" A third alternative solution, one Conwell implicitly rejected, was to "establish the simple protectorate over it and spend millions more in caring for it."[54] Conwell's position concerning Cuba did not change over the years. By the end of 1901, he still felt that the island was too small to maintain independence—that it was an easy prey for expansionists. Germany in particular was seen as the potential predator. But if Cuba were to become an American state this danger would end.[55]

Especially fascinating was Conwell's opinion of American immigration policy. One would naturally assume, given his harsh attitude toward Roman Catholic countries as being especially ignorant, that he would wholeheartedly support strict immigration quotas levied on the Southeastern European countries, to say nothing of the quotas and restrictions laid on pagan Orientals. Quite the opposite was the case, however. Conwell enthusiastically supported open immigration and scathingly denounced American immigration policy. A member of Congress apparently asked the Temple minister to write a critique of current immigration laws. Conwell did not write the booklet but did deliver sermons on the issue. The immigration laws at the time (1923) had quota limits for foreigners of every class and origin, all of which Conwell opposed. Not only did Conwell see quota restrictions denying America the larger labor force needed for its bourgeoning industrial capacity, but he believed it was shortsighted by keeping out good men and women regardless of origin who would be useful to America. Moreover, quota policies were perceived as selfish. While restrictions would temporarily raise wages of the laboring class by keeping labor in short supply, it would in time force a rise in labor costs and hurt production. Such restrictive policies made no sense to him since the country was in a growth cycle with a need for millions of immigrants. America could support "at least two hundred million more inhabitants,"[56] he said. The only legitimate immigration restrictions were to keep out the evil, the diseased, the beggers, and bring in "only the righteous and the helpful ones."[57] Conwell was also critical of America's unwillingness to treat Japan and China as equals in immigration laws. Such discrimination was seen as detrimental not only to the labor needs of America but also to the missionary enterprise because of the ill-feeling such a policy engendered in foreign Orientals who were potential candidates for Christian conversion.[58] Contrasted with many of his ministerial colleagues and thousands of Protestants, Conwell did not share the paranoia over the influx of pagans and Catholics (and many didn't make that distinction) into America. Rejecting the fear of those who believed that immigrants served as a fifth column for the Papacy he was disturbed to hear "the severest and harshest language used by members of my own denomination [Northern Baptist] concerning the Roman Catholic Church."[59] Such denominational behavior was "un-American and un-Christian and un-Godlike." Roman Catholics in the military had heroically participated with the Protestants in the Spanish—American war, planting the American flag on Cuban hillsides. Such hate campaigns against Roman Catholics could only serve to weaken and destroy the American influence for good in the world.

The only immigrant-related issue that was of concern to Conwell was the number of immigrants in the United States at the outbreak of World War I; fifteen million foreign-born in the United States with twenty million children totaling thirty-five to forty million people who had allegiance to some other country. Compounding the concern was the poor economic and social condition of the immigrants, which implicitly could give rise to disloyalty to the United States or at least apathy toward their adopted land. Not knowing English, confronted with strange customs, living in dwellings that were disgraceful and overcrowded, the poorest classes of Europe came with higher expectations that can be met, segregated in the cities; these were the conditions that worried Conwell, conditions not the fault of the immigrant. The solution? Each state should allow no more than can be assimilated and cared for, but again welcome with open arms, hearts and minds "every man, women and child from any foreign land, as long as they are so situated that they can comply with American institutions, as long as they understand American liberty, and American responsibilities."[60]

What accounts for Conwell's liberal view of immigration? At first glance this is a puzzling qustion, but his attitude makes considerable sense when one considers his pro-business stance and its thirst for cheap labor. As for the influx of "ignorant" Catholics and pagans, Conwell still assumed the optimistic stance of Protestants that these immigrants would be converted and absorbed into a Protestant

America. Moreover, even though poor and Catholic, any immigrant willing to endure the risks and hardships of immigrating to American was made of the stuff this country desired.

These are the foreign policy issues of concern to Russell Conwell. But what is the significance of Russell Conwell delivering his perception of proper foreign policy through benediction? Surely the pulpits across the land heralded much the same message. The attitude of the Protestant clergy in general concerning foreign policy issues is well documented. What is so special about Conwell?

It is instructive to get an added dimension of the ministry of Russell Conwell. He was a prisoner to the fame of his "Acres of Diamonds" lecture. Consequently, historians overlook not only the much broader message that he conveyed, including his foreign policy opinions in his sermons, but also the influence of this broader message by virtue of the name recognition he enjoyed due to "Acres of Diamonds" fame. While his influence on shaping popular opinion on foreign policy issues cannot be quantified, it is instructive to note that he was in the vanguard advocating American intervention anywhere in the world, motivated by his conviction that the United States had an obligation to aid the oppressed wherever the oppression. This call to arms, motivated by altruism, was commonly heard throughout the Protestant press of his day,[61] and it is likely that Conwell's influence played a role in helping to shape Baptist opinion in particular, and Protestant opinion in general, because of his prestige.[62] Temple Baptist was turned into a center of agitation for intervention on behalf of Cuba. Conwell made several visits to the island, established a Cuban Relief Fund, and members of his Church volunteered to help with the National Christian Relief Association organized at the Philadelphia YMCA.

Church trustee Edward O. Elliott whose life as trustee spans the ministry of Conwell, felt that the Temple minister pioneered the way leading to United States intervention in Cuba and occupation of the Philippines.[63] Indeed Conwell's activites in the 1890s on behalf of Cuba have been compared to Henry Ward Beecher's agitation activity against slavery in the 1850s. Both used their churches as centers of activity for their respective crusades. Beecher using Plymouth Church as a site for a mock slave auction, and Conwell using Temple Baptist as a site not only for massive rallies but for a reception held in honor of Evangeline Cisneros, the daughter of the Cuban leader rescued from a Spanish prison.[64] Before her arrival Conwell prepared the way with the sermon, "The escape from Cuba." Once the Spanish-American War was won, and so easily, it was the enthusiasm of the clergy and religious press to "uplift, civilize and Christianize the Philippines" that, along with other pressures, caused President McKinley to go along with the tide and take territory.[65].

The Temple minister is interesting and worth studying also because he was such a mirror of the times. Whatever criticism one may wish to level at the man, he was acting in character and should be interpreted and enjoyed in that light. Perry Miller's words to those who make it a habit to rake the Puritans over the coals for their prudery are applicable to those who scorn Conwell. There is only one thing worse than praising the Puritans as harbingers of religious liberty, says Miller, and that is to berate them for their intolerance. The Puritans came to this country because they knew they had the Truth. For them to be tolerant was to be theologically wishy-washy, and unfaithful to the Call. Similarly, one might say that there is one thing worse than to give blanket praise to Conwell for his attitude toward the poor, and that is to berate him for his unabashed nationalistic fervor. The marvel is that he was as moderate as he was in the jingoistic context of his times. The Temple minister fit comfortably within two moods of the country as described by Richard Hofstadter. On the one hand was a mood of protest and humanitarian reform, populim, and utopianism; on the other hand was a mood of national self-assertion, aggression, and expansion. The motif of the first was sympathy, of the second was power.[66] With exceptions, Conwell expressed both moods as described at the beginning of this essay. His humanitarian impulse justified aggression on behalf of the oppressed. Of course the residual benefits of material prosperity, power, and prestige of the nation sweetened the pot and indicated the blessing of God in these holy ventures.

Furthermore, a study of Conwell's foreign policy opinion through sermon is useful because he represented a strong voice that was in the center politically on foreign policy issues. As such his was a moderating voice between two extremes. Rejecting the expansionism of a Josiah Strong on the one hand, and denouncing the do-nothingism of an Anti-Imperialsim League on the other, he consistently called for intervention, housecleaning, and withdrawal for the sake of the principle of self-determination. Clearly, America was to be the moral policeman of the world. It is also clear that while his enthusiasm for American power, technical expertise, education, and moral soundness knew no bounds, his nationalism was not a blind fervor devoid of the prophetic. Conwell praised and damned heroes and villians alike.

Finally, Conwell's foreign policy opinions are worth remembering since they expressed values to which much of American Christianity can relate today. Curiously, he was a preacher advocating such a range of foreign policy attiudes that both Fundamentalists and Liberals today would be able to find points of agreement with him were they aware of his diverse message. This is not to say that all of American Christianity can relate to all of Russell Conwell. But there are conwellesque opinions that will warm the cockles of any New Right adherent, and opinions which even liberal Protestantism and Catholism will cheer. This might be considered a rather remarkable athletic achievement if we were considering stretching exercises. Since that is not the case, suffice it to say that Conwell represented significant rootage here to consider.

For the New Right, which would include Fundamentalists and many Evangelicals, Conwell would be admired not only as the precursor to a power of positive thinking ministry, for which he is best known, but for some of his values that are perceived as lost today and needing to be found by America. Conwell's anti-League of Nations posture on the basis that Christian America should not be unequally yoked with unbelievers is a page taken out by the Fundamentalists of the New Right in their opposition to the United Nations. Other pages from Conwell taken by the New Right would be his peace-through-strength emphasis, and American responsibility to make the world Christian and democratic, becoming again the Christian moral leader of the world. Until this day occurs, like Conwell the Fundamentalists in particular see the rest of the world as pagan and hence depraved.

Mainline Protestantism and Catholicism would be comfortable with Conwell's conviction of the need for close interdenominational cooperation, including cooperation with Roman Catholics in working for peace in the world, and for applying pressure and influence on the government regarding foreign policy issues. Conwell's caution of not being unequally yoked to nonbelievers applies only to non-Christian religions, but certainly not to Roman Catholics. His adamant opposition to expansionism would be applauded by the main liners as would be his emphasis on the need to provide education, technical assistance, and food to parts of the world in need.

I suspect also that Conwell represents a ministry that attempted to fuse the emphasis of individual salvation with a broader Christian social concern. Conwell could possibly be seen as being sympathetic to "the camps of both the Moodys and the Rauschenbusches."

This as well as his middle-ground position on foreign policy issues is significant, it seems to me, for two reasons. The first comes from a commmon observation that during Conwell's lifetime the Social Gospel movement, which in the 1890s had enjoyed support from both conservative and liberal clergy, split asunder following the Great War over the issue of evolution and biblical inerrancy. The Fundamentalists, who formed out of this controversy, showed their aversion to the liberals by rejecting not only evolution and biblical criticism, but any social teachings of the gospel as well in deference to an emphasis on individual salvation. It seemed that there was no middle ground any more. It is my observation, however, that Russell Conwell came close to representing a continuation of this middle ground well into the 1920s, at least in the realm of his foreign policy statements, and perhaps even in his social philosophy as well. Martin Marty observes the growing gap between Fundamentalists and Liberals when he states that nobody tried to stand in the camps of both the Moodys and the Rauschen-busches with the exception of Benjamin Fay Mills whom he cites as the last of those who tried "to follow the joint vocation of evangelist and agent of social change."[67] Benjamin Fay Mills died in 1916, Conwell in 1926. It could be that a significant voice in Protestantism extended this dual emphasis as well as a moderate foreign policy voice through the heart of the Fundamentalist movement and controversy of the 1920s.

A second reason this study seems significant stems from a current observation that the camps of both the evangalist and the social reformer are coming together again as during the Social Gospel heyday in the current Protestant evangelical movement. Such a movment is marked by a middle ground position between the ravings of extreme Fundamentalists on the one hand who would bring on Armageddon, and the seeming "peace at any price" accommodationists on the other hand. The present day Evangelicals are distinguished not only by their fusion of evangelistic fervor with calls for significant social change, but also by their moderate position that is horrified by the thought of Armageddon yet still advocates a generally hard-line stance against the Communist world.

Perhaps Conwell represents another link in that thin middle ground thread during a time when the bulk of Protestantism was either in the Moody camp or the Rauschenbusch camp. Perhaps his middle ground stance in foreign policy helps to explain why at one time he had a foot in America's more bellicose side and at another time lashes out at inordinant pride, calling for national repentance and humility. And perhaps Conwell represented that thread nearly connecting the Social Gospelers of the 1890s in all of their breadth of emphasis with the Evangelicals of the 1980s.

The breadth of Russell Conwell's ministry in general may come as a surprise to those who have viewed him narrowly. Moreover, while on balance he leans on the political continuum a bit to the right, he showed surprising flexibility and good sense for his day, and understanding him helps us to understand ourselves just a little bit better.

— 10 —

Civil Religion in a New Context: The Mexican-American Faith of César Chávez

Spencer Bennett

In the midst of the attempt to regain perspective on the connection between religion and politics in American life, some have turned to the analysis of American civil religion. Decidedly an umbrella term, civil religion is generally described as a belief in a framework of national symbols, rituals, traditions, and institutions that, in expressing the common ethos of a people, also reveals a dimension of purposeful and transcendent ultimacy. American civil religion owes a great deal to the development of American Christianity in its symbolism, but it is quite divergent in its sources. In its often neutral language about God in the political process it is indebted to the Enlightenment. In its colorful use of popular imagery and artifacts it belongs under the category of folk religion. And because American civil religion has to provide common ground of belief for so many diverse ethnic populations, it can correctly be called an exercise in religious pluralism.

It is the ethnic dimension of civil religion that I would address here. Many of the symbols so far ensconced in our public religion come from the notion of America as the "New Israel" as that idea was inculcated in the experience of national events and persons. The writing of the Declaration of Independence and the Constitution, the agony of the Revolutionary and the Civil Wars, and the crystalizing of patriotism in those wars in the speeches of Tom Paine and Abraham Lincoln, the deaths of the Kennedys and Martin Luther King: all of these represent aspects of a national belief in the sanctification of an American destiny.[1] But the other side of that coin is that all of these events had as their origins the perspectives of minorities who came to represent the majority view.

For example, the civil religion of the American Revolution was a mosaic of symbols, similies, metaphors, and analogies that owed its origins to the Puritan heritage of its leaders. For the colonists, the concept of the Old Testament God who leads the children of Israel out of the wilderness becomes a forceful metaphor for their own struggle with the British. The analogy explains their temporary losses (due to lapses in conventional morality), the need for patience and perseverance (consistent with forty years in the wilderness), and gives them hope that, whatever the odds in numbers (like the odds of the ancient Israelites), the final victory is theirs. Yet, Old Testament images are not the only source of inspiration for these patriots. It is well known that the images of nature through the influence of Deism were strong in the thinking of Jefferson, Adams, et al. Catherine Albanese in her book, *Sons of the Fathers, The Civil Religion of The American Revolution,* makes a case for the liberty tree as a galvanizing symbol of the Revolution.[2] It served not only as a convenient reference for the hanging in effigy of British officials, but also as a paradigm for the thirteen colonies branching out from the trunk of union.

But because these metaphors are so well entrenched in public civil religion, we forget the character of the English and particularly the English Puritan experience which supplied them. To put this another way, how could a Mexican-American relate to the liberty tree or the ancient biblical text so prominent in colonial experience given his/her radically different background? For the predominant motif of the American Revolution was the ancient tribe of Israel, a downtrodden people who would emerge through their faith, victorious over superior forces. In doing so they would overcome a wilderness which hampered their efforts at liberty and with their victory be given the promise of prosperity for themselves and their future generations. All the assumptions of the European mindset function here. The Lord of human history or the Jehovah of Battles who would lead them onward, the importance of the prophet Joshua personified in George Washington, the manipulation of nature to human ends (stories about the freezing and thawing of earth to let the colonists pass where the British bogged down), and the political power many felt God endowed upon the people in the Declaration of Independence—all of these were seen as signs of God's favor.

Contrast this centralizing motif with that of the origins of the Mexican people two hundred and fifty years earlier. There the controlling metaphor is the Lady of Guadalupe, borne out of a combination of Indian lore and Spanish Catholicism.[3] She was first seen by an Indian peasant, Juan Diego, at the ancient Aztec shrine of the goddess of the moon outside of Mexico City in 1531. Her discovery was a sign that the gods of nature had survived the holocaust of the

Spanish invasion. Before that first vision of the "brown lady," the Indians and the *mestizos,* the children of the Spanish and the Indians, were outcasts with no place in church, society or government. With her as protectress, the way was open for them to be included in all three. She ensured for the Indian that his old Aztec gods retained some of their power through her, since the Lady revealed herself at the shrine of the moon goddess, *Tonantzin,* whose shrine was later to become the Basilica of Guadalupe. Like the liberty tree for the English colonists, the Virgin becomes an icon. The rays of the sun, a central force in Aztec worship, still radiate from behind her in portraits of her.[4] She stands upon the moon, a tribute to the sacred place at which she reveals herself. Finally she is brown and consequently the patroness of a mixed race. To those despised by Spanish and Anglo alike, she promises salvation and protection under the law.

It is clear that the Virgin of Guadalupe through Mexican-American culture brings an added dimension to American civil religion. For one thing, her character is feminine. She brings an element of passive reflection into focus as a national attribute. Where the God of the American Revolution, in Anglo terms, is active and male as are the bearers of his revelation, the Virgin in her femininity protects a people who have been ravished and oppressed in the Conquest and who will continue to suffer in the future. Her identity is not with a people who rise to power but with the poor who are victimized. She promises not authority, but the protection of the law and orderly process in a world which is otherwise lawless and full of violence. The thrust of this image is not the control over nature so prominent in the lore about the God of the American Revolution but of sanctuary for the poor and oppressed in a world where natural forces are arbitrary and cannot be controlled.

Finally, the revelation of the Virgin is through mystic vision, while the God of the American Revolution makes Himself known through the word. From hundreds of Protestant pulpits, ministers invoked through sermons the identification of the colonial cause with God's purpose for the new nation. In these sermons the patriots were admonished by the interpreted norms of Old Testament law to keep the faith and perform accordingly. But in Juan Diego's vision flowers, as the symbol of nature, and music, as the language of the human heart, are instrumental in creating the necessary conditions for the Virgin's appearance. Instead of drawing parallels to the biblical text for the creation of a people, the context is the coming together of two worlds, the Aztec and Spanish Catholicism. The Mexican-American is planted in a tradition where he cannot forget the integral part nature played in the metaphysics of his pre-Columbian ancestors. In that tradition endurance and submission to natural forces were part of religion and had their counterparts in the Christian vitures of humility and penance. Reflection, meditation, and introspection become important elements in Mexican religion and subsequently in the accompanying civil religion. Furthermore, "flower and song" religious rituals and the cycles of nature relate to each other.

But it might be argued that the parameters of the discussion so far do not extend beyond the limits of orthodox Catholicism to the issue of American civil religion. After all, colonial civic piety became such only when Sam Adams took religious symbols into the coffee houses and saloons of Boston and hammered them into a call for civic action. If ministers recruited from their pulpits, there still could be no civil religion unless the populace, outside the dictates of formal religion, embraced and transferred the symbols of their own political and military actions in the name of nation rather than church. That this transition took place we know from the currency that such terms as the "New Israel" still have at public functions in our time. But is the same true of Mexican-American religion? Has there been a transference of its piety into the political self-consciousness of an emerging people so that they consider the heritage of their world view a legitimate part of the accepted civil religion of our time?

At least as Mexican-American civil religion functions, the answer has to be yes. If the symbolism of the above comes to focus in the Virgin of Guadalupe, she is always present on national holidays, and her presence is required at personal celebrations such as marriages and first communions. In the Southwest, she can be found everywhere in icon form from groceries (in the form of votive candles) to buses (planted right in front of the driver). But beyond this, she became the inspiration for one facet of the civil rights movement of the 1960s as the patron saint for the American Farm Workers Union in the United States, where, in her person as a phenomenon of civil religion, she was eminently functional.

The Religious Dimension
of the United Farm Workers' Struggle

On 10 March 1968 after a fast of twenty-five days, a small Mexican-American, César Chávez, so weakened by hunger that he could not hold his head up, sat in an overstuffed chair on the back of a flatbed truck before 8,000 farm workers, supporters and a few politicians in a park in Delano, California. To make this scene even more unusual, beside this *campesino,* seated in another overstuffed chair, was an Irish-American, Robert F. Kennedy, looking uncomfortably out of place. Neither Kennedy nor Chávez spoke to the crowd that day; instead James Drake of the California Migrant Ministry, assistant to Chávez in the United Farm Workers' Organizing Committee, read the text of Chávez's speech.

It is hard to believe that the simple, if impressive, act of a fast of twenty-five days by one man could draw such a crowd, especially when Chávez insisted that his fasting was a personal act of religious sacrifice, assuredly and singularly his.

> I undertook this fast because my heart was filled with grief and pain for the suffering of the farm workers. The fast was a first for me and then for all of us in this Union. It was a fast for nonviolence and a call to sacrifice. . . . It is my deepest belief that only by giving our lives do we find life. I am convinced that the truest act of courage, the strongest act of manliness is to sacrifice ourselves for others in a totally nonviolent struggle for justice. To be a man is to suffer for others. God help us to be men.[5]

These would have been strong words in a male culture raised upon *machismo* and stronger yet to an audience whose origins lay in a civilization created out of the violence of foreign conquest. But they should have seemed exceedingly strange to farm workers struggling to create more equitable conditions for themselves in the fruit and vegetable fields of southern California only to experience beatings, intentional hit-and-runs, false arrests, insecticide sprayings, and numerous other harassments from the growers, Teamsters, and deputy sheriffs in the San Joaquin Valley for the last six years.[6] Yet, it was the faith of this quiet-spoken man that made the farm workers' movement in California as much an enterprise in public religion as an exercise in civil rights for an oppressed minority.

Of course Chávez shared his vision of nonviolence as a means for securing justice with Martin Luther King, who would be assassinated a month later (and Kennedy a month after that). Both men shared as well the rhetoric of the public pulpit and the strategies of nonviolence. But there were differences in backgrounds and talents that make the nuances of leadership for the United Farm Workers under Chávez stand out with a singular character. For one thing, King was a rhetorician in the true sense of the word, an exhorter, a preacher, one who drives others to actions by the moral authority of his pronouncements. Chávez, on the other hand, was a model and example, who by his ascetic actions of fasting and penitential marches created in others the desire to emulate him. Second, the theology of the Southern Christian Leadership Conference was largely that of Protestant liberalism (strongly dosed by the realism of prophetic black experience), a belief that God's grace, with the help of nonviolent strategy, could break the power of racism. Sit-ins and marches were calculated to bring opponents to self-awareness. They would come to realize that the demonstrators would not hate them, no matter how much brutality was inflicted upon them. In contrast, the philosophy behind *La Causa* stressed the role of confession, penance, and acts of contrition that the farm workers might be strengthened for further suffering and cleansed of any residual hatred toward their enemies. While the key symbol for Christian blacks in the movement was the empty cross (a scandal turned into victory), the symbol for thousands of Mexican-American migrant workers was the Lady of Guadalupe, who, in her "brownness" protects those like her— the humble poor of Mexico and the Southwest.

Like King, Chávez's background is steeped in religion, but his is a background rich in a Southwest Catholicism in contrast to the black Protestantism of the deep South. Chávez's early religious training came from his mother, who insured that his catechism was heavily laced with social teachings about nonviolence and the poor. Her patron saint was St. Eduvigis, a patroness of those in poverty, on whose birthday Mrs. Chávez would send her childeren to the streets to find a hobo to bring home for dinner. Chávez claims that feeding the poor was a lifelong habit of hers.[7] His formal religious training came from his grandmother, "Moma Teller." It was good enough that the priest in Yuma, twenty miles away, allowed César and sister Rita to take their first communion without the usual catechetical classes. César's religious training was serious and strict (Moma Teller would hit him with a cane if he giggled during the Rosary), but reinforced by the warmth and generosity of his mother it was lasting, as Chávez himself admits:

> Since those days, my need for religion has deepened. Today I don't think that I could base my will to struggle on cold economics or on some political doctrine. I don't think there would be enough to sustain me. For me, the base must be faith.[8]

The other influence upon Chávez was as much an issue of social justice as that of religion. This was his association with Father Donald McDonnell from 1950 on in the barrio of *Sal si puedes* (Escape If You Can) in San Jose. McDonnell and Father Thomas McCullough were assigned to the Spanish Mission Band, a group of priests serving the thousands of Mexican-Americans in the rural and urban areas of Northern California. Although McDonnell and McCullough performed their spiritual duties in saying the mass in the migrant camps and barrios, they were strongly affected by the living conditions of the poor and spent a lot of time listening to and aiding these *braceros,* wetbacks and local workers in the fields. Both men believed strongly in the social teachings of the church expressed in the papal encyclicals *Rerum Novarum* and *Quadragessimo Anno* which upheld the right to a living wage and the right of workers to organize unions. McCullough introduced Dolores Huerta, the woman who would become a legend in *La Causa*, to the Community Service Organization, a privately funded social action agency operating out of San Jose, and thus launched her on a new career as a social worker.

McDonnell was saying mass in a ramshackle Puerto Rican hall when he met Chávez. Through McDonnell Chávez received his first experience in working with small groups and internal organizations when he and McDonnell organized a burial party for a fundless Mexican family. Under McDonnell's direction, Chávez also began a reading program which made him aware, for the first time, of the church's teachings on social justice, the lives of the saints, and the history of farm labor in California.

> As Father McDonnell followed legislation very closely he introduced me to the transcripts of the senate La Follette Committee hearings held in 1940 in Los Angeles. I remember three or four volumes on agriculture describing the Associated Farmers, their terror and strike breaking tactics and their financing by banks utilities and big corporations. These thing began to form a picture for me.[9]

It is important to see Chávez's early training as rooted in practical experience with respect to his orientation toward social justice and the strategies necessary to make it a reality. Where Martin Luther King came from the theory of his graduate work at Boston, primarily the works of Gandhi and Reinhold Niebuhr, to the hard situation of racism in Montgomery, Chávez, a migrant worker himself, lived under the hard conditions of the fields as he read the social gospel of Catholicism late into the night. This meant that, unlike the civil rights movement in the South where blacks had to create social situations (the Woolworth sit-ins) to break the chains of segregation, the United Farm Workers were in no way middle class nor were they concerned about the social implications of race. The economics of oppression came ready-made to Chávez and his followers. The more progressive element in the church merely supplied the rationale for lived and felt hardships in the fields as unjust under the teachings of Christ. The Southern Christian Leadership Conference, although aware of the economic plight of blacks, would address that fact in a different way and at a different level than the farm workers. This was so partially because of class but also because of the religious differences between the two groups, as well as the fact that civil rights in the South began as an urban movement while the Mexican-American effort was agricultural from the beginning.[10]

It was out of his religious background and his experience with the poor that Chávez forged the strategic and symbolic elements that would come to represent the United Farm Workers. But it is not the case that the movement simply represented the social justice arm of the Catholic Church anymore than the SCLC came to represent black Protestantism. Both gorups moved into a mode of prophecy that had as its goal an appeal to national conscience. Both agencies attempted to convince the larger public that the symbols of their respective movements were in keeping with the values of the natioan as they had been inculcated into the metaphors of earlier historical situations and became part of the accepted civil religion by the majority. The evidence that the civil rights movement was not denominational and local but was ecumenical and national is complicated but vital. One piece of evidence is that in both cases support from the institutional churches has been fragmentary at best and nonexistent or for the opposition most of the time. While many national religious organizations supported the grape strikes from 1965 on, many local priests, ministers, and laity opposed the farm workers.[11] Chávez's frustration over the oppositon from within the church is all the more understandable when seen against the social and economic injustices the workers suffered at the hands of the grower.[12]

But equally true, both the SCLC and the UFW are only implicitly religious in orientation and composition—much like civil religion at the national level. The latter included priests such as Mark Day at the administrative level as well as Jim Drake, a Presbyterian minister, who served as a personal aide. But there were others, like the playwright Luis Valdez who was not a believer and a host of Jewish volunteers including Marshall Ganz who found Chávez's personal brand of Catholicism baffling. What brought these supporters together was the conviction that the plight of the migrants and the solution to that plight was a national social issue where the pressure of the courts and national conscience should be brought to bear on the growers. To achieve this, Chávez and his followers would have to attract support through reference points and symbolic strategies that, through the media, could create instant recognition and empathy before a national audience.

Among the farm workers themselves the key symbol became the Virgin of Guadalupe. This because she is as much a presence in popular religion of Mexican-American culture as she is an icon of the church.[13] Because of her association with both Mexican revolutions she is not only a source of cultural pride but a metaphor for the struggle among the poor for economic justice. Chávez's use of her for the marches, strikes, and celebrations of the United Farm Workers was a natural reminder of the long history of the Mexican and the Mexican-American peoples. It is she who has the honored place in the shrines of the movement and who is carried at the head of all processions and parades along with the union banners and the United States flag. She represents for the farm workers the marriage of the promise that the poor have a place in God's plan in their daily struggle for recognition and justice.[14] Chávez first enunciated this in his Sacramento march letter of 1966, where he drew upon the traditional pilgrimage to the Basilica of Guadalupe in Mexico by the religiously devout to explain the farm workers' march from Delano to Sacramento during the Lenten season. Pilgrims make their way to the shrine of the Virgin with sacrifice and hardship as an expression of penance and commitment and with the hope of "some sincerely sought benefit of body or soul." So was the Delano march a pilgrimage of penance: "public penance for the sins of the strikers, their own personal sins as well as their yielding perhaps to the feelings of hatred and revenge in the strike itself."[15]

Two factors that are very much a part of the rituals of civil religion are evident here. Chávez points to a recognizable and cherished symbol of past tradition and future hope in the Vigin. All of his followers may not be devout Catholics but the cultural implications and the political meaning of the Guadalupe become clear as he rehearses her epic. Throughout American history the necessity for political leaders to do just this kind of rehearsal with recognized and accepted analogies has become part of the pattern of public piety. Jefferson's appeal during the American Revolution for days set aside for fasting and prayer, Lincoln's constant reminders of the Puritan heritage in his Civil War speeches, and indeed the required reference to the original concept of America as the "city upon a hill" in all presidential inaugural addresses—all of these testify that, no matter how little Americans understand about the actual circumstances of the Plymouth Colony, the majority of citizens identify with the conviction of divine mission behind that original enterprise. Beyond that to the biblical notion of Israel itself, Americans are stirred by the idea that their tradition is that of the minority which achieves victory through God's guidance and help.

Chávez calls upon a similar pattern of images. Like the promise that came in Juan Diego's first vision of the Virgin, where the Indian and his children were to have a place in church and society, the Mexican-American farm worker believed that Delano was his cause: "his great demand for justice, freedom and respect from a predominantly foreign cultural community in a land whre he was first."[16]

There is a variation here to be sure; the growers who would identify with that earlier vision of persecution under a foreign government are now subject to indictment under the terms of their own arbitrary power. The Mexican-American has replaced them in the national epic. For just as the Indian was the bedrock of Mexican society and yet was despised by the Spaniard, so were the farm workers first in the rich and fertile California lands where they now toil for foreign landlords who despise them. But both groups receive legitimization and authority under the mantle of the Virgin. Juan Diego's vision has apparently come full circle in the UFW's view of its own destiny.

Just as the larger meaning of the Virgin's presence at UFW events is implied but vital, it can also be argued that there was an implicit understanding that the theme of the "New Israel" as a wandering band who carried God's authority with them in the ark of the covenant is part of Chávez's understanding of the UFW mission. For the use of the Virgin as a portable shrine conveys this meaning. She was carried to the strike locations where she served not only as the focal point for the masses given nightly for the strikers but also as a drawing card for Mexican strikebreakers imported from the border. First used during the strike against DiGiorgio farms in May of 1966, the "station wagon" Lady became a common sight. The shrine proved an attraction for the cautious but devout Mexican aliens working in the field. At noon during the first day of its presence, eight strikebreaking women skipped lunch to attend a prayer vigil. Chávez recalls:

> The same evening about fifty women came. The next evening half the camp was out, and from then on, every single day, they were out there. Every day we had a mass, held a meeting, sang spirituals, and got them to sign authorization cards. Those meetings were responsible in large part for keeping the spirit up of our people inside the camp and helping our organizing for the coming battle.[17]

As with the original colonists (primarily Jefferson and Franklin) there were skeptics about the blatant use of religious symbolism as part of the rationale for gathering support and making public statements. Some, like Jerry Kircher, saw the use of a portable shrine as strictly a functional tool for winning union allegiance, claiming when the union got the contracts "we won't need Our Lady." Kircher was convinced that Chávez was not taking advantage of the Church because "it's as if he knew that to get from where the farm workers were to where they had to go, they needed help."[18] (Catherine Albanese makes the same comment about colonists who during the Revolution invoked stronger authority images of God than they did afterwards when they felt more in control of their own government and destiny.) But others associated with the UFW were less sure of this forecast and its accompanying philosophy. Like Stokely Carmichael and other young blacks with regard to Martin Luther King's notion of humility in the SCLC, Luis Valdez, a nonbeliever, Marshal Ganz and other Jewish coworkers were bothered by the presence of the Virgin and by Chávez's acts of self-denial. They initially saw not the slightest need for atonement on the workers' part since they were obviously the victims. And they did not like nor did they understand the aura of Mexican Catholicism evident in the presence of the shrine at union gatherings.[19]

The second element in American civil religion has been the consecration of suffering as the means by which values are validated as transcendent in origin. The travails and hardships of the Puritans, the price paid in blood in all wars, the toils of the pioneers—all of these are seen as necessary for the credentialing of political acts as sacral in nature. One only has to note the conclusion of Lincoln's Second Inaugural to realize how firm the belief of struggle as sacral event is rooted in the American mind. Chávez was able to convince many of his sincerity and of the UFW's authenticity as the union which should represent the workers through his many acts of self-denial. For him, the 1966 march to Sacramento was a sacrificial pilgrimage; he had (deliberately?) begun the march with the handicap of a worn-out pair of shoes that soon made his feet into a mass of blisters. And while the fast that Chávez undertook from 14 February to 10 March 1968 created great consternation among his volunteers, he saw it as absolutely necessary. For him, the fast was an act of repentance for his and the workers' ill-will toward the growers and an absolution of those harsh attitudes.

The messianic element in this certainly came from Chávez's Mexican background. And some rejected it in the same way they thought Martin Luther King's tactics were self-aggrandizing. But those close to Chávez understood. Dolores Huerta recalled:

> Poor César! They just couldn't accept it for what it was. I know it
> is very hard for people who are not Mexican to understand, but this

is part of the Mexican culture—!the penance, the whole idea of
suffering for something, of self-inflicted punishment. It's a tradition
of long standing.[20]

Jim Drake saw it from a slightly different angle. "Mexicans believe that
from suffering you get strength rather than death," and "this is expressed
in penitential acts."[21] Chávez found this to be the case in his fast. "After
seven days it was like going into a different dimension. I began to see
things in a different perspective, to retain a lot more, to develop
tremendous powers of concentration."[22]

But he also believed his fast to be a positive demonstration of the
principle of nonviolence. Responding to the increased violence of the
Teamsters during the strike and the nationwide boycott against
Guimarra farms, Chávez saw his fast as a strategy to demonstrate the
passive resistance of the movement. In the statement officially issued
by the UFW's Organizing Committee on February 25 the language was
religious in terms of the meaning of the fast.

> It is an act of the spirit which reaches to every man's need to escape
> living death and to begin giving of himself for the sake of other men.
> It is a personal act which beckons to each of us to participate in the
> nonviolent world-wide struggle against man's inhumanity to man.[23]

It was also a masterful strategy in rallying support for the group
at a time of low morale. When Chávez took to his bed at "Forty Acres,"
his headquarters just outside of Delano, supporters came from miles
away to attend the nightly masses, many setting up tents (like the
children of Israel around Moses) and camping there for the duration
of the fast. Support came at all levels of society and in all forms:
offerings from the workers themselves, verbal encouragement from
Robert Kennedy from Washington, and fifty thousand dollars from the
United Auto Workers by Paul Schrade at the mass concluding the fast.
Meanwhile Chavez, in his tiny bedroom, elicited greater dedication from
his cohorts and made new converts daily from those who visited him.

Meanwhile Chávez's opponents accused him of manipulation. The
growers, frustrated and baffled by his self-proclaimed acts of penance,
his commitment to nonviolence and his success, reacted variously.
Some insisted that he secretly left Forty Acres nightly and ate heartily
(Chávez's brother, Manuel, kidded guests exclaiming: "Don't bother
him now, he's eating.")[24] A parody of the Apostle's Creed found its
way into public places after the fast. "I believe in César Chávez, creator
of all the Troubbbleee(sic) and Hell, and the United Farmers (sic)

organization. . . ."[25] And finally officials of the California Grape and Tree Fruit League lamented: "How does one cope with an adversary so determinedly bucking for sainthood?"[26] Yet, if there was an element of calculation in the creation of the myth of self-sacrifice in César's leadership, the myth itself is an essential aspect in adding new saints to the pantheon of those enshrined in the lore of civil religions. Suffering is present and martyrdom is often the form it takes for minority groups to get the attention and the conscience of a national audience.

Finally the role that the daily masses played in the UFW has to be seen as much as a public religious symbol as one representing the Catholic Church. It was public in the sense that it created for the Mexican-American sacred space, as it was celebrated in the fields, much like the sacred space of the liberty tree for the Anglo colonists of an earlier period. Jim Drake, who participated in many of the masses, claimed that:

> When we celebrate the Eucharist in a field or beside a picket line, with real grapes and real bread, it has the kind of earthy meaning that it had in the Indian villages before all the cathedrals were built. Of the strike, people are saying, "We've always suffered. Now we can suffer for a purpose."[27]

The separations between religions, classes, and ethnic groups were erased in these masses. Instead of the usual vestments with the emblazoned cross, priests wore newly designed stoles with the black thunderbird, now the emblem of the UFW as well as of the ancient Aztecs, pinned against a red background. And like the fast and the marches, the masses pulled together divergent groups in the movement. Tensions between the Filipinos and the Mexican-Americans lessened as they celebrated the universal meaning of the mass. Doubt about the power of religious acts to create political and social solidarity was also dispelled for Anglo followers as they attended the masses night after night. Jerry Cohen, the union lawyer, noted: "No matter what their religious background, anyone interested in farm workers, or with any sense about people could see that something was going on that was changing a lot of people"[28] Chávez was even successful in getting fundamentalist Protestant Mexican-Americans, initially suspicious of his Catholicity, to participate in the worship services.[29]

The large masses came at the end of particulary long battles for the union when they got the attention of the state legislature in the Delano march or won contracts from growers. These were events of the whole community as a form of thanksgiving and public catharsis. For the mass was followed by speeches from Chávez, Huerta, and other leaders, and, after that, a fiesta where a combination of victory dance, feast day, and religious ritual were all wrapped up in one event. As such they represent the diverse elements of public and particular celebration so common and necessary in civil religion. The ritual of the mass kept the connection between the institutional church and the UFW alive. The presence of the *La Causa* banner and the speeches brought religion and politics together as the victories in the fields were rehearsed. The shrine of the Virgin of Guadalupe insured the cultural relevance of religion. And the plays by the resident migrant workers' theater group, *El Teatro Campesino,* recreated the social tensions and dynamics between social and economic classes in the drama of the strikes. As such they added an element of prophecy in the ironic mode of street theater. All of these factors worked together to provide an event that was at once local and universal, an occasion that was both religious and political, and a celebration that spoke to national priorities in its small victories over sectional economic injustices.

Conclusion

Some critics of American civil religion claim bankruptcy for the proposition because it is so predominantly Anglo-American in its values. Yet a case can be made for the rejuvenation of old forms if we take into consideration the contributions minority groups make to the proposition of a public religion which serves the needs and stimulates the conscience of the larger citizenry. In such a development two aspects need be considered. One is the evolution of natural symbols and paradigms within the minority tradition which can be recognized by the group itself as characterizing its traditions. These must be vital symbols which pervade daily life and secular as well as sacred existence and are political as well as religious. Second, such symbols as exist and the narratives which go with them must be able to be introduced into the public forum in such a way that memory will be evoked for a larger, more national audience—memory of their own epic but also of other more established contributions to civil religon. Memorial Day is an example, where to the memory of the American Revolution has been added that of the Civil War and those which followed, thus adding new cultural and ethnic dimensions of sacrifice with the passing years. (Viet Nam and its place in the solemnity of Memorial Day is only now being absorbed: for the sacrifices there a different ethnic mix from previous wars, but also must be seen in the light of what was essentially a military defeat.)

That Mexican-American culture has its own particular contributions to make to civil religion is clear from the above. To the male sovereignty of God, long a theme in our designation of God during war as the Jehovah of Battles, is added the femininity of God through the Virgin of Guadalupe. It is she who as protectress of the poor gives legitimacy to political battles fought on other grounds than military expeditions. in the reflective nature of nonviolent strategies for achieving justice, i.e., the fast, marches, and nonresistant forms of civil disobedience, we see a contrast to the designation of a national God discovered in the whirlwind of armed conflict. Yet, if we look into the Anglo traditions within American history we can find that more meditative side of civil religion as well in the call for repentance during the Revolution, the abolitionist movement during the Civil War, the Anti-Imperialist League during the early years of the nineteenth century, and the civil rights movement of our time as it has been represented by the ACLU and the Anti-Defamation League.

Civil religion, to this point, has largely been identified with a manifest destiny which includes the domestication and control of the wilderness as an expression of individuality. The twentieth century has reaped the harvest of this attitude in the devastaton of our natural resources and pollution of our environment. But in the Mexican-American tradition, harmony with the natural world, through the Indian influence, is a larger theme. This minority brings to civil religions a consciousness of nature as sacred and its seasons as sacral times, especially evident in the Farm Workers' use of the mass as agricultural celebration with fruits and vegetables on the altar. It would seem crucial that the national conscience be stirred by this alternate vision of human destiny, and there are other precedents for it in the history of American agricultural communes and Native American life.

Finally, the mystical character of civil religion has received little attention although it looms as a large reality. Much emphasis has been put upon the written and spoken word as the medium of revelation, and this is reflected in our national shrines of the Archives, which house the Constitution and the Declaration of Independence, and the Capitol. But the idea of visual pageantry is central in Mexican-American life and the public gathering where dance and music convey as much meaning, if not more, than human speech. Art and drama, the stuff of popular culture, say more about the heartbeat of public values than the solitary pronouncements from the White House. Historians of civil religion are beginning to turn to other less documentary forms in their analysis of the topic. Studies seem to require as much anthropological as sociological inquiry.

But in all of this the point is to restore a sense of perspective to the articulation of civil religion as the public religion of the whole nation. Minorities, as the above study shows, forge unique responses through symbolization to the hardships pressed upon them, and they believe that the rest of America can appropriate their meaning for a renewal of purpose. If for no other reason than extending the definition of national justice, Mexican-Americans, blacks, Polish-Americans, Japanese-Americans, et al. should be included in the definition of civil religion. But beyond this claim upon conscience is a claim upon history. "The New Israel" does not begin and end with the Anglo-American saga; indeed, that saga is not even complete in itself without the discussion of social and cultural interaction with other ethnic groups and its consequences for perceptions from without and within. Rather, the United States, if it is to keep this image of humility before God which so constitutes the idea of ancient Israel (slaves made into a holy people), must look to the diversity of experience among all her peoples if the notion of civil religion is to remain a useful and prophetic concept.

— 11 —

Religion and Nationalism
in the United States

Phillip E. Hammond

Tocqueville's profoundest insight about the United States in *Democracy in America*[1] was his observation that the selfish motives unleashed by democracy were, in the U.S., kept in check in several ways, chief of which were citizens' "habits and mores." Churches—and voluntary associations generally—constituted the major agencies nourishing these mores because they provided ways for self-interest to be tempered with community concern. A wealthy family, for example, could build a monument to itself by endowing a hospital; the family name became enshrined, and the community got a health care facility. Recognizing that mere good will was not quite the basis of the donor's motives, Tocqueville coined the phrase "self-interest rightly understood" to characterize such motives. The institutional arrangements of America, he said, encouraged this orientation.

This orientation is necessarily the product of two antithetical forces, as Tocqueville clearly saw. Selfishness does not disappear as altruism takes over; rather, community concern becomes a way of activating self-interest. Society benefits not from canceling out individuals' self-concern, then, but by providing channels for its expression that result in a wider welfare than occurs through simple aggrandizement of self. A kind of tension is thus built into American democratic culture, at least as long as the forces of self-interest do not overwhelm community welfare or the forces of society do not overwhelm individual initiative and reward.

One of the clearer analyses of American culture in the above terms is S. M. Lipset's *The First New Nation*,[2] wherein the intrinsic tension between individual achievement (and its reward and recognition) and equality (and its emergence and enforcement) provides the organizing theme of the book. In essence, Lipset argues, encouragement of achievement through reward and recognition serves to create inequality, while efforts to extend egalitarianism through collective programs serve to discourage individual initiative. Because of the simultaneous strength of these two values, however, neither can dominate for long before a countermovement gets underway to strike a balance. The revolving door exchange of Democratic and Republican Presidents is but one manifestation of this phenomenon.

The question can be raised as to what keeps such doors revolving. Why does not one of these value orientations overwhelm the other? Tocqueville was quite explicit on this score: various sects may worship in distinctive manners, he said, "but all preach the same morality."[3] That is to say, the mutually counteracting forces of achievement and equality, of self-interest and community welfare, were promulgated as God-given; it was *right* that people be simultaneously selfish motivated and collectively concerned.

It is true that Tocqueville visited America at a time (1831) when powerful emotional religious forces (sometimes called the Second Great Awakening) has spread widely throughout the still largely Protestant population. The resulting sameness the Frenchman found in American religion, despite the proliferation of sects, therefore left an over-powering image in his aristocratic Roman Catholic mind. Remarkably, however, Lipset, writing more than a century later, still saw Americans as pervasively motivated by a common denominator religion and still saw that common denominator religion as a moderating force keeping both achievement and egalitarianism in check.

The First New Nation appeared just before the cultural revolution of the 1960s and 1970s, however. The religious pluralism that was not even present for Tocqueville to observe, and which, though present for Lipset to observe, was not culturally disruptive, has since become problematic indeed. It is not that theological doctrines have proliferated, but rather the various sects no longer "preach the same morality." Americans are profoundly divided on big moral issues, and they know it. Moreover, they are also divided on the legitimacy of those agencies—churches, schools, courts—that might in the past have adjudicated differences by reference to a common denominator religion. The "public square" is "naked," Richard John Neuhaus[4] tells us, stripped of any God about whom Americans in general are agreed. In principle, therefore, self-interest may no longer be rightly understood; it may grow unchecked until the collective welfare is overwhelmed. Conversely, collective welfare, in the name of justice, could stamp out individual liberty. Achievement may prevail at the expense of equality, or possibly the reverse will be true. In either case, so this view has it, the habits and mores can no longer hold in check the value tension inherent in American culture.

Of course, just as Tocqueville noted a century and a half ago, other forces than the habits and mores can also counteract unbridled democracy—whether pure self-interest or despotic statism. Thus, for example, America remains a relatively open, mobile society, allowing at least some of the frustrated people to move on rather than get swept up by authoritarian currents. More importantly, perhaps, the U.S. remains a federated government, with separation of powers, including an independent judiciary and a Bill of Rights reasonably immune to legislative corrosion. Not surprisingly, therefore, the day-by-day operation of our society appears relatively unchanged in spite of the breakdown of normative consensus. The mechanism of a "same morality" may no longer function, in other words, but other mechanisms still do, and we have moved neither toward a libertarian, "Yuppie" heaven nor toward a fascist, "Christian" hell.

In a recent book, *Religion in American Public Life*,[5] A. James Reichley offers a particularly clear scheme for understanding the above state of affairs. Historically, he says, the tension between "egoism" and "authoritarianism" (i.e., self-interest vs. any vision of imposed social order) had been moderated by a "theism" generally agreed upon by all involved. The humane civility resulting from this mutual accommodation between egoism and authoritarianism was thereby further transformed into a "theist-humanism" because of Americans' common religious orientation. In the past at least, the public square did not ignore God but took account of divine forces. Now, however, the best that can be effected is a "civil" humanism, a social order that leaves out mention of God.[6] Charges—chiefly by conservative Protestants—are made that "secular humanism" is thus being chosen in preference to the traditional theistic humanism. Whatever the merits of such an argument regarding "choice," continued use of theistic humanism as a presumed overarching ideology would appear no longer possible in such a religiously pluralistic society.[7] People—at least people in official positions—cannot choose to articulate their actions with reference to the traditional theistic humanism. To do so would be potentially to offend some whom they officially represent.

In his 1967 essay, "Civil Religion in America,"[8] Robert Bellah provided a term to describe the phenomenon others have labeled theistic humanism or common denominator religion. His term "civil religion" rather quickly became the label of scholars, and, while many bastardized its meaning by viewing it as merely synonymous with patriotism, it nevertheless communicated a profound idea: Americans have access to an ideology which is sensitive to both individual self-interest and the collective welfare, while at the same time both are subject to rules not of human origin. American history can be read in terms of how readily American citizens availed themselves of this civil religion. A certain suspicion is called for, however.

It is *not* the case that at times when the civil religion was invoked, Americans acted wisely, and when it was not invoked, the outcomes were unfavorable. Certainly the general public, and even some scholars, find it difficult to conceive of civil religion that is corrupting and misguided as well as ennobling and wise. But whether the judgment is good or bad is not the issue; the issue is whether a course of action is urged or justified in the name of an ideology having the nation-state as the principal actor in a drama believed to be written and directed by transcendent forces. Using this criterion, one can note that the American civil religion has been invoked to differing degrees at different times, and one can further note that when it has been invoked, the degree of responsiveness has differed. That is to say, the American civil religion has waxed and waned, both in terms of how *much* it has been appealed to, and in terms of how *appealing* it was found to be. Two other essays in the present volume illustrate these points with remarkable clarity.

Russell Conwell, Warren Vinz tells us, is mistakenly perceived—because of the incredible popularity of a single lecture delivered many times—as having been simply a spokesman on behalf of self-interest. Material success is one's right, he seemed to say. However he was more, Vinz insists, as can be seen in his attention to "issues of national and international importance in an age of burgeoning industry, big-time military power, and domestic and international political and economic hardball." It is clear from his numerous sermons, articles, and books that he had a clear vision of the good society as well as a vision of the good life.

> The Temple minister fits comfortably within two moods of the country. . . . On the one hand is a mood of protest and humanitarian reform, populism, and utopianism; on the other hand a mood of national self-assertion, aggression, and expansion. The motif of the first is sympathy, the second is power.

Significantly, however, both moods are expressed as if they are not merely for the good of the nation and its individual citizens but God-ordained as well; divine blessings flow from such courses of actions.

Conwell is appealing not just to a Protestant God, moreover. If, as late as the end of the nineteenth century, his speech is filled with

Christian allusions—Christian principles, Christian American, etc.—it is probably because Conwell was not sensitized to non-Protestant sentiments about such language. It is certainly not because he fashioned his audience to be exclusively Protestant.

And yet if Conwell's invocation was to the God of American civil religion and not just to a Christian, Protestant, Baptist God, is is not clear that his invocation was broadly appealing. Vinz suggests that Conwell had the attention of highly placed politicians, and certainly his popularity as a public preacher is beyond question. As was asserted above, however, the question of which ideology is being appealed *to* is different from the question of how appealing the ideology *is* to the people to whom it is addressed. What can be seen clearly in the career of Russell Conwell is an instance of a vibrant civil religion in operation. For those at least to whom it was appealing, it was a living faith. Its existence was not in doubt, nor were its structure and content vague in the minds of those who articulated it.

Spencer Bennett's description of the Mexican-American faith of César Chávez offers a contrasting view of the American civil religion. In this instance we see not a creed whose existence, structure, and content are uniformly accepted and taken for granted, but rather a creed still being formed, being doubted by some, argued over by others, and entirely unrecognized by yet others. If the creed articulated by Chávez remains simply the ideological motivation for the United Farm Workers, then it will not be civil religion in the sense we are using that term. No matter how vibrant and brilliantly expressed, unless the transcendent theory encompasses, and is embraced by, otherwise contending factions, it cannot be considered *civil* religion. The difficulties faced by Chávez and described so poignantly by Bennett reflect just this situation.

The point can be put crudely: César Chávez would have no hope of winning the moral support of Americans generally by offering a particularistic ideology, a creed so peculiar to farmworkers that, in motivating them, it leaves everyone else unmoved. Thus, some of Chávez's own lieutenants "were bothered by Chávez's acts of self-denial and sacrifice," Bennett writes. "And they did not like or understand the primitive aura of Mexican Catholicism evident . . . at union gatherings."

If the engine power of the farmworkers is therefore to be widely effective, it obviously must employ images, build upon concepts, and otherwise merge into the faith already implicitly held by those to whom appeal is being made. Chávez, it would seem, knows this and is trying to get under the umbrellas of American civil religion but without giving up the most powerful elements of the creed held by his followers. He is trying, in effect, to add rural Mexican Catholic ingredients to an ideological mix largely composed of Yankee Protestant Enlightenment flavors. How can that happen?

It is one of the virtues of Bennett's essay that, in laying out the farmworkers' story as it does, an answer—perhaps the only answer—can be seen. The answer is not the symbol of the Virgin of Guadalupe, for, while non-Catholics may tolerate her, they will not resonate to her. Nor can the symbol be the cross, because the American civil religion is not Christian. What can and does motivate the farmworker and non-farmworker alike is the theme of sacrifice, symbolized in this instance by fasting and penitential marching perhaps, but readily recognized also in the heroic efforts of the Revolutionary colonists, the Civil War dead, those who fought wars to save democracy, and the brave civil rights demonstrators who stood up to dogs, cattle prods, even lynch mobs. In the name of civil righteousness, many have sacrificed before; farmworkers in their quest for justice stand in *that* tradition, even if they are accompanied by crucifixes and the Dark Virgin.

We return, then, to the subject with which this essay began—the "habits and mores," the self-interest rightly understood, the common morality taught by all the churches. We live at a time when such ideas often times sound remote. The God of one faction is not the God of another, and a third faction—with full rights of citizenship—may reject the idea of God altogether. How then might a group, convinced of its own righteousness, convince others? Here is where enter the twin issues discussed above: Can a civil religion be invoked? And, if it is, will its appeal be broad enough? The naked public square may be owing to the absence of God in the civic arenas, in other words, or it may be that the gods being invoked are not recognized as such.

— 12 —

Millennial Politics in Contemporary Peru

Gustavo Benavides

The interaction between religion and the pursuit and maintenance of political power, or—to put it differently in order to avoid the danger of hypostasizing "religion"—the sacralization of political activities, has a long history in Peru. The earliest of the pan-Andean cultures, Chavín, already shows the intimate connection between the elaboration of the theology and the emergence of complex social formations.[1] The establishment of the Inca empire with its capital in Cuzco was accompanied by the development of a system of social control in which religion played an important role.[2] Finally, the destruction of the empire in the sixteenth century, which led to the exploitation of the native population, was carried out by a military force representing not only the Spanish Crown but also Christendom. Defining themselves as Christian, the conquerors of Peru proceeded, on the one hand, to make use of the native population as a labor force, and on the other, to carry out extensive campaigns in order to Christianize the heathens. Conquest, domination, and control were, then, not only military and political, but also religiously legitimized actvities.[3] But the sacralization of the struggle for power was not restricted to the Christian Spaniards: already in the sixteenth century, around 1560, when the military victories of the conquerors were still fresh in the memories of the survivors, a millenarian movement, the *Taqi onqoy* (or *Taqi ongo*, literally "dancing sickness") spread through the land. According to Cristóbal de Molina, writing before 1575, the defeated believed that the sanctuaries and divinities (*huacas*) destroyed by the Spaniards would come back to life, the Spaniards themselves would be killed, their cities destroyed, and their memory would vanish.[4] That was not the case, and under Toledo the earlier indigenous theocracy was replaced by what Pierre Duviols has called a totalitarian, brutal, colonial theocracy, which engaged in the systematic attempt to uproot non-

Christian religious practices and beliefs.[5] Sacralization, then, was at work on both sides, especially a particular variety of sacralization: millennialism—the belief that the old order will come to an end and a new age will begin.[6] It is important to remember that the discovery, conquest, and settlement of American by Europeans had taken place to a certain extent within the millenarian atmosphere. The influence of Joachinism had been pervasive during the Middle Ages, and in fact Columbus himself had read and been influenced by Joachim of Fiore, whose prophecies he had included in his own *Libro de las profecías*.[7] It is also known that some of the members of the religious orders who went to what is known under the ideologically charged name of the "New World," particularly the Franciscans, were influenced by millenarian expectations. There were in fact attempts by Franciscans to separate Indians from non-Indians in order to preserve the purity of the former.[8]

From the beginning of the interaction between Europe and the Andean world, we find that conquest, millenarian hope, cultural and physical genocide, self-defense, consolidation of political power, and control were articulated to a lesser or greater extent in religious terms. This does not mean that any of the events mentioned above were "fundamentally" or "ultimately religious"; such a view is based on the premise of an independent, identifiable, religious sphere, and forgets that with the possible, but by no means certain, exception of industrial society, it is impossible to identify a specific religious sphere, separated from the political, military, and other domains. It is not the case, for example, that the conquest of America was an enterprise fueled by the mysticism that produced St. John of the Cross and St. Teresa, as one author has maintained, carrying to its logical, if absurd, conclusion, the culturalist thesis.[9] An examination of the rebellions that took place in the eighteenth century, particularly the great movement under Tupac Amaru II, shows that rebellion against Spanish domination was not the product of a disembodied "messianic ideology of the Andean world," as it has been suggested;[10] the rebellions were the result of the confluence of many causes, with the economic ones playing a crucial role.[11] At the same time, it is true that elements of Andean mythology interacting with Christian beliefs concerning the death and resurrection of Christ were used to interpret the series of events that had punctuated the destruction of the empire and gave rise to a utopian ideology which is still visible today.[12]

The Andean elements that contributed to the elaboration of a utopian response include a perception of the world in dual terms: the world above (*hananpacha*) and the world below (*hurinpacha*), "world" (*pacha*) meaning both space and time, time-space, universe, earth.[13] This dualism of complementarity was at work both at the highest levels of reality, as well as in everyday matters such as the division of towns and villages into a *hanan* (above) and a *hurin* (below) section. Once the Inca empire came in contact with the Spaniards it was necessary to integrate the newcomers into this hierarchical universe. However, the conquerors did not fit into any of the positions in which the Andean classificatory system would have placed them. Whereas from the point of view of the vanquished it was a matter of reorganizing and thus saving the world and placing the Spaniards and themselves in it, from the point of view of the conquerors it was a matter of acquiring complete domination of the physical world and of destroying the Andean cosmos.[14] But even this complete destruction could be understood in Andean terms as a *pachacuti*,[15] a situation of chaos, a transition from one age to another, a world turned upside down: a situation that has to be brought to an end.

It is in this attempt to recreate the world and undo the conquest that, not quite paradoxically, Christian elements are assimilated and used. The central component of Christian mythology was indeed well suited for the purpose, since it was not difficult for the people of the conquered empire to understand their suffering in terms of original sin, a concept which in the edifice of Christian theology has as its counterpart the incarnation, execution, and resurrection of the Son of God. The theme of death, resurrection, and redemption was used to make sense of the situation of the defeated people, and the death, by strangulation (actually *garrote*), of the last Inca, Atahualpa, in 1532, and of a noble rebel, Tupac Amaru I, in 1572, were placed in a mythological context in which death would be followed by resurrection and redemption. The two deaths, perceived as one,[16] gave rise to the myth of Inkarrí (Inca-Rey:Inca-King), the beheaded being whose head, buried either in Spain or in Lima, is according to some versions growing a body, or, according to others, waiting to be reunited with its body.[17] The dismembered Inkarrí is thus an emblem of the fractured reality of the Andean world and his hoped-for wholeness stands for a reversal of the actual situation of fracture and incompleteness.

It should be clear, however, that the confrontation between those who soon would be known under the generic name of "Indians" and Spaniards was not a mere clash of classificatory systems, resolved in the shadowy world of mythology through the resurrection of an *Urmensch*-like archetype of the Andean world; on the contrary, the confrontation involved military conquest, appropriation of land, indiscriminate killing, extraction of labor from the survivors, forced conversion to Christianity, and "extirpation of idolatries."[18] The onslaught, then, having taken place at all levels had to be answered at all levels: through rebillion, mass suicide,[19] movements such as the *Taqui onqoy* and, finally, through the assimilation and use of the instruments, both physical and ideological, brought by the conquerors. Ultimately, the assimilation of the central mythologeme of Christianity is not fundamentally different from the use of horses and gunpowder by the Indian armies: both had proven to be more effective than the physical and ideological weapons of the Inca empire. Horses, guns, and Christianity could be accepted, mastered, if necessary transformed, and then used against the original owners of the weapons. Therefore, if the myth of Inkarri came into being in the seventeenth century,[20] that does not mean that the great rebellion of Tupac Amaru II was a lonely exception at the end of the eighteenth; the myth and the rebellions tried to accomplish through different means—at times antagonistic, at times complementary—the task of undoing the conquest.[21]

That members of a subject people accept and use the religion of the dominant group is not infrequent in the history of colonial and other types of domination. An examination if the literature dealing with messianic and millenarian movements, cargo cults, and slave rebellions, provides many examples of the utilization by rebel groups of the suitably interpreted religion of the oppressors.[22] One would be tempted to use the term "syncretism" to refer to these cases of interpretation and appropriation, but this concept ultimately seems to be less a useful analytical tool than a case of theological obfuscation, since it presupposes the existence of pure religions and of universally valid canons of interpretation, when, in fact, the canons themselves are the result of protracted conflicts and are continuously subject to theological and to other challenges. What was said above about the difficulty of identifying a specific "religious" sphere applies also to the problem of identifying the "essence" or "limits" of a given religion. After all, just as the Christian God is the result of the confluence of Near Eastern, Roman, and Greek elements, and, in Mexico at least, the Virgin of Guadelupe was originally a figure who incorporated elements from the Aztec goddess Tonantzin, so did Inkarrí incorporate elements from the mythology of Christianity and the notion of *pachacuti*, all of this in the context of the situation of oppression in which the Andean people found themselves. The roles played by these divine or mythical beings and by these religions were never exclusively "religious"; the function played by Christianity during the first three centuries of its existence until the conversion of Constantine included the creation of a sense of identity among certain groups in the Roman *ecumene*[23] and, as Wardman has argued, that of a religion whose God "began his official existence within the Roman system as a victory-god."[24] Likewise, the Virgin of Guadalupe was born as a Nahuatl-speaking divinity whose apparition to Juan Diego, an Indian, could be understood as the acceptance of the recent converts into the Christian community, while at the same time preserving the old gods. Later, in the seventeenth century, the Spanish conquest of Mexico was justified theologically "on the ground that it allowed the Virgin to become manifest in her chosen country, and to found in Mexico a new paradise."[25] Less than two centuries later, however, when the war of independence made it necessary to fight the Spanish armies while preserving the religion the Spaniards brought, the myth was further developed when Servando Teresa de Mier claimed that the image of the Virgin had been brought to Mexico by the apostle Thomas long before the Spanish conquest.[26]

Unlike Mexicans, Peruvians did not create a symbol of national identity for the simple reason that Peruvians, or rather, the Peruvian ruling groups, did not attempt—or did not want—to create a sense of national identity. If one compares the role played by the Virgin of Guadalupe in Mexico with that of, for example, the Lord of Miracles (*Señor de los milagros*) in Peru, one realizes that the cult of the latter is largely confined to the coast, primarily during the month of October when the massive processions in his honor take place.[27] Inkarri, on the other hand, is an underground and fractured figure both literally and metaphorically, unknown to most of the established urban population (in fact, anthropologists have collected versions of the myth generally in rural areas or among recently urbanized groups).

The absence of a unified symbolic system[28] makes it necessary that various institutions provide at least an illusory sense of community. Of the two main candidates, army and church, the Catholic church as institution can hardly function as a vehicle for national identity as all the countries surrounding Peru are also Catholic. The position of the armed forces would seem to be no more promising, particularly when one consideres that the great figures in the war of independence—San Martín, Bolívar, Sucre—were foreigners, and when one further remembers that the most important was since independence was one in which Peru was thoroughly defeated by Chile.[29] Nevertheless, the armed forces have managed to transform a military defeat into a series of heroic actions (which they no doubt were), nurturing both a cult of military heroes—Grau and Bolognesi— and a revanchist attitude toward Chile, which allows the armed forces to consume a large proportion of the national budget in extravagant military spending.[30] But clearly neither are armed forces, nor the carefully nurtured cult of military heroes, not the sporadic occasions in which Peruvian soccer teams compete in international events, can create a unified symbolic system. Peru is a country divided by class, cultural, linguistic and ethnic lines, in such a way that with the partial exception of the sense of unity created by the institutions and civic rituals mentioned above, the diverse groups that compose Peruvian society have had to maintain or develop their own ritual activities.

In the rural areas, particularly in peasant communities, the ritual calendar is based on a system of duality and complementarity not fundamentally different from what has existed in the Andean world for centuries.[31] As is generally the case in agricultural societies, Andean ritual is closely related to agricultural labor and in more general terms is concerned with ecological regulation.[32] These rituals deal at the same time with the maintenance of social solidarity through the distribution of religious *cargos, compadrazgo* relationships, etc. There are other rituals, however, not directly concerned with group cohesion or with ecological regulation, but rather with the dramatization of the position of peasant groups in Peruvian society. Given the peculiar characteristics of this society, these rituals have to take care of several contradictory requirements. In the broadest terms, the rituals are used in order to make visible the desire for ultimate harmony the country; on the other, they have to dramatize the actual position of subordination of peasant, "Indian," groups. This second function should also be considered as having at least two components: (1) to make the subordinate position visible, since this is, after all, what corresponds to reality; (2) to reveal the frustration that this situation generates and, at the same time, to imagine a utopian situation in which harmony is achieved or positions are reversed. It should be noted that the different functions are both contradictory and overlapping; for instance, it could be argued that to postulate the existence of harmony in the country is the same as to hope for a utopian situation in which harmony is finally achieved. But this is not so: the existence rituals in which subordinate groups celebrate their inclusion in an all-encompassing "Peruvian" society simply indicates the acceptance of the reality represented by the state, its courts of law, police, military conscription, etc., a reality in which the groups that compose society have unequal access to wealth and the exercise of power. One the other hand, "utopian" rituals reject this merely formal sense of nationhood and invent situations in which reality is either turned upside down or turned into one of real equality. Rituals that dramatize subordination and conflict are the link between the other two: they, like religion in general, function as the symbolic field, as the battleground where history—past, present, and future— is fought out.

These ritual battles have indeed been fought since the seventeenth century. Manual Burga, who has studied what he calls the "crisis of Andean identity," has described how in 1656, in Chilcas, during the festivity of the Ascension of the Virgin Mary, and Indian initiated the process of appropriation of Spanish culture involving both concealment and parody. His performance consisted in riding a wooden horse whose hind parts were covered by the robe of the Virgin. Another example, this one of a clear oppositional type, took place in Mangas, where a confrontation between "Incas" and Indians representing Spaniards was staged. It is at this point, according to Burga, that Andean ritual choreography takes the decisive step, finding, through the use of rituals and the past, a new mechanism by which "identity through oppposition" could be created.³³ Identity through opposition is also what is asserted during the rituals reenacting the capture of Atahualpa by the Spaniards, celebrated in Chiquián and observed by Alberto Flores Galindo in August 1984. But the issue in the case of Chiquián (and no doubt in many others) is *whose* identity. As Flores Galindo remarks, in the rituals celebrated in the early nineteenth century the Inca was the most important figure, while now it is the Spanish side, represented by the "Captain," that has the upper hand.³⁴ Thus identity is less identity as a Peruvian, than it is identity as a member of a group with a specific position in the ethnic-economic-social structure of the country, and is therefore fundamentally a claim to economic resources and political powers.

Dramatization of ethnic and political conflict is certainly not restricted to Peru. Remaining within the areas where Indian cultures came in contact with Spanish conquerors and colonizers, we find the same tension between subordination and confrontation, between unity and division in, for example, the southwest of the United States, in southern Mexico, and in Bolivia. In the United States, the most thoroughly studied of these celebrations takes place in the city of Santa Fe, where parades and processions whose center is the Virgin Mary as *la conquistadora* constitutes a symbolic field where ethnic and social conflicts are played out. Many of the tensions and ambiguities found in Peru are also found in Santa Fe: the maintenance and reinforcement of a Hispanic social elite through the recruitment of eligible men into the Caballeros de Vargas (and their female counterparts); the celebration of Spanish superiority in relation in Indian culture, but while also celebrating the coexistence of the two (and later three) cultures. An important difference is that in Santa Fe, because of the annexation of formerly Mexican territory by the United States, the upholding of "Hispanic" identity is carried out against the background of an older but subordinate "Indian" and a recent but dominant "Anglo" culture.[35] In Mexico, the tension between Indian groups and the superordinate Mexican culture, studied in the Oaxaca area by Eva Hunt,[36] is expressed ritually and theologically given the impossibility of expressing conflict openly.[37]

In all these cases we find that the creation of myths and symbols, the performance of rituals, and the elaboration of "syncretistic" theological systems, are not mere epiphenomena: they are attempts to visualize and often to modify through symbolic confrontation the position a group occupies in the social system. These activities are the result of the intersection of power and symbolic relationships:[38] the exercise of power mediated through the meanings generated by social actors and the creation of meaning not against the background of other disembodied meanings in a world understood as text, but within the world made of ecological, economic, and political constraints.

II

To move from an examination of millenarian movements in the Andean world to a discussion of what is probably the most important development in contemporary Catholic theology would seem to require a radical change in approach. After all, millennialism and utopia, "syncretism" and rituals of protests, historization of myth and mythification of history appear to some as the domain of anthropologists and other students of "exotic" phenomena, whereas Liberation Theology, as a form of theology—misguided to some, redeeming to others—would appear to require the traditional methods employed in the analysis of religious texts. Thus one could follow what could be called the inquisitorial approach, and ask whether the writings of, for example, Gutiérrez conform to the Christian revelation as interpreted by the Holy See, or one could follow the history-of-theology (-philosophy, -ideas, and so forth) approach and, less concerned with dogmatic faithfulness than with tracing influences and identifying new developments, one could place these teachings in their intellectual setting as perhaps the unavoidable outcome of the confluence of the new valorization of "the World" in mid-twentieth-century Catholic theology with the changes and expectations brought about by the Second Vatican Council (the Council itself having been influenced by mid-twentieth-century theologians like Teilhard de Chardin, Henri de Lubac, Congar, and others). But theology is never just theology, and it is not necessary to be a theologian (or a believer) to deal with theological writings. Liberation Theology emerged during a critical period in Latin America, and particularly Peruvian, history. The years between the encounter at Medellin (1968) and the one in Puebla (1979)[39] saw not only the publication of the major works by Gutiérrez, Assmann, and Segundo;[40] these were also the years during which the economic situation of the continent worsened considerably, and during which the external debt began to grow apparently out of control. Politically, countries moved to the left or to the right, abandoning the complacency of the previous years. Chile elected a socialist president who managed to remain in power for three years until he was overthrown and killed in a military coup which imposed a brutal dictatorship still in power today; in Argentina, Brazil, and Uruguay, military regimes engaged in generalized repression.[41]

In Peru, the corrupt and inefficient government of Fernando Belaúnde was overthrown by the armed forces in 1968, leading to the establishment of a reformist military government under a general, Juan Velasco Alvarado, who because of his humble origins and reformist policies became as popular with segments of the lower classes as he became unpopular with the middle and particularly the upper classes, for whom the name Velasco became synonymous with plebeian domination, if not communism. Unfortunately, many of the changes that took place during the "first phase" of the military government were carried out in a manner that was both authoritarian and inefficient; furthermore, the traditional military thirst for expensive weaponry was indulged in without restraint, aggravating the already precarious economic situation. Nevertheless, the years of the *primera fase* were virtually the first time that a government with a semblance of popular support had exercised power in the country. This opening, brought about by forces that had traditionally served the interest of the oligarchy, had significant political consequences; the Velasco regime showed that the people (in the pejorative sense of *"el pueblo"*) could exercise power through leaders with whom they could identify. Particularly, the Andean population was granted a certain degree of recognition; for the first time in Peruvian history the language of a large segment of the population, Quechua, was given official status (so that, for example, Quechua speakers could hear for the first time a summary of the news read in that language on national television, an event that was welcomed with derision by many Spanish speakers for whom Quechua is less a language than an incomprehensible sign of backwardness[42]). Significantly, the most important symbol of Andean resistance, Tupac Amaru II, was promoted as symbol of national identity by the government instead of Pizarro, the Spanish conqueror.

Writing and doing pastoral work in this context, the creators of the Theology of Liberation were attempting to come to terms theologically with the events that were taking place around them. It has been claimed that Liberation Theology is not theology at all, but rather a particularly perverse form of Marxism propagated by misguided priests;[43] against this view it should be said that these theologians are following a traditional theological procedure: on the one hand, they are approaching "the World" using as code the Christian canon—the Bible, the Fathers, papal encyclicals, writings of contemporary theologians—and on the other, they are functioning, loosely, within the limits of ideology, Marxism. It would appear that in using Marxist sources and interpretive procedures, Christian theologians are being unfaithful to the spirit of Christianity, given the fact that Marxism is an atheistic system. In reality, however, there is no more reason to interpret, for example, the book of Exodus in a feudal, capitalist, or fascist context than in a Marxist one. Ultimately, that is the function of religious texts and religious utterances: to serve as the almost empty vessels from which, precisely because of their relative emptiness, an almost unlimited number of interpretations can be extracted. What Gutiérrezz, Segundo, Assmann and others have done is neither new nor non-permissible in a religious context. What Liberation Theology does is to articulate grievances, conflicts, and hopes in a language that can be understood and can therefore be effective. To talk about alienation and surplus, dependence and capitalism, socialism and conscientization will have a certain effect among educated groups, but even among these groups to talk about liberation and exodus may awaken a deeper response. In this sense, theological texts are not fundamentally different from rituals; insofar as both are signifying structures, they can be used to organize floating meanings endowing the resulting structures with a sense of inevitability which otherwise might be lacking.[44] This process of fixation is what we call "sacralization," stressing, however, that we are dealing not with a static, clearly delimited, reified, "religion," but rather with processes. That these processes are being carried out by group with frequently diametrically opposed interests should surprise no one. In fact, as indicated earlier, texts and rituals are precisely the spaces within which opposing interpretations state their claims.

Given the fundamental ambiguity of Christianity regarding political issues, the question as to whether the interpretation proposed by the

Theology of Liberation is a valid one makes sense only from the point of view of someone who is already theologically committed; all that is left to the non-theological observer is to verify the theological plausibility of Liberation Theology. From that standpoint, one has to recognize that the interpretations of the Hebrew and Greek scriptures advanced by Gutiérrez, Segundo, and others do not do violence to the texts (or, to put it positively, their interpretations do as much violence to these texts as others have done through almost two millenia of Christian history). It indeed seems to be the case that Christianity can be understood as recognizing only one history, "one human destiny, irreversibly assumed by Christ, the Lord of history."[45] Likewise, the events narrated in the book of Exodus make it impossible to consider the liberation of the Israelite tribes from Egypt as a fundamentally "spiritual" affair. Concerning the issue of violence—certainly the most politically charged in a continent in which violence is systematically exercised against the lower classes—the examples from the New Testament adduced by Segundo show that the use of violence can be theologically justified in a Christian context.[46]

More examples could be given, but our point is not to present the main teachings of Liberation of Theology, but simply to point out that this politically radical interpretation of Christianity, which maintains that "liberation" should be understood not as a mere "spiritual," "otherwordly," escapist salvation, but as an "integral" liberation, is perfectly plausible in a strict theological sense. The only arguments that can be advanced against Latin American Liberation Theology in a theological context are other interpretations of the same more or less closed corpus of scriptures. It is true that certain interpretations will be preferred by the church hierarchy, but what will ultimately decide which interpretation is a valid one from the point of view of the hierarchy will not be theological arguments—themselves open to interpretation—but dogmatic pronouncements backed by the power to exclude individuals from the ritual economy of Catholicism. Thus far, the attitude of the Vatican concerning political and economic issues has been ambiguous; on the one hand, the pope has decried the political and economic conditions in which most Latin Americans live, but on the other he has warned priests against becoming involved in political activities[47] (that his own prouncements are political seems to have escaped him). Concerning specifically the Theology of Liberation, the strategy of the Vatican has been to neutralize the most revolutionary components of this movement, while declaring that the concerns expressed by the Liberation Theologians are the same concerns the church has embodied for centuries. Thus on 6 August 1984 cardinal

Joseph Ratzinger, Prefect of the Sacred Congregation for the Doctrine of the Faith, issued a document entitled *Instruction on Certain Aspects of the "Theology of Liberation."* In this document we find many of the themes developed by the Liberation Theologians, although spiritualized and domesticated. Ratzinger starts by saying, "The gospel of Jesus Christ is a message of freedom and a force of liberation," but then he goes on to say, "Liberation is first and foremost liberation from the radical slavery of sin."[48] Ratzinger's view of liberation is thus summarized in the first six lines of the *Instruction*: misery, injustice, violence, hunger, etc., are real and to be deplored, but the meeting of "the aspiration of liberation and the theologies of liberation" can be understood "only in light of the specific message of Revelation, authentically interpreted by the Magisterium of the Church."[49] Furthermore, whereas slavery is to be condemned, "the most radical slavery is slavery to sin" ('sin' not to be restricted to "social sin").[50] While poverty is condemned, Ratzinger informs us that suffering is not to be equated with poverty or with political oppression. Most importantly, "it is from God alone that one can expect salvation and healing. God, and not man, has the power to change the situation of suffering."[51] Ratzinger closes his *Instruction* with a call to all the church: "with boldness and courage, with farsightedness and prudence . . . pastors will consider the response to this call a matter of the highest priority, as many already do."[52] To demand both boldness and prudence may appear as unreasonable, but this demand accurately summarizes the position of the hierarchy: on the one hand, the no-doubt sincere desire for an improvement of the conditions in which many Catholics live, and on the other, the absolute refusal to consider the legitimacy of any challenge to the power of the church or any radical political change.[53]

As is generally the case with these confrontations, Ratzinger's pronouncements have been interpreted differently by the various groups involved in these politico-hermeneutical struggles; for some sympathizers of Liberation Theology, the *Instruction* implies a general acceptance of the principles of this theology; the opponents point out that many of the central components of Liberation Theology have been rejected. The essential ambiguity of this document has been further complicated by a Pastoral Message of the Peruvian Bishops in which the prelates, moving away from Ratzinger's position and apparently resisting pressures from the Vatican, issued a much more positive assessment of Liberation Theology.[54] Finally, when the pope visited Peru in February 1985 he delivered several speeches, including one in Ayacucho, the stronghold of the rebel group, Shining Path, whose ideology we will discuss below. In Ayacucho the pope said: "Although injustice and misery can be circumstances likely to give rise to bitterness and hatred, they alone are not enough to explain the phenomenon; they are not the real source. Hatred and violence are born in man's heart, from his aberrant passions and convictions, from sin."[55] As it was to be expected, the pope said that "Christianity recognizes the noble and rightful struggle for justice at all levels, but it calls for justice to be promoted through understanding, dialogue, effective and generous work, coexistence, and excluding solutions that follow the paths of hatred and death."[56] In Lima, the pope praised the activities of the sixteenth-century archbishop St. Toribio de Mogrovejo, who, according to the pope, "was an authentic precursor of Christian liberation" in Peru, and who "on the basis of his full fidelity to the Gospel, denounced the abuses of unjust systems applied to the Indians," although "he did not do so with political aims in view nor for ideological reasons, but because he discovered serious obstacles to evangelization in such abuses.[57] In other words, the pope praised the activities of a member of the hierarchy who in the first years after the destruction of the Inca empire did not question Spanish domination, but merely denounced the abuses resulting from it, and that because such abuses interfered with pastoral activities.

The opposition between the Liberation Theologians and the Vatican would seem, then, to be radical. The situation, however, is not so simple. After all, both the Vatican and the Theology of Liberation function under the assumption that Latin American is and must remain Catholic, no matter what political changes take place. In a sense in fact, Liberation Theology is more radical than the hierarchy in this regard, because whereas the hierarchy would appear to be prepared, however reluctantly, to retreat into the realm of the spiritual if the political situation were to warrant it, the Theology of Liberation by insisting on the idea of one history and one world rejects the secularization model and refuses even to consider relinquishing the privileged position of Catholicism in Latin America. Elsewhere we have argued that the ultimate aim of Liberation Theology is to secure the survival of the church in a continent likely to undergo radical changes.[58] Indeed it may be the case that revolutionary theologians are ultimately protecting the institution they seem to threaten, and this may be the reason for the contradictory measures taken by a Vatican that cannot afford to endanger its chances of survival in an area of the world in which forty percent of all Catholics live.

This paper, however, is not primarily concerned with the ways in which the Theology of Liberation may ultimately serve the interests of the church as institution; in the context of an examination of the utopian functions of religion; it is more important to examine the discourse of Liberation Theology as utopian discourse. It is often forgotten that the same religious formulations (whether presented in a dogmatic or an a mythological manner) can be understood differently by members of priestly hierarchies, by the lower clergy, and by the various strata of lay followers.[59] Whether a spiritualized and domesticated version of Liberation Theology is accepted as valid by the Vatican, or whether the Liberation Theologians themselves retreat into the realm of "spirituality" (as the most recent work by Gutiérrez seems to indicate), the fact is that lay and clerical adherents of this movement are likely to continue on their own religio-political paths, regardless of the direction theological leaders may take. Theological formulations merely open up old texts, point out possible ways of interpreting sacred stories, put in motion hermeneutical—and therefore political—enterprises. Once theological (or mythical) forms of discourse have begun functioning, the forms themselves may transform possible political choices into necessary forms of action.[60]

In the case of Liberation Theology the rejection of the separation between an otherwordly—spiritual—history and a worldly one requires a canon interpretation that integrates apparently disparate aspects of reality; it also requires a demystifying interpretative approach and the constant attempt to uncover and neutralize ideological constructs.[61] This the Liberation Theologians achieve by using traditional theological and philosophical "hermeneutical" procedures; Juan Luis Segundo, for instance, engages in an elaborate four-step "hermeneutical circle," but for all the "exegetical suspicion" he exercises, the fourth step brings us back predictably to traditional theology and to a renewed religious commitment.[62] In general terms, what seem to be central to utopian movements-both those classified as being based on mythological represenations and those, like Liberation Theology, based on theological exegesis—is the perception of reality as one, without distinguishing religious from non-religious aspects, and an attitude of exegetical suspicion. In the case of those millenarian movements studied by anthropologists, the distrust by colonized peoples of interpretations of the Bible offered by missionaries can be radical and may be expressed not only be rejecting specific teachings, but it may involve—as with the Melanesians studies by Worsley—the belief that the white man has concealed a secret (sometimes declared to be the first page of the Bible), a secret whose possession explains the dominant position of the colonizers.[63]. What is significant in this exegetical procedure is the coexistence of acceptance and rejection in the attitude of the colonized toward the religion of the colonizer, a phenomenon we have already encountered in our discussion of the emergence of "syncretistic" myths and rituals in Peru.

Strictly speaking, the situation in which the Liberation Theologians find themselves is not fundamentally different from that of seventeenth-century Andean mythmakers or twentieth-century Melanesians; in all these cases one has to appropriate (or reappropriate) what the other claims as its own. But whereas in the seventeenth century the difference between self and other is relatively clear and Christianity is still the religion of the other, in the twentieth century the boundaries between self and other are more ambiguous and Christianity has become one's own religion. Nevertheless, the struggle to wrestle Christianity from the other is still on: no longer from the other as conqueror, *extirpador de idolatrías*, as the conservative theologian who, like Ratzinger, still acts as an inquistor. No one believes any longer that one of the pages of the Bible has been kept hidden by the other, or that a secret formula is being withheld; now it is a matter of interpreting correctly the sacred text.

It will be argued that there is an immense distance between the fantasies of deprived peoples and the refined theologies of a *Hochreligion*. But the reason for this distinction is itself a theological one. From a strictly non-theological position this separation is untenable: either one grants to millenarian mythologies and to millenarian theologies the capacity to articulate utopian hopes, or one denies that to both; in any event, it is not justifiable to proceed in a crypto-theological manner and establish confessionally biased distinctions. In fact, it must be stressed that the exegetical procedures used by the Papuans were not fundamentally different from those used by Liberation Theology. As Worsley points out, the Papuans "select not those passages [of the Bible] enjoining resignation in the face of hardship and miseries on this earth but those which imply 'muscular Christianity,' the righting of wrongs by the faithful themselves. They do not believe in the perpetuation of a universe in which there is for ever to be a miserable life on earth and an ultimate heaven after death . . . . They seek to make heaven on earth, in the here and now." And just as Liberation Theologians identify the tribes of Israel, the chosen people, with the poor, so do the Papuans believe that "It is the native people themselves who must be the Chosen, for they are simple peasants and herdsmen, people whose customs . . . are often similar to those depicted in the Old Testament. Like the Jews, also, they have laboured under oppression and wait to enter the Promised land."[64]

On the other hand, it should be emphasized that the application of labels such as "messianism," "millennialism," and "myth" to phenomena not usually studied by anthropologists must not be understood as an attempt to explain away Liberation Theology and analogues movements; to say that both Melanesians involved in cargo cults and Liberation Theologians reject coventional versions of Christianity does not erase the complexity of Liberation Theology; if anything, it forces us to recognize the many implications of cargo cults, millenarian movements, rituals of protest, etc. Unfortunately, there is a tendency among some anthrolopologists and particularly among some practitioners of the so-called "history of religious approach" to exoticize phenomena that are not in the least exotic and thus to deprive them of their political significance. This is done, for example, by proclaiming the need to "understand—and only to understand—the "world view" of alien groups; by inventing a totally idealized *homo religiosus* who is constantly attempting to recapture a lost *illud tempus*; by uncritically assuming the division of the world into "sacred" and "profane" realms; by indulging in bland calls for enumenism and pluralism. In fact, as the preceding pages should have made clear, religious phenomena are never simply "religious" the religiousness of a movement emerges when choices are transcendentally grounded and when a given discourse assumes forms that appear both as fixed and as infinitely open to interpretation. But it is not solely the skillful manipulation of fixity and openness that will determine which group will define what Christianity—or, more specifically, what Catholicism— is. The labor of interpretation takes place in a world in which changing political and economic conditions open up new choices: increased secularization, conversion to Protestantism, hope for apocalyptic deliverance.

III

Although there is no comprehensive treatment of the phenomenon of conversion to Protestantism in comtemporary Peru, it is clear that the number of conversions to various Protestant groups has increased considerably during the last two decades. Converts generally come from groups attempting to move upwards in the strongly hierarchical Peruvian society, and it seems safe to assume that the rejection of Catholicism and the embrace of Protestantism implies a rejection not only of a particular version of Christianity but also of the traditional values of a Spanish cultures which is now perceived as having been defeated by a Protestant United States. Conversion, perhaps more than most religious phenomena, is able to condense in a single signifying act a large number of apparently unconnected concerns. Thus, for a Peruvian, conversion to Protestants may signify the rejection of hierarchical social and ecclessiastical structures perceived as necessarily connected; it may indicate also either upward social mobility, or at least the fact that such mobility is being sought; politically, conversion may imply the abandonment of explicit political activity and the retreat into the emotional gratification provided by, for example, Pentecostal groups (although it should be remembered that, in the case of Guatemala at least, the fact that a Protestant general assumed the presidency did not involve a retreat of the military into the spiritual realm, but rather a tactical change in the genocidal strategy pursued by the army). In any event, conversion to Protestantism in the Peruvian context does not seem to be significantly different from conversion to Protestantism in other Latin American countries,[65] or indeed from conversion to Catholicism in, for example, Vietnam.[66]

Like ritual, conversion is polysemous, going beyond narrowly conceived religious concerns. It may be the case that the experience of being spiritually reborn is, likely mystical experience, a religious—or existential—event, but one should be aware that the term "experience"—religious, mystical, or otherwise—is simply a label whose appearance in a given context neither solves nor clarifies anything. "Experience" is in fact the name given to something that is produced as the result of the intersection of many factors. The experience of conversion, for instance, may involve, in the case of Peruvian who has decided to become Protestant, a complex system of rejections and acceptances which at a certain point coalesce producing a mental—but never just "mental"—state which we may choose to call the experience of conversion. The roled played by economic, social, and ultimately political factors in this process is crucial. After all, it must be remembered that people convert to sects originating in the United States and certainly identified with that country; therefore, all the contradictory responses that the United States evokes in a Peruvian—and in general in a Latin American—are likely to be present also in the attitude toward a Protestant sect.

Explicit millennialism is also found in contemporary Peru. In *Europa y el País de los Incas,* Alberto Flores Galindo mentions the case of several prophets and preachers, some in the Amazon region, others on the northern coast, and others in Lima. In the capital, the prophet Ezequiel Ataucusi embodies in his very name the tensions we have been examining; Ezequiel (Ezekiel in English) is the name of one of the Old Testment prophets, while Ataucusi is a Quechua name. The Peruvian prophet, who heads the group *Israelitas del nuevo pacto* (Israelites of the new convenant), preaches in the capital where he seems to be particularly popular among the so-called *informales*, a large segment of the population of the shantytowns (*barriadas, pueblos jóvenes*) that surround the city, and who engage in economic activities that because of their "informal" nature are neither taxed nor regulated by the government. It would seem that the convergence of Old Testament images and the revalorization of the Indian component of the nation is an important aspect of Ezequiel Ataucusis' activity (a preacher whose appearance resembles that of an Old Testament prophet as depicted in popular editions of Bible stories[67]). This convergence of Christian and Andean elements is found, as we have already seen, in the "syncretistic" rituals of rebellion during the colonial period and in the learned elaborations of Liberation Theology, and what was said before concerning the dangers involved in referring to these developments using the vocabulary of the anthropology of religion is still valid. To place these movements at the same level does not imply that any of them has been explained; placing them together fundamentally recognizes their politico-religious nature and the similarity of their attitude towards the complex relation between Christianity and the Andean world.

Of the movements examined in this paper, *Sendero luminoso* (Shining Path) is the one whose millenarian component is the most difficult to identify. Shining Path is a rural-urban guerrilla movement which announced itself to the world in 1980, claiming to be the true representative of Marxism-Leninism-Maoism.[68] Since 1980, *Sendero* (as the group is known in Peru) has waged guerilla warfare against the government as well as against those regarded as informants and collaborators with the state. The Peruvian government has responded with increasing levels of violence—including disappearances, mass killings, torture, and rape—against those accused of belonging to *Sendero* or of being its sympathizers. Unfortunately, due to the deep-seated class prejudice and racism prevalent in Peruvian society, the disappearances, mass executions, torture, and rape committed by the armed forces have elicited only a limited amount of protest among the dominant urban groups, for whom *Sendero* is one more example of the irrational and treacherous savagery of 'the Indians.'"[69] Whether the violence started by *Sendero* is the unavoidable response to the structural violence organized and administered by the "second phase" of the military government under General Morales Burmúdez, and later by the reelected Fernando Belaúnde, is open to question, but is not to be dismissed out of hand as most Peruvian politicians do.[70] What is true is that after General Valesco was deposed by the armed forces in an internal coup, the government headed by Morales Bermúdez undid many of the reforms begun by Velasco, in order supposedly to control an economic situation that had reached catastrophic conditions (and which was caused to a great extent by irresponsible weapon purchases). In 1980, after twelve years of military government, the president ousted by the armed forces in 1968, Fernando Belaúnde's Terry, was reelected in an atmosphere of relative hope. However, Belaúnde's was an administration whose high officials had spent the years of military rule in the United States, working for international corporations and other institutions whose interests they faithfully administered when they reached power. The economic crisis that started during the military years worsened during the Belaúnde administration, plunging the country into economic chaos and condemning large segments of the population to misery. The monetarist economic policies pursued by Belaúnde and his ministers aggravated the economic situation, flooded the country with imports, and consequently devastated domestic industrial production. Furthermore, a large proportion of the income generated by exports was used to pay the interest on the external debt and for even more military expenditures, which during the civilian Belaúnde administration constituted a larger percent of the gross domestic product than during the years of military government.[71]

This is not the place to review the vast literature concerning the causes of revolution, particularly of peasant revolutions.[72] We will refer to this literature only insofar as it sheds light in the genesis and development of *Sendero luminoso*, without attempting to solve the controversy between the so-called "moral economy" and "political economy" approaches. The reconstruction of the history of the emergence and development of *Sendero* given by Degregori, González, Favre, and McClintock, and their attempts to place this history in a causal perspective shows some agreement. In the first place, there is a general consensus regarding the significance of the integration of the Ayacucho region into the national market economy.[73] Students of peasant revolutions have emphasized the effects that an increased market participation have in the lives of peasants, even if not everyone agrees with Wolf's contention that peasants try to keep the market "at arms length"[74]; more specifically, social scientists have shown how it is precisely the process of monetarization that tends to trigger millenarian movements.[75] Another factor that contributed to the emergence of *Sendero* is the establishment (actually reopening) of the

University of Ayacucho (Universidad Nacional San Cristóbal de Huamanga) in 1959; the University became the meeting point between "culture brokers"—intellectuals, professors—and the students, some of whom belonged to provincial urban elites, while others had rural backgrounds.[76] But certainly neither the integration of Ayacucho into the capitalist system nor the establishment of the University would have been sufficient to account for the emergency and success of a group such as *Sendero* if the political and economic situation of the region and the country had been different.[77] McClintock, Degregori, and González have emphasized the fact that Ayacucho is (with Apurímac) one of the two poorest *departamentos* in Peru and have given detailed information about illiteracy, life expectancy, nutrition, number of physicians per capita, etc., coming to the conclusion that some provinces of Ayacucho constitute fourth-world islands in a third-world country. If we turn our attention to the political situation of the country, we find that *Sendero* emerged around 1970, when the "revolutionary" wing of the armed forces was in power; the movement came into being, then, at a time of accelerated social change, and came of age during the transition from the reformist "first phase" and the conservative "second phase" of the military government. It was during the second phase that several events, generally recognized as leading to revolt, took place; these are the repression or cancellation of political gains, the lack of fulfillment of the expectations raised by the agrarian reform, and then the sudden downturn in the economy.[78] The effects of the sudden economic crisis in a region such as Ayacucho, already partially integrated into the market economy, were particularly painful. These abrupt economic and political reversals contributed to make *Sendero's* message more plausible and therefore more appealing among university students, many of whom maintained contact with the peasant communities from which they originated. Because of their intermediary position, the students were able to function as cultural mediators, and contributed to the formation of peasant-urban networks, establishing a situation of interdependence between revolutionaries and peasants.[79]

Sendero luminoso is not, then, a purely peasant revolutionary movement. On the contrary, it has emerged, as Degregori has remarked, in the interstices between rural and urban areas,[80] appealing to intermediary groups, no longer rural and not yet entirely urbanized— Favre's "uprooted" (*desarraigados*)[81]—population groups whose increase in "cognitive capacity"—to use Singelman's formulation—is not matched by an increase in economic and political opportunities.[82] It is in this no-man's-land that the millennial component of *Sendero* must be sought. It is true that both Lumbreras and Favre have rejected "millenarist" explanations of *Sendero*, emphasizing rather the effects of the economic and social dislocation mentioned above. Favre has in fact said that to refer to *Sendero* in millenarist terms is to engage in exorcism.[83] Favre is correct. As we have emphasized more than once in this paper, labels such as "messianism" and "millennialism" lend themselves to being used in a substantive fashion, so that those who employ them may be tempted to believe that they have reached the "essence" of the phenomena they are trying to explain. When dealing with radical peasant revolts in the Andean world, for example, some misguided anthropologists may be tempted to explain their occurrence not as the result of the confluence of economic and political factors but rather as the sudden, and quite unexplainable, activation of an alleged "messianic ideology of the Andean world," forgetting that, as Adas has warned, "the assertion that millenarian expression is adopted because there is a tradition of millenarian expectation is at worst tautological and at best ex post facto."[84] Millenarian ideologies and their leaders arise in the space between two or more social formations, that is to say, in periods of transition. The *Taqi onqoy*, the myth of Inkarrí, the revolts caused by the system of *repartos*, the activities of the prophet Ezequiel Ataucusi, have emerged as the response to dislocations in the lives of more or less extended groups caused by Spanish imperialism, by the introduction of a market economy, and by an abrupt process of rural uprooting and urbanization. These ideologies can be seen as creative and to a great extent rational attempts to come to terms with new situations.[85] In the case of *Sendero luminoso*, however, we do not find any explicit millenarian components. *Sendero* presents itself as a Marxist, scientific, anti-utopian ideology, whose purpose is the destruction of the bourgeois state and the establishment of an egalitarian society. Furthermore, *Sendero* is not an exclusively rural movement; in fact, as stated before, it developed in an urban setting, the city of Ayacucho, and more specifically in an academic environment, the Unversidad Nacional San Cristóbal de Huamanga. *Sendero's* leader, Abimael Guzmán, "President Gonzalo," was a philosophy professor, author of a thesis on Kant. Nevertheless, as Favre himself has noted, *Sendero* functions within a culture in which oral traditions are still important and has access to a symbolic language which, if hermetic to outsiders, can be understood by those who have access to traditions transmitted orally.[86] Furthermore, the very fact that Guzmán was an intellectual, a professor of philosophy in a provincial university, where his students were mostly the sons and daughters of displaced provincial elites on the one hand

and of peasants on the other, forces us to place him in the category of cultural mediator, a catagory from which leaders of millenarian movements have traditionally emerged.[87] It is not, then, that Guzmán's intellectual activities, or his not being a peasant or an Indian, move him away from the phenomenon of millenarianism; on the contrary, it is the fact that Guzmán is neither a peasant nor an Indian—his *nom de guerre,* "Gonzalo," reminds one of Francisco Pizarro's brother, Gonzalo, who headed an insurrection against the Spanish Crown— which places him in that structurally ambiguous position that enables him to articulate the ideology of a movement that emerges in periods of transition.

A possible consequence, then, of the confluence of a Marxism reified into infallible science on the one hand and of oral tradition on the other could be the incorporation of elements of the Andean symbolic system into the ideological vision proclaimed by *Sendero.* Thus it is possible that conceptions such as that of a cataclysmic change, a *pachacuti,* may be assimilated into an ideology which quite consciously seeks to destroy the present corrupt social order. In his account of *Sendero,* Werlich writes that in 1970 Abimael Guzmán was expelled from the "Red Flag" group, accused of "occultism," that is, of using local customs and messianic traditions to build support among the peasantry.[88] In fact it is difficult to imagine that Guzmán and his followers would have disregarded the vast storehouse of myths and symbols of the rural "little tradition" which could be turned against the dominant, urban, Hispaic culture (including the political parties that constitute Izquierda Unida, which are considered as accomplices of the repressive state). Scott has shown how traditionally exploited rural groups create an alternative symbolic universe in which values and representations of the dominant culture are inverted, parodied, and profaned, and Wolf has remarked that oppressed peasant groups perceive the world as reversed, a perception that leads to millenarian expectations.[89] It is precisely this alternative symbolic universe and the perception of a world turned upside down and of a dismembered Inkarrí which which be available to the ideologists of *Sendero.* This does not mean that the myth of Inkarrí produced *Sendero luminoso* or that *Sendero* is "essentially" a "messianic" or "millenarian" movement; it means rather that floating meanings could have been manipulated, transformed, and incorporated into a "scientific" ideology, very much as Christian myths and symbols were assimilated into the Andean rebellions of the eighteenth century. This also means however, that, just as the leadership of *Sendero* could utilize traditional Andean symbols, so could certain members of the movement reinterpret and assimilate the theories of Marx, Engels, Mao, and the Peruvian Marxist theoretician José Carlos Mariátegui into an ideological framework àt least partially constituted by Andean traditions. What was said earlier about the possible existence of diverse goals among the leaders and the followers of the Theology of Liberation applies also to movements such as *Sendero luminoso*: beneath the illusory solidity of a movement one can find different visions of the world, competing symbolic universe, conflicting goals.

It should be emphasized that this discussion of *Sendero luminoso* is largely conjectural. Nevertheless, an examination of a book entitled *Tiempos de guerra*, containing extracts of writings of Abimael Guzmán printed in verse form, may give the reader access to some of the symbols used by this movement. The compiler of the book, Rosa Murinache, writes that, convinced of the high values of these documents, she decided to deal with them as if they were poetic material. This she did by selecting the most valuable thoughts (*"los pensamientos más altos"*), placing them in poetic form without adding a single word to the original text.[90] The texts are of an apocalyptic nature and speak of light as a creative, generative, principle: of masses ready, waiting for the light; of light turning into steel. Guzmán writes about an optimism caused by the movement's participation in the "divinities of the modern world: mass, class, Marxism, Revolution." He writes about "The vanguard of the proletariat . . . assaulting the heavens, the darkness and the night" and populating the earth with light and happiness. One text says; "The time has arrived, comrades, the time has arrived. It is time for the great rupture." This rupture is achieved through the revolution, conducted by the "the Party that is the light of the Universe." It is certainly possible that the imagery of light, darkness, revolution, and rupture could have been used in a non-Andean context, and that the notion of "grcat rupture" has nothing to do with the idea of *pachacuti*. Yet it is difficult to believe that either leaders or followers would have been unaware of the mythical resonances of these images.[91] A parallel to this possible confluence of Marxist and Andean imagery can be found in the so-called Lenin epic that emerged in Muslim Central Asia before 1930. According to the Russian sources used by Sarkisyanz, stories concerning Lenin's revolutionary activities were placed in a traditional Islamic contact, so that, for instance, Lenin was regarded as Muhammad's descendant, and his political struggles were seen in a religious context.[92] A similar confluence of Leninism and religion can be found in Mongolia, where according to the *Anglo-Russian News* in 1929, it was believed that "Lanan (Lenin) Bahadur is a descendant of Djinghiz Khan . . . whose lost teachings he has found. . . . He wandered about through the deserts and steppes until he discovered the lost teachings of Djinghiz Khan at Samarqand. These taught him the art of world conquest and from these he also learned that Moscow belonged to his ancestors. He conquered the city and revived the old Mongol teachings.''[93] It could be said that, just as the Russian Revolution was not caused by Islamic or Buddhist messianic representations, but could have nevertheless used them on certain occasions, so it is conceivable that a movement such as *Sendero luminoso* could use elements from the symbolic universe of the Andean world, even if we agree that *Sendero* is not the product of an alleged "messianic ideology of the Andean world."

This brief examination of millenarian elements in Peruvian politics should serve as a reminder of the fact that "religion" is never simply "religious," being rather a component—at times central, at times subordinate—in the pursuit of social power. Given the uncertainty of the economic situation and political situation in Peru, it is reasonable to assume that movements such as the ones discussed in this paper will continue arising and attracting a significant proportion of the population, particularly of those newly urbanized groups for whom Peru is an elusive idea, if not a foreign land.

Notes

Chapter 1. Gustavo Benavides.

1. Max Weber, *Wirtschaft und Gesellschaft* (1922) (Tübingen 1975), p. 28; "Macht bedeutet jede Chance, innerhalb einer sozialen Beziehung den eigenen Willen auch gegen Widerstreben durchzusetzen, gleichviel worauf diese Chance beruht."

2. Steven Lukes, *Essays in Social Theory* (New York 1977), pp.3–29; id., "Power and Authority," in Tom Bottomore and Robert Nisbet, eds., *A History of Sociological Analysis* (New York 1978), pp. 633–76.

3. See, besides Lukes, Gerhard E. Lenski, *Power and Privilege, A Theory of Social Stratification* (Chapel Hill 1966, repr. 1984); Dennis H. Wrong, "Problems in Defining Power" and "Force and the Threat of Force as Distinct Forms of Power" in Wrong, *Skeptical Sociology* (New York 1976), pp. 163–95; Anthony Giddens, " 'Power' in the Writings of Talcott Parsons" and "Remarks on the Theory of Power" in Giddens, *Studies in Social and Political Theory* (London 1977), pp. 333–49; id., *Central Problems in Social Theory* (Berkeley 1979) esp. pp. 88–94; J. G. Merquior, *The Veil and the Mask, Essays on Culture and Ideology* (London 1979), esp. pp. 1–38 (on power and ideology); Michael Mann, *The Sources of Social Power,* vol. 1 (Cambridge 1986) (on societies as power networks).

4. On this issue see Frank Parkin, "Social Stratification," in *A History of Sociological Analysis,* pp. 599–632. In a discussion of stratification in which W. R. Runciman argues against ignoring the three separate dimensions of "class," "status" and "power," he nevertheless acknowledges "the closeness of fit between the three dimensions alike in industrial and pre-industrial societies"; see W. R. Runciman, "Class, Status and Power?" *Sociological Studies* 1 (1968), repr. in Runciman, *Sociology in its Place and other Essays* (Cambridge 1970), pp. 102–40, esp. p. 132ff. For an overview of conceptions of power see Raymond D. Fogelson and Richard N. Adams, eds., *The Anthropology of Power, Ethnographic Studies from Asia, Oceania and the New World* (New York, San Francisco and London 1977); and also Benedict R. O'G. Anderson, "The Idea of Power in Javanese Culture," in Claire Holt, ed., *Culture and Politics in Indonesia* (Ithaca 1972), pp. 1–69, an exemplary study.

5. Louis Dumont, "A Fundamental Problem in the Sociology of Caste," *Contributions to Indian Sociology* 9 (1966), repr. in Dumont, *Religion/Politics*

197

and History in India (Paris and The Hague 1970), pp. 152–65, esp. p. 155; id., Préface à l'édition "Tel" of *Homo hierarchicus* (Paris 1979) pp. i–xl, esp. pp. iii, vii–viii, xiv, xxv.

6. L. Dumont, *Homo hierarchicus. Le système des castes et ses implications* (Paris 1966), new ed. "Tel" (Paris 1979), ch. 2; but see Owen M. Lynch, "Method and Theory in the Sociology of Louis Dumont: A Reply," in Kenneth David, ed., *The New Wind, Changing Identities in South Asia* (The Hague and paris 1977), pp. 239–62.

7. See, from the point of view of a textual indologist, Madeleine Biardeau, "Le sacrifice dans l'Hindouisme," in M. Biardeau and Charles Malamoud, *Le sacrifice dans l'Inde ancienne,* Paris 1976, pp. 25n, 52; for similar conclusions from an anthropological perspective see Susan Wadley, "Power in Hindu Ideology and Practice," in *The New Wind,* pp. 133–57, esp. pp. 136–41; see also Barrington Moore, *Social Origins of Dictatorship and Democracy,* Boston 1966, p. 458.

8. The intimate connection between untouchability and poverty is examined in André Béteille, "Pollution and Poverty," in J. Michael Mahar, ed., *The Untouchables in Contemporary India* (Tucson 1972), pp. 411–20; cf, p. 419; "A kind of cumulative causality keeps the poor isolated because of their 'unclean' habits, and keeps the isolated poor because they lack access to the means of material advancement. At the bottom of the hierarchy, material deprivation and ritual impurity reinforce one another. The poor are unclean, both physically and ritually." Béteille's thesis is confirmed in Joan P. Mencher, "On Being an Untouchable in India: A Materialist Perspective," in Eric B. Ross, ed. *Beyond the Myths of Culture* (New York 1980), pp. 261–94; Mencher also discusses the Untouchables' attidude toward hierarchy (see note 10 below).

9. See Jayant Lele, "The *Bhakti* Movement in India: A Critical Introduction," in *Tradition and Modernity in Bhakti Movements* [International Studies in Sociology and Social Anthropology 31] (Leiden 1981), pp. 1–15.

10. On *jāti* mobility see David G. Mandelbaum, *Society in India* (Berkeley 1970) vol. 2, pp. 442ff, and *passim.* On anti-Brahmanic attitudes see Moore, *Social Origins of Dictatorship and Democracy,* p. 455ff; Mencher, "On Being an Untouchable in India," p. 272ff. Ideological fragmentation and resistance is discussed in Nicholas Abercrombie, Stephen Hill, and Bryan S. Turner, *The Dominant Ideology Thesis* (London 1980); James C. Scott, *The Moral Economy of the Peasant, Rebellion and Subsistence in Southeast Asia* (New Haven 1976), esp. pp. 219–40; id., "Protest and Profanation, Agrarian Revolt and the Little Tradition," *Theory and Society* 4 (1977): 1–38, 211–46; id., "Hegemony and the Peasantry," *Politics and Society* 7 (1977): 267–96; id., *Weapons of the Weak, Everyday Forms of Peasant Resistance* (New Haven 1985); esp. pp. 304–50.

11. Lucian W. Pye, *Asian Power and Politics, The Cultural Dimensions of Authority* (Cambridge 1985), p. 275. (Students of Buddhist and Indian logic in general will be amused by the statement found on p. 133.)

12. On the role of Buddhism in the legitimation of power (and warfare) in Theravada countries see Bardwell L. Smith, ed., *Religion and the Legitimation of Power in Thailand, Laos and Burma* (Chambersburg 1978), and *Religion and the Legitimation of Power in Sri Lanka* (Chambersburg 1978). Attitudes towards nirvana in Theravada countries are discussed in Robert C. Lester, *Theravada Buddhism in Southeast Asia* (Ann Arbor 1973), p. 86; Melford E. Spiro, *Buddhism and Society* (New York 1970), pp. 59, 79ff; Kitsiri Malalgoda, *Buddhism in Sinhalese Society 1750–1900* (Berkeley 1976), p. 15. For a study of Buddhist, particularly Mahayana approaches to violence and war see Paul Demiéville, "Le bouddhisme et la guerre," Post-scriptum à l'*Histoire des Moines guerriers du Japon* de G. Renondeau,]Bibliothèque de l'Institut des Hautes études Chinoises XI] (Paris 1957), pp. 347–85, repr. in P. Demiéville, *Choix d'études bouddhiques* (leiden 1973), 261–99.

13. A detailed study of attempts to define "religion" is impossible here; although the references that follow are by no means complete, they provide a sample of the most influential contributions in the last three decades. From an anthropological perspective see: Raymond Firth, "Problem and Assumption in an Anthropological Study of Religion," *Journal of the Royal Anthropological Institute* 89 (1959): 129–48 (cf. p. 31: "religion may be defined as a concern of man in society with basic human needs and standards of value, seen in relation to non-human entities or powers"). Robin Horton, "A Definition of Religion and its Uses," ibid., 90: 1960, 201–26 (cf. pp. 210–11: "Religion can be looked upon as an extension of the field of people's social relationships beyond the confines of purely human society"). Jack Goody, "Religion and Ritual: The Definitional Problem," *British Journal of Sociology* 12 (1961): 142–64; Clifford Geertz, "Religion as a Cultural System," in Michael Banton, ed., *Antropological Approaches to the Study of Religion* (London 1966), pp. 1–46; Melford E. Spiro, "Religion: Problems of Definition and Explanation," ibid., pp. 85–126 (cf. p. 96: "an institution consisting of culturally patterned interaction with culturally postulated superhuman beings"). Sociological contributions include: Peter Berger, *The Sacred Canopy* (Garden City 1967); Thomas Luckmann, "Religion in der modernen Gesellschaft," in Jakobus Wössner, ed., *Religion in Umbruch* (Stuttgart 1972), pp. 3–15; Jakobus Wössner, "Religion als soziales Phänomen," ibid., pp. 16–46; Günter Dux, "Ursprung, Funktion und Gehalt der Religion," *Internationales Jahrbuch für Religionssoziologie* 8 (1973): 7–67; Karel Dobbelaere and Jan Lauwers, "Definition of Religion—A Sociological Critique," *Social Compass* 20 (1973/1974): 535–51; Th. Luckmann, "über die Funktion der Religion," in Peter Koslowski, ed., *Die religiöse Dimension der Gesellschaft* (Tübingen 1985), pp. 26–41 (almost identical to his 1972 article). Lucid explorations of the religion-ideology complex are Pierre Bourdieu, "Genèse et structure du champ religieux," *Revue française de sociologie* 12 (1971): 295–334, Stephan Feuchtwang, "Investigating Religion," in Maurice Bloch, ed., *Marxist Analyses in Social Anthropology* (London 1975), pp. 61–82; Bryan S. Turner, *Religion and Social Theory. A Materialist Theory* (London 1983); Robert Bocock and

Kenneth Thompson, eds., *Religion and Ideology* (Manchester 1985); Kenneth Thompson, *Beliefs and Ideology* (London and New York 1986). Contributions from historians of religion include: Ugo Bianchi, "The Definition of Religion," in Bianchi, et al., *Problems and Methods of the History of Religions* (Leiden 1972), pp. 16–26 (Bianchi stresses the need to take into account historical continuities); Hans G. Kippengerg, "Diskursive Religionswissenschaft," in Burkhard Gladigow and H. G. Kippengerg, eds., *Neue Ansätze in der Religionswissenschaft* (Munich 1983), pp. 9–28, esp. pp. 24–28 (on religion as discourse); and W. Richard Comstock, "Toward Open Definitions of Religion," *Journal of the American Academy of Religion* 52 (1984): 499–517; Comstock applies theoretical developments from linguistics and literary theory, and emphasizes the need to take into account the role of metonymic relations between "religious" and "secular" texts.

14. On whether dietary regulations are due primarily to classificatory processes (Mary Douglas, *Purity and Danger* [New York 1966]) or to nutritional and ecological concerns see Marvin Harris, *Cultural Materialism* (New York 1979), and *Good to Eat* (New York 1985).

15. "Ultimate concern" and "Absolute" are examples of Topitsch's empty formulae; see Ernst Topitsch, "Über Leerformeln," in *Probleme der Wissenschatstheorie, Festschrift für Viktor Kraft* (Vienna 1960), 233–64; Michael Schmid, *Leerformeln und Ideologiekritik* Tübingen 1972). On the strategies of theological language see Hans Albert, *Das Elend der Theologie* (Hamburg 1979).

16. Edmund Leach, "Anthropology of Religion: British and French Schools," in Ninian Smart, et al. eds., *Nineteenth Century Religious Thought in the West* (Cambridge 1985), vol. 3, pp. 215–62, cf. p. 255; in his *Social Anthropology* (Oxford 1982), Leach uses "cosmology" as the equivalent of the anthropologists' "primitive religion." See also Werner Cohn, " 'Religion' in Non-Western Cultures," *American Anthropologist* 69 (1967): 73–76; id., "On the Problem of Religion in Non-Western Cultures," *Internationales Jahrbuch für Religionssoziologie* 6 (1969): 7–19.

17. The process of sacralization is analyzed in Roy A. Rappaport, "Ritual, Sanctity, and Cybernetics, *American Anthropologist* 73 (1971): 59–76, repr. in *Reader in Comparative Religion* (New York 1979), pp. 254–66 (abridged); id., "Sanctity and Lies in Evolution," *Ecology, Meaning, and Religion* (Richmond 1979), pp. 223–46.

18. On the role of priests see Bourdieu, "Genèse et structure du champ religieux." The problem of religious evolution is discussed in Klaus Eder, "Die Reorganisation der Legitimationformen in Klassengesellschaften," and Rainer Döbert, "Zur Logik des Übergangs von archaischen zu hochkulturellen Religionsystemen," both in K. Eder, ed., *Die Entstehung von Klassengesellschaften* (Frankfurt 1973), pp. 288–99 and 330–63; also Lenski, *Power and Privilege*, pp. 128–29, 173, 209, and esp. 256–66; Mann, *Sources of Social Power*, vol. 1, p. 158.

19. The irreducible nature of religion and *a fortiori* of religious experience has an almost dogmatic status in the study of religion. See, however, Firth, "Problem and Assumption," p. 136; Horton, "A Definition of Religion," pp. 206–207, and Wayne Proudfoot, *Religious Experience* (Berkeley 1985).

20. The religion-power complex is studied in Pierre Bourdieu, "Genèse et structure du champ religieux"; id., *Ce que parler veut dire, L'économie des échanges linguistiques* (Paris 1982); Maurice Bloch, "Symbols, Song and Features of Articulation. Is Religion an Extreme Form of Traditional Authority?" *Archives européennes de sociologie* 15 (1974): 55–81; Burkhard Gladigow, "Kraft, macht, Herrschaft, Zur Religionsgeschichte politischer Begriffe," in *Staat und Religion* (Düsseldorf 1981), pp. 7–22.

21. *La regalità sacra* [Supplements to *Numen* IV] (Leiden 1959); Luc de Heusch, et al., *Le Pouvoir et le Sacré* (Brussels 1962); Haralds Biezais, ed., *The Myth of the State* [Scripta Instituti Donneriani Aboensis VI] (Stockholm 1972); Burkhard Gladigow, ed., *Staat und Religion* (Düsseldorf 1981); Günter Kehrer, ed., *"Vor Gott sind alle gleich," Soziale Gleichheit und soziale Ungleichheit und die Religionen* (Düsseldorf 1983); Otto Heinrich von der Gablentz, "Religiöse Legitimation politischer Macht," in Carl-Joachim Friedrich and Benno Reifenberg, eds., *Sprache und Politik, Festgabe für Dolf Sternberger* (Heidelberg 1968), pp. 165–88; B. Gladigow, *Macht und Religion, Formen der Herrschaftslegitimierung in den antiken Religionen,"* in *Spielarten der Macht* [Humanistische Bildung 1]] (Stuttgart 1977), pp. 1–31; Herbert Frey, "Religion as and Ideology of Domination," in *Religion and Rural Revolt,* pp. 14–30. See also Lenski, *Power and Privilege,* pp. 1–10, 260.

22.See Guenter Lewy, *Religion and Revolution* (New York 1974); János M. Bak and Gerhard Benecke, "Religion *and* Revolt?"; and Ivan Varga, "The Politicisation of the Transcendent," both in Bak and Benecke, eds., *Religion and Rural Revolt* (Manchester 1984), pp. 1–13 and 470–81; Bruce Lincoln, ed., *Religion, Rebellion, Revolution* (New York 1985).

23. See note 10 above.

24. The historical roots of Christian and Muslim attitudes toward gender are studied in John Davis, "The Sexual Division of [Religious] Labour in the Mediterranean," in Eric R. Wolf, ed., *Religion, Power and Protest in Local Communities* (Berlin 1984), pp. 17–50.

25. Besides the indispensable writings of Noam Chomsky (especially *The Fateful Triangle,* Boston 1986) and Edward Said (*The Question of Palestine,* New York 1979), see Anton Shammas, "A Stone's Throw," *The New York Review of Books* 25, n. 5 (31 March 1988): 9–10, and 25, n. 12 (28 July 1988): 42.

26. See Arthur Hertzberg, "The Illusion of Jewish Unity," *The New York Review of Books* 25, no. 10 (16 June 1988): 6–12.

27. On the history of the development of American civil religion see

Maureen Henry, *The Intoxication of Power. An Analysis of Civil Religion in Relation to Ideology* (Dordrecht 1979); on Beveridge and Bryan see pp. 91ff. Henry's own theology is stated on pp. 224–27.

28. Robert N. Bellah, "Civil Religion in America," originally published in 1967, repr. in Bellah, *Beyond Belief* (New York 1970), pp. 168–89; the passage quoted appears on p. 186. See also Bellah, *The Broken Covenant* (New York 1975), and Robert N. Bellah and Phillip E. Hammond, *Varieties of Civil Religion* (San Francisco 1980). The ideological background of the concept of civil religion and the social position of its proponents is examined in Michael W. Hughey, *Civil Religion and Moral Order. Theoretical and Historical Dimensions* (Westport 1983); on Bellah see pp. 157–70.

29. On South Africa one may consult T. Dunbar Moodie, *The Rise of Afrikanerdom. Power, Apartheid, and the Afrikaner Civil Religion* (Berkeley 1975); J. Alton Templin, *Ideology on a Frontier. The Theological Foundation of Afrikaner Nationalism 1652–1910* (Hartford 1984); Leonard Thompson, *The Political Mythology of Apartheid* (New Haven 1985). On the Philippines, David R. Sturtevant, *Popular Uprisings in the Philippines 1840–1940* (Ithaca 1976), *passim*; Hans-Jürgen Greschat, "Religiöser Nationalismus auf den Philippinen," in *Humanitas religiosa, Festschrift für Haralds Biezais* (Stockholm 1979), pp. 242–51.

30. See notes 20 and 21 above. It is therefore rather surprising to discover that "power" has just been "restored" to religion by some sociologists; see James A. Beckford, "The Restoration of *Power* to the Sociology of Religion," in Thomas Robbins and Roland Robertson, eds., *Church-State Relations, Tensions and Transitions* (New Brunswick and Oxford 1987), pp. 13–37 (an otherwise valuable study).

Chapter 2. Ninian Smart.

1. The term "Buddhist modernism" has been used by Heinz Bechert, "Theravada Buddhist Sangha: Some General Observations on Historical and Political Factors in its Development," *Journal of Asian Studies* 29/4 (August 1970): 761–78. Gananath Obeyesekere has used the expression "Protestant Buddhism" to cover much the same thing, in "Religious Symbolism and Political Change," Modern *Ceylon Studies* 1 (1970): 46–47.

2. Jayatilleke's *The Message of the Buddha* was posthumous, and edited by Ninian Smart (London: Allen and Unwin, 1975).

3. "Sri Lanka: The Evolutionary Dialectics of a Buddhist State," in Carlo Caldarola, *Religion and Societies: Asia and the Middle East* (Berlin 1982).

4. François Houtart, *Religion and Ideology in Sri Lanka* (Colombo 1974).
5. For the general Indian experience see Paul Hiebert, "India: The

Politicization of a Sacred Society," in Caldarola, *Religion and Societies,* pp. 289–331. For one of the more militant of the alternatives to the modern Hindu ideology, see Ninian Smart, *Prophet of a New Hindu Age* (London 1985) (with Swami Purnananda).

Chapter 3. Lina Gupta.

1. P. C. Chatterjee, *Secular Values for Secular India,* (New Delhi, Paula Press: 1972), p. vii.

2. *U. S. News,* 6 April 1987, p. 34.

3. Donald Eugene Smith, *India as a Secular State,* (Princeton 1976), p. 495.

4. See Teja Singh, *Guru Nanak and His Mission,* (Amritsar, 1963).

5. See Chajju Singh, *The Ten Gurus and Their Teachings,* (Lahore 1903).

6. See Avatar Singh, *Ethics of the Sikhs,* (Patialia 1970).

7. Smith, *India as a Secular State,* p, 439.

8. See Indubhusan Banerjee, *Evolution of the Khalsa,* (Calcutta 1972).

9. Khushwant Singh, *The Sikhs,* (London: George Allen & Unwin Ltd., 1953), p. 178–80.

10. Quoted in Chatterjee, *Secular Values for Secular India,* p. 291.

11. Smith, *India as a Secular State,* p. 441.

12. Ibid., 440.

13. See Khushwant Sings, *The Sikhs.*

14. See Kailash Chader Gulati, *The Akalis Past and Present,* (New Delhi 1974).

15. A new alphabet which was used for the sacred writing of the Sikhs.

16. Quoted in Harbans Singh, *The Heritage of the Sikhs,* (New York: Asia Publishing House, 1965), p. 302.

17. See *Constitution of India* as modified November 1977.

18. M. V. Pylee, *India's Constitution,* (New York: Asia Publishing House, 1979), p. 126.

19. Chatterjee, *Secular Values for Secular India,* p. 2.

20. *After Partition, Modern India Series* No. 7, p. 45.
21. Smith, *India as a Secular State,* p. 133.
22. Ibid., 108.

23. Ibid., 110.

24. Ibid., 112.

25. Ibid., 439.

26. Ibid., 443.

27. Ibid., 444.

28. Chatterjee, *Secular Values for Secular India,* p. 294.

29. See Kuldip Nayar and Khushwant Singh, *Tragedy of Punjab,* (New Delhi: Vision Books, 1984).

30. See P. B. Gajendragadkar, *The Constitution of India, Its Philosophy and Basic Postulates,* (New York: Oxford University Press, 1969).

Chapter 4. Stephan Feuchtwang.

1. I owe a great debt of thanks to Dr. Soo Ming-wo for help in compiling these materials, with financial assistance from the City University, London.

2. Leo Strauss, *Spinoza's Critique of Religion* (New York: Schocken, 1965); John Bossy, "Some Elementary Forms of Durkheim," *Past and Present* 95 (May 1982).

3. Judith Berling, "Religion and Popular Culture: The Management of Moral Capital in *The Romance of Three Teachings,*" in David Johnson, Andrew J. Nathan, Evelyn S. Rawski, eds., *Popular Culture in Late Imperial China* (Berkeley: University fo California Press, 1985); Daniel Overmyer, "Values in Chinese Sectarian Literature: Ming and Ch'in *pao-chüan,*" ibid.

4. Ann S. Anagnost ("Politics and Magic in Contemporary China," *Modern China* vol. 13, no. 1 [January 1987]) following are some of the same clues as I am, makes a similar point: the statements are "not really about feudal superstition at all but are playing on the negative imagery of this category to project other messages of concern" (p. 42), and she concludes that this has the effect of turning what is described into an anti-state activity and a kind of popular alternative or resistance. An example of this is the case of a spirit-medium promising the imminent dawn of a new kingdom (Anagnost, "The Beginning and End of an Emperor: A Counter-representation of the State," *Modern China* vol. 11, no. 2, [April 1985]). Her otherwise rich and subtle analyses make use of a surprisingly bald concept of the state and hegemony. I will pay closer attention to policy and concept than she has.

5. *Ningxia Ribao,* 19 October 1982 (BBC Summary of World Broadcasts, Part 3: Far East, 7175, 5 November 1982). [BBC Summary of World Broadcasts, Far East will be referred to as FE.]

6. G. W. F. Hegel, *Phenomenology of the Spirit,* translated by A. V. Miller, (Oxford: Clarendon Press, 1977), paragraphs 541–43.

7. E.g. *Hongqi* (Red Flag), 1 May 1986 (FE 8264, 21 May 1986).

8. *Fujian Ribao,* 13 January 1982 (FE 6935, 23 January 1982). My stresses.

9. E.g., *Banyuetan* (Fortnightly Talks) 1 (1982) and 6 (1982).

10. *Hongqi,* 16 June 1982 (FE 7074, 10 July 1982).

11. *Hongqi,* 1 May 1986 (FE 8264, 21 May 1986).

12. *Hongqi,* 16 June 1982 (FE 7074, 10 July 1982).

13. *Shehui Kexue* (Social Studies) 4 (1985): 79.

14. See reports in, for instance, *Nanfang Ribao* (Southern Daily) 3 May 1981, 5 November 1981, 5 June 1982,; *Banyuetan* 23 (1982); Nanning Radio, 11 July 1982; and *Zhongguo Fazhibao* (China Law News) 31 December 1986, p. 2.

15. In Tibet, according to a personal communication from Dr. Michael Aris, for which many thanks.

16. *Guangming Ribao* (Enlightened Daily) 20 April 1981.

17. *Nongcun Gongzuo Tongxun* (Rural Work) 1 (1982): 45.

18. See Elizabeth Croll, *The Politics of Marriage in Contemporary China* (Cambridge University Press 1981), and Kay Ann Johnson, *Women, the Family and Peasant Revolution in China* (University of Chicago Press 1983).

19. Delia Davin, "The Employment and Status of Peasant Women," in S. Feuchtwang, A. Hussain, and T. Pairault, eds., *Transforming China's Economy in the Eighties,* 2 vols., (London: Zed Press, 1987).

20. *Zhongquo Fazhi Bao* (China Law News) 31 December 1986, p. 2.

21. Changsha Radio, 22 October 1979.

22. *Renmin Ribao,* November 1981.

23. *Minzhu yu Falu* (Democracy and the Legal System) 7 (1982): 43.

24. *Guangming Ribao,* 24 March 1983, p. 2.

25. *Zhongguo Funu* (China Women) 12 (1981).

26. *China Youth,* 29 January 1983.

27. *Nangfang Ribao,* 5 May 1981.

28. *Zhongguo Fazhibao,* 31 December 1986, p. 2.

29. *Banyuetan* 23 (1982).

30. *Banyuetan* 7 (1981).

31. Guangzhou Radio, 28 March 1981.

32. *Beijing Review* 15 (1981).

33. *Banyuetan* 15 (1981): 9–11.

34. *Beijing Ribao* (FE 7256, 12 February 1983).

35. *Guangming Ribao,* 19 March 1983, p. 2.

36. *Hongqi,* 1 May 1986 (Fe 8264, 21 May 1986).

37. *Zhongguo Fazhibao* (China Law News), 31 December 1986, p. 2.

38. In an observation of the rampant growth of "superstitious activities" (*mixin huadong*), an article printed in *Shehui* (Society), no. 6 (20 December 1986) gives three main reasons for their revival. One is the low level of scientific knowledge in the countryside. The second is where cadres stress the economy and prosperity at the expense of ideological work. And the third is cadres not making a clear distinction between the policy of freedom of religious belief and the policy of suppression of superstitious activities by ideological work. They "wrongly assume superstitious activities to be the exercise of religious freedom."

39. Anagnost, "Politics and Magic in Contemporary China."

Chapter 5. Alexandre Bennigsen.

1. Z. Sirajitdinov, "Sviashchennyi kamen' schastia ne podarit" ("The Holy Stone will not bring happiness"), *Komsomoletz Usbekistana* (Tashkent), 10 October 1986.

2. *Pravda Vostoka* (Tashkent) 5 and 7 October 1986, quoted in *Keston News Service,* no. 262 (30 October 1986): 9.

3. *Kommunist Tajikistana* (Dushanbe) 31 January and 12 February 1987.

4. The incident was described in the Tajik language newspaper *Tojikistoni Soveti,* 9 April 1987.

5. V. G. Pivavarov, "Sociological Research on the Problems of Customs, Culture, National Traditions and Religious Beliefs in the Chechen-Ingush ASSR," *Voprosy Nauchnogo Ateizma* (Moscow), vol. 17. (1975): 316.

Chapter 6. M. W. Daly.

1. Ali A. Mazrui, "The Black Arabs in Comparative Perspective: The Political Sociology of Race Mixture," in Dunstan M. Wai, *The Southern Sudan: The Problem of National Integration* (London 1973), p. 72.

2. For the curiously anti-climactic atmosphere of the day see G. N. Sanderson, "Sudanese Nationalism and the Independence of the Sudan," in Michael Brett, *Northern Africa: Islam and Modernization* (London 1973), pp. 97–110.

3. See M. W. Daly, *Empire on the Nile: The Anglo-Egyptian Sudan, 1898–1934* (London 1986), pp. 308–12.

4. Abdullahi Ahmed An-Na'im, "On Sudanese Identities", paper delivered to a workshop at the Woodrow Wilson International Center for Scholars, Washington, D.C., February 1987.

5. Manifesto of the Sudan People's Liberation Movement, 31 July 1983.

Chapter 7. Shahin Gerami.

1. Yahya Nuri, *Huquq va Hudud-e Zan dar Islam* (Tehran 1961), p. 22.

2. Ibid., 242.

3. Levy Reuben, *The Social Structure of Islam* (Cambridge 1957), p. 99, quoting the thirteenth-century Sunni jurist al-Baydawi.

4. All translations of Koranic excerpts are from the translation by M. H. Shakir (New York 1982).

5. Murtiza Mottahari, *Nizam-i Huquqi Zan dar Islam* (Tehran 1974), p. 164.

6. *Hjab* literally means partition, but the word generally refers to a type of clothing that protects a woman from the eyes of men, except for her husband and some blood relatives (father, brother, son, and so forth).

7. Murtiza Mottahari, *Masalleh-e Hejab* (Qum n.d.), p. 78.

8. See Mottahari, *Nizam,* pp. 160–61.

9. Susan Moller Okin, *Women in Western Political Thought* (Princeton 1979), p. 82.

10. *Hadith:* tradition; refers to actions and sayings attributed to the Prophet Muhammad and his family.

11. A. Ferdows and A. Ferdows, "Women in Shiat Fiqh: Images through the Hadith," in G. Nashat, ed., *Women and the Revolution in Iran* (Boulder 1983), pp. 55–68.

12. Mottahari, *Masalleh,* p. 221.

13. Ibid.

14. Moller Okin, *Women,* p. 82.

15. Ferdows and Ferdows, "Women," p. 58.

16. Mottahari, *Nizam,* p. 163.

17. Ali Shariati, *Fatimah Fatimah Ast* (Fatimah is Fatimah) (Tehran, n.d).

18. Shahla Haeri, "Women, Law, and Social Change in Iran," in J. Smith, ed., *Women in Contemporary Muslim Societies* (London 1980), pp. 209–35.

19. Eliz Sanasarian, *The Women's Rights Movement in Iran: Mutiny, Appeasement, and Repression from 1900 to Khomeini* (New York 1982), p. 62.

20. World Bank, *World Tables: Social Data* (Baltimore), 3d ed., vol. 3, p. 44.

21. Sanasarian, *The Women's Rights,* p. 10.

22. World Bank, *World Tables.*

23. See Mary Hegland, "Aliabad Women: Revolution as Religious Activity," in G. Nashat, ed., *Women,* pp. 171–95; and Patricia Higgin, "Women in the Islamic Republic of Iran: Legal, Social and Ideological Changes," *Signs* 10, no. 31, (Spring 1985): 477–94.

24. See G. Nashat, "Women in the Ideology of the Islamic Republic," in her *Women,* pp. 195–217; and Farah Azari, "The Post-Revolutionary Women's Movement in Iran," in F. Azhari, ed., *Women in Iran* (London 1983), pp. 190–225.

25. Ettelaat, Kordada, no. 15880 (June 1979): 5.

26. G. Hojatti Ashrafi, *Majmue-h Comel-e Qavanin v-Mogharrat-e Jazai* (Tehran 1985), pp. 14m–24m.

27. Ministry of Justice, *Rouznameh Rasmi-e Jumhuri-e Islami-e Iran,* No. 11694 (April 1985): 1.

28. *Iran Times,* 21 February 1986.

29. Azari, *The Post Revolutionary,* p. 220.

30. A. Tabari and N. Yeganeh, *In the Shadow of Islam* (London 1982), p. 238.

31. *Iran Times,* 5 September 1986.

31. Ibid., 17 January 1986.

33. Ibid.

34. Ibid., 6 June 1986.

Chapter 8. William M. Batkay.

1. See Norman L. Zucker, *The Coming Crisis in Israel: Private Faith and Public Policy* (Cambridge, Mass. 1973). I am deeply grateful to David Geithman and Maurie Sacks for reading earlier drafts of this article, and for advice and encouragement; to Montclair State College for providing hours of released time in fall 1986 for writing; and to Arnold and Frances Hagler for allowing me access to their newspaper files.

2. See Charles S. Leibman and Eliezer Don-Yehiya, *Religion and Politics in Israel* (Bloomington, Ind. 1984); Zalman S. Abramov, *Perpetual Dilemma: Jewish Religion in the Jewish State* (Rutherford, N. J. 1976); and Alice and Roy Eckardt, *Encounter with Israel: A Challenge to Conscience* (New York, 1970).

3. See, e.g., Emile Marmorstein, *Heaven at Bay: The Jewish Kulturkampf in the Holy Land* (London 1969); Rael Jean Isaac, *Party Politics in Israel: Three Visions of a Jewish State* (New York 1981); Daniel Meijers, " 'Civil Religion' or 'Civil War': Religion in Israel," in Eric R. Wolf, ed., *Religion, Power and Protest in Local Communities: The Northern Shore of the Mediterranean* (Berlin 1984), pp. 137–61.

4. See Zucker, *Coming Crisis,* for the Conservative approach; and Isaac, *Party and Politics*, for the movements' increasing restiveness.

5. See Ephraim Tabory, "Reform and Conservative Judaism in Israel: A Social and Religious Profile," in *American Jewish Yearbook 1983* (Philadelphia 1983), pp. 41–61.

6. For statistics see Tabory, "Reform"; Charles S. Liebman, *Pressure without Sanctions: The Influence of World Jewry on Israeli Policy* (Rutherford, N.J. 1977); Zucker, *Coming Crisis;* Jack Weinshanker, "President's Column," *United Synagogue of America New Jersey Region Newsletter,* Spring 1986; Herbert Rosenblum, *Conservative Judaism· A Contemporary History* (New York 1983); and The Jewish Theological Seminary of America, *Celebrate a Century of Achievement* (n.d.), marking the centennial of the seminary.

7. Wendy Elliman, "The Reform Movement: A Report," *The Israeli Economist* 36 (March 1980): 18–19; David Rudge, "Conversion Battle Threatens Reform Settlement in Galilee," *Jerusalem Post International Edition,* 1 August 1986; and Jewish Theological Seminary, *Celebrate.*

8. See Rosenblum, *Conservative Judaism;* Elliman, "The Reform Movement"; and Tabory, "Reform and Conservative Judaism."

9. On the Baeck Center see Tabory, "Reform and Conservative Judaism"; and Elliman, "The Reform Movement".

10. On leasing public space see Amnon Rubinstein, "Law and Religion in Israel," *Israel Law Review* 2, no. 3 (July 1967): 380–414. On the woman

convert see Haim Shapiro, "Reform Convert Wins Court Order," *Jerusalem Post International Edition,* 26 April 1986; and "High Court Bans Inscribing 'Converted' on ID Cards," *United Jewish Federation of MetroWest Jewish News,* 11 December 1986.

11. For an overview and examples see William Frankel, *Israel Observed: An Anatomy of the state* (London 1980); Rosenblum, *Conservative Judaism;* and Liebman, *Pressure.*

12. See Richard G. Hirsch, "Mercaz," *Conservative Judaism* 34, no. 6 (July-August 1981): 35–41; *MERCAZ: Movement to Reaffirm Conservative Zionism* (n.d.); and "Temple Schedules Shabbat Speaker," *United Jewish Federation of MetroWest Jewish News,* 6 November 1986.

13. On the press see, e.g., Joseph Heckelman, "Israel's Delegitimized Majority," *Jerusalem Post International Edition,* 9 August 1986. For the increasing sharpness of public comment see, e.g., "Reform, Conservative Leaders Blast Ruling on IDs for Converts," *United Jewish Federation of MetroWest Jewish News,* 3 July 1986. On identity cards see Thomas L. Friedman, "Uproar in Israel over Converts' ID's [*sic*]," *New York Times,* 25 June 1986.

14. On electoral bargaining see Daniel J. Elazar, "Religious Parties and Politics in the Begin Era," in Robert O. Freedman, ed., *Israel in the Begin Era* (New York 1982), pp. 102–20; and Eliezer Don-Yehiya, "Religion and Coalition: The National Religious Party and Coalition Formation in Israel," in Asher Arian, ed., *The Elections in Israel, 1973* (Jerusalem 1975). On the "Who is a Jew?" issue see Moshe Samet, "Who is a Jew? (1978–1985)", *Jerusalem Quarterly* 37 (1986): 109–39.

15. For American Conservative and Reform contributions to Israel see Liebman, *Pressure;* for Conservative Zionism see Abraham Karp, "A Century of Conservative Judaism in the United States," *American Jewish Yearbook 1986* (Philadelphia 1986), pp. 3–61.

16. Cf. Rabbi Ralph Pelcovitz's letter to the editor, *Jerusalem Post International Edition,* 23 August 1986.

17. Between 1969 and 1975, for example, about thirty thousand Americans came to Israel in this category: See Kevin Avruch, *American Immigrants in Israel: Social Identities and Change* (Chicago and London 1981), table 3.1.

18. See Harold R. Isaacs, *American Jews in Israel* (New York 1967), for pre-1948 immigration figures; for post-1948 data see Daniel Shimsoni, *Israeli Democracy* (New York 1982). See also Avruch, *American Immigrants,* table 3.1.

19. For the geographic origins of Conservative and Reform Jews in Israel see Tabory, "Reform and Conservative Judaism"; and Avruch, *American Immigrants,* table 3.11. On the rabbinic leadership of non-Orthodox

congregations see Tabory; and Frankel, *Israel Observed.* On the motives of American Conservative rabbis in moving to Israel see "Conservative Rabbis and Israeli Life: A Mini-Symposium," *Conservative Judaism* 31, no. 3 (Spring 1977): 259–76.

20. Yitzhak Hildesheimer, an official of an Orthodox Zionist organization, claims that "much more than 50 percent of [immigrants] are Orhtodox": letter to the editor, *Jerusalem Post International Edition,* 3 May 1986.

21. See Eytan Gilboa, "Attitudes of American Jews Toward Israel: Trends over Time", *American Jewish Yearbook 1986,* pp. 110–25.

22. On the importance of the formative processes in the *Yishuv* see Frankel, *Israel Observed;* Sam Lehman-Wilzig, "Religion and State in Israel," *The Israeli Economist* 36 (March 1980): 17–19; Sammy Smooha, *Israel: Pluralism and Conflict* (Berkeley 1978); and Dan Horowitz and Moshe Lissak, *Origins of the Israeli Polity: Palestine under the Mandate* (Chicago 1978). For the Reform perspective on this issue see Elliman, "The Reform movement."

23. See Samet, "Who is a Jew? (1958–1977)," *Jerusalem Quarterly* 36 (1985): 88–108, and "Who is a Jew? (1978–1985)"; Ira Sharkansky, *What Makes Israel Tick: How Domestic Policy-Makers Cope with Constraints* (Chicago 1985); Liebman and Don-Yehiya, *Religion and Politics*; Abramov, *Perpetual Dilemma*; and Eckardt, *Encounter.* Liebman, *Pressure*, p. 117, also argues that Conservative and Reform leaders lack a specific vision of Israel, and that, in their view, it is not "proper, necessary, or legitimate for one to pursue self-interested objectives there."

24. See "Will Charge Orthodox Rabbi with Disrupting Congregation," *United Federation of MetroWest Jewish News,* 30 October 1986. Cf. Albert S. Axelrad, "Reflection on Religious Pluralism and the State of Israel," *Conservative Judaism* 34 (May-June 1981): 41–47.

25. Jack J. Cohen, "Religion in Israel: II," *Jewish Frontier* 34 (November 1967): 9–15; Mendel Kohansky, "Reform Judaism Meets in Israel [*sic*], *Midstream* 14, no. 9 (November 1968); and Joshua D. Haberman, "The Reform Rabbinate and Israel," *Judaism* 33, no. 3 (1984): 282–88.

26. See Charles S. Liebman, "Diaspora Influence on Israeli Policy," in Moshe Davis, ed., *World Jewry and the State of Israel,* vo. 2 (New York 1977), pp. 313–28.

27. Liebman, "Diaspora Influence"; Zucker, *Coming Crisis.*

28. The phrase was coined by Zbigniew Brzezinski.

29. See, e.g., Pelcovitz's letter to the editor; and Haim Shapiro, "Storm over Identifying Converts," *Jerusalem Post International Edition,* 5 July 1986.

30. On the Orthodox rabbinate's concern with endogamy see, e.g., Shapiro, "Storm." Cf. Edwin Samuel, "Religious Conflict in Israel," *Jewish*

Heritage 8 (Fall 1965): 35. On the centrality of power considerations see Cohen, "Religion in Israel: II," pp. 9–15; and Zucker, *Coming Crisis.* For a broader explanation of Orthodox rejection of non-Orthodox religious marriages see Solomon Poll and Ernest Krausz, eds., *On Ethnic and Religious Diversity in Israel* (Ramat Gan, Israel 1975), p. 12.

31. See Lehman-Wilzig, "Religion and State"; and MERCAZ; Murray Zuckoff, "Peres Issues Appeal for Jewish Unity", *United Jewish Federation of MetroWest Jewish News,* 20 November 1986; and Samet, "Who is a Jew? (1958–1977)" and "Who is a Jew? (1978–1985)." For related examples of Conservative and Reform deference to Israeli government appeals see Rosenblum, *Conservative Judaism;* Liebman, *Pressure;* and Zucker, *Coming Crisis.*

32. The argument about "self-esteem" is Rabbi Perry Raphael Rank's in an unpublished sermon at Congregtion Shomrei Emunah, Montclair, N.Y., October 1986. On the Conservative and Reform perception of what is "real" Judaism see Heckelman, "Israel's Delegitimized Majority"; and Janet Aviad, *Return to Judaism: Religious Renewal in Israel* (Chicago and London 1983), pp. 6, 165. For the ramifications of the Orthodox background of early Conservative leaders see Rosenblum, *Conservative Judaism;* Elliot Dorff, *Conservative Judaism: Our Ancestors to our Descendants* (New York 1977); and Marshall Sklare, *Conservative Judaism: An American Religious Movement* (New York 1972). See also Gerson Cohen, "From *Altneuland* to *Altneuvolk*: Toward an Agenda for Interaction between Israel and American Jewry" in Davis, ed., *World Jewry,* pp. 237–57.

33. See Steven M. Cohen, *American Modernity and Jewish Identity* (New York and London 1983), for examples of recent surveys.

34. Lerner's comments are in *Conservative Judaism* 29, no. 4 (Summer 1975): 5, quoted in Rosenblum, *Conservative Judaism,* p. 104. Tannenbaum's view was expressed in an unpublished lecture to Congregation Shomrei Emunah, Montclair, N.Y., 30–31 May 1986. See Samet, "Who is a Jew? (1978–1985)," for Agudat Israel's perceptions.

35. See Sklare, *Conservative Judaism.* Rabbi Irving Greenberg argued that by the mid-1960s the Conservative movement was reproducing itself from within its own ranks: see "Toward Jewish Religious Unity: A Symposium," *Judaism* 15, no. 2 (Spring 1966): 132–63. On Reform support for Habad see Haim Shapiro, "Herzog to Reform Jews: Get into Politics," *Jerusalem Post International Edition,* 7 June 1986.

36. For survey data on religious self-identification see, e.g., "Smith Poll for 'The Jerusalem Post' Finds: 67 Per Cent Find Ultra-Orthodox Unacceptable," *Jerusalem Post International Edition,* 5 July 1986; and Lawrence Meyer, *Israel Now: Portrait of a Troubled Land* (New York 1982), chapter 9. On traditional Jewish religious symbols and practices in Israel see Liebman and Don-Yehiya,

Religion and Politics, and the survey evidence in Chaya Zuckerman-Bareli, "The Religious Factor in Opinion Formation among Israeli Youth," in Poll and Krausz, *Ethnic and Religious Diversity,* pp. 53–89. For a detailed examination of Israeli civil religion see Leibman and Don-Yehiya, *Civil Religion in Israel: Traditional Judaism and Political Culture in the Jewish State* (Berkeley 1983). Cf. Myron Aronoff, "An Interpretation of Israeli Political Culture," paper presented at the 1985 annual meetings of the American Anthropological Association, 4–8 December 1985.

37. See Jonathan S. Woocher, "Sacred Survival: American Jewry's Civil Religion," *Judaism* 34, no. 2 (Spring 1985): 151–62; Cohen, *American Modernity*, table 8.1; and Liebman, *Pressure,* p. 114.

38. Woocher, "Sacred Survival"; Judith N. Elizur, "The Image of Israel at Thirty-Six," *Judaism* 33, no. 3 (Summer 1984): 263–82; Cohen, *American Modernity*, table 8.1; Irving Greenberg, "The Interaction of Israel and American Jewry—After the Holocaust," in Davis, *World Jewry*, pp. 259–82. For an illustration of the lack of concern mentioned here see "Parents of Israelis Set Mini-Convention," *United Jewish Federation of MetroWest Jewish News,* 30 October 1986.

39. Shapiro, "Herzog to Reform Jews"; Rosenblum, *Conservative Judaism*; Liebman, *Pressure*; and Zucker, *Coming Crisis.*

40. See, e.g., *MERCAZ.*

41. On the "invisibility" of non-Orthodox forms of religious Judaism in Israel see Liebman and Don-Yehiya, *Religion and Politics*; Smooha, *Israel*; Zucker, *Coming Crisis*; Georges R. Tamarin, *Forms and Foundations of Israeli Theocracy* (Tel Aviv 1968); and Nathan Rotenstreich, "Secularism and Religion in Israel," *Judaism* 15, no. 3 (Summer 1966): 259–83. On the founding generation see Tom Segev, *1949: The First Israelis* (New York, 1986), especially part 3. On Israeli religious perceptions see also Harvey Molotch and others, "American Jews and the State of Israel," *Center Magazine* 16, no. 3 (May-June 1983): 8–26. Shlomo Deshen's masterful overview does not even mention Conservative or Reform Judaism: "Israeli Judaism: Introduction to the Major Patterns," *International Journal of Middle East Studies* 9 (1978): 141–69.

42. See Sharkansky, *What Makes Israel Tick,* for an insightful overview.

43. Axelrad, "Reflections."

44. Elazar, "Religious Parties"; and Frankel, *Israel Observed.* See Elliman, "Reform Movement," for some examples of explicitly political bargaining for some of these concessions.

45. Elazar, "Religious Parties"; and Frankel, *Israel Observed.*

46. See Shapiro, "Herzog to Reform Jews", for an Israeli view of the importance of politics to non-Orthodox chances for recognition. On interest

groups in Israel see Asher Arian, *Politics in Israel* (Chatham, N.J., 1985); and Yael Yishai, "Interest Groups in Israel," *Jerusalem Quarterly* 11 (Spring 1979): 128–44. On the proposal for a Conservative Zionist party see Tsvi Bisk, "The Conservative Movement in Israel," *Conservative Judaism* 37, no. 2 (Winter 1983–84): 28–33; Robert Gordis, *Understanding Conservative Judaism* (New York 1978), chapter 13; and Myron M. Fenster, "Religion in Israel," *Congress Bi-Weekly* (13 January 1969): 12.

47. Liebman and Don-Yehiya, *Religion and Politics;* and Frankel, *Israel Observed.*

48. See Kohansky, "Reform Judaism"; and Cohen, "Religion in Israel: II."

49. This point was raised first by Arian in *Ideological Cleavage in Israel* (Cleveland 1968).

50. For the postage-stamp affair see "MK Upset by 'Non-Orthodox' Stamps," *Jerusalem Post International Edition,* 7 December 1985; and "Yeshiva University Boycotts Ceremony," Ibid., 31 May 1986. The quotations are from Frankel, *Israel Observed,* p. 217, and Zucker, *Coming Crisis,* p. 91.

51. For a thorough discussion of the Baka dispute and its precedent-setting resolution see Edwin Black, "The Baka Accord," *United Jewish Federation of MetroWest Jewish News,* 13 November 1986 and 20 November 1986; on the establishment of the Conservative seminary in Jerusalem see Ralph Mandel, "Israel," *American Jewish Yearbook 1986,* p. 345.

52. Jewish Theological Seminary, *Celebrate.*

Chapter 9. Warren L. Vinz.

1. Russell Conwell, "Mexico," *Temple Review* 27, no. 44 (19 December 1919): 3. [*Temple Review* is hereinafter cited as *TR*.]

2. Ibid.

3. Esther 4:14.

4. Henry May, *Ideas, Faiths, and Feelings* (New York and Oxford: Oxford University Press, 1983), p. 175.

5. *TR* (24 October 1895): 519.

6. Conwell, "America's Danger," *True Philadelphian* 2 no. 3 (24 June 1898): 347.

7. Ibid.

8. Conwell, "Freedom That Is Slavery," *TR* 9, no. 23 (7 March 1902): 481.

9. Ibid.

10. Conwell, "Opportunities in National Unrest," *TR* 27, no. 14 (4 April 1919): 3.

11. Conwell, "The Influence of Our Nation," *TR* 12, no. 9 (27 November 1903): 3.

12. Ibid.

13. Ibid., p. 4.

14. Ibid.

15. Ibid., p. 5.

16. Ibid., p. 14.

17. Conwell, "Patriotic Sons of America," *TR* 17, no. 14 (16 October 1908): 4.

18. Conwell, "Rule of the Majority," *TR* 21, no. 22 (3 April 1913): 6.

19. Conwell, "Thanksgiving for Victories," *True Philadelphian* 2, no. 19 (5 August 1898): 524.

20. Ibid.

21. Ibid.

22. Conwell, "Theodore Roosevelt," *TR* 27, no. 10 (21 November 1919): 1.

23. Conwell, "The Saviour at the Panama Canal," *TR* 23, no. 44 (9 December 1915): 3.

24. Matthew 6:29.

25. Conwell, "The Saviour," pp. 4, 5.

26. Ibid., p. 5.

27. Ibid.

28. Ibid., p. 6.

29. Conwell, "God's Care of the Nation," *TR* 7 no. 24 (15 March 1901): 523.

30. Conwell, "Mexico," p. 3.

31. Ibid.

32. Ibid., p. 4.

33. As an aside, before delivery of this sermon, Conwell reminded the congregation of its responsibility to study the issue of the League and vote accordingly. While Conwell publicly supported woman's suffrage he hardly gave it a ringing endorsement when he declared "Every one of you women who now *have* the right to vote and every one of you men who *should* vote must study this question so that you may vote right." Underlining mine.

34. Conwell, "An Unfair Partnership," *TR* 31, no. 2 (5 October 1923): 276.

35. Ibid.

36. St. Paul.

37. Matthew 28: 16–20.

38. Conwell, "An Unfair," p. 276.

39. Ibid.

40. Ibid., p. 278.

41. Conwell, "German Indemnity," *TR* 25, no. 43 (14 December 1917): 3–6.

42. Baptist reaction to Turkish massacres is recorded in Robert G. Torbet, *A Social History of Philadelphia Baptist Association, 1707–1940* (Philadelphia: Westbrook Publishing Co., 1944), pp. 219–20.

43. Conwell, "The Second Battle," *TR* 28, no. 18 (30 April 1920): 2.

44. Ibid., p. 4.

45. Conwell, "Rule of the Majority," *TR* 21, no. 22 (13 April 1919): 4.

46. Conwell, "Patriotic Hearts," *TR* 25, no. 35 (16 November 1917): 4, 5.

47. Conwell, "Rule," p. 4.

48. Conwell, "Limits of Liberty," *TR* 30, no. 25 (23 June 1922): p. 4.

49. Conwell, "Mexico," *TR* 27, no. 44 (19 December 1919): 5.

50. Conwell, "Thanksgiving for Victories," *True Philadelphian* 2, no. 19 (5 August 1898): 524.

51. Ibid.

52. Ibid., p. 525.

53. Ibid.

54. Ibid.

55. Clyde Kenneth Nelson, *The Social Ideas of Russell Conwell,* unpublished dissertation, University of Pennsylvania (1968), p. 380.

56. Conwell, "Loving One's Other Self," *TR* 31, no. 35 (2 November 1923): 305, 306.

57. Ibid.

58. Conwell, "The Kingdom of God a True Democracy," *TR* 27, no. 6 (18 January 1919): 7.

59. Conwell, "America's Danger," *True Philadelphian* 2, no. 13 (24 June 1898): 353.

60. Conwell, "Church Aid to Patriotism," *TR* 24, no. 4 (27 January 1916): 11.

61. Julius W. Pratt, *Expansionists of 1898* (Gloucester, Mass.: Peter Smith, 1959), pp. 279–316.

62. Robert G. Torbet, *A Social History of the Philadelphia Baptist Association 1707–1940* (Philadelphia: Westbrook Publishing Co., 1944).

63. Nelson, p. 358.

64. Ibid., p. 364.

65. Pratt, p. 316.

66. Richard Hofstadter, *The Paranoid Style of American Politics* (New York: Alfred A. Knopf, 1965), p. 150.

67. Martin Marty, *Righteous Empire* (New York: Harper & Row, 1970), p. 186.

Chapter 10. Spencer Bennett.

1. Robert Bellah, *The Broken Covenant: American Civil Religion in Time of Trial* (New York: Seabury Press, 1975), 3–35.

2. *Sons of the Fathers: The Civil Religion of the American Revolution* (Philadelphia: Temple University Press, 1976), 58.

3. For an analysis of the Virgin as a symbol in Mexican civil religion see Eric R. Wolf, "The Virgin of Guadalupe: A Mexican Nation Symbol," in Lieri Isauro and Durna H. Russell Bernard, ed., *Introduction to Chicano Studies* (New York: Macmillan, 1973), 246–52.

4. Miguel León-Portilla has to date written the best treatment of Aztec metaphysics in *Aztec Thought and Culture* (Norman, Oklahoma: University of Oklahoma, 1963).

5. Winthrop Yinger, *César Chávez: The Rhetoric of Nonviolence* (Hicksville New York: Exposition Press, 1975), 46–47. Yinger includes a number of important documents by Chávez and the UFWOC: the fast speech, the Sacramento March letter of 1966, a fast letter to the National Council of Churches, an open letter text on nonviolence, and a Good Friday letter dated 23 April 1969 to one of the growers, refuting the charges of violence by the workers in the grape boycott. Printed in *The Christian Century*, the letter has been compared to Martin Luther King's "Birmingham" letter written in 1963 to refute those ministers who charged that his nonviolent tactics were responsible for racial violence.

6. The most thorough, if least interpretative, account of the trials of the United Farm Worker's Organizing Committee is found in Jacques E. Levy, *César Chávez: Autobiography of La Causa* (New York: W. W. Norton and Company, Inc., 1975).

7. Peter Matthiessen, *Sal Si Puedes: César Chávez and the New American Revolution* (New York: Random House, 1969), 220.

8. Levy, 27.

9. Ibid., 91.

10. Joan London and Henry Anderson, *So Shall Ye Reap*, (New York: Thomas Y. Crowell, 1970), 141. London and Anderson show the inadequacy of earlier organizing tactics in the area of rural labor when Norman Smith of the UAW was sent to California and failed with principles which had been successful in organizing auto workers in Detroit in the 1930s.

11. See the growers' sponsored publication, *Clergy Views of Delano and the Grape Boycott* (Fresno, California: Rudell Publishing Co., n. d.).

12. Mark Day, *Forty Acres: César Chávez and the Farm Workers* (New York: Praeger Publishers, 1971), 58–59.

13. Peter Williams claims: "Popular religion is generated when the official religion proves inadequate for those for whom it is prescribed or when social confusion reaches such a point that no institutionalized religion is adequate to interpret the ultimate relation of the group or the individual to the cosmos." *Popular Religion in America* (Englewood Cliffs: Prentice-Hall, 1980), 16.

14. Wolf, 251.

15. Yinger, 106–107.

16. Ibid.

17. Levy, 227.

18. Ronald B. Taylor, *Chávez and the Farm Workers* (Boston: Beacon Press, 1975), 169.

19. Matthiessen, 127–28.

20. Levy, 277.

21. Matthiessen, 137.

22. Levy, 276.

23. Yinger, 111.

24. Levy, 279.

25. Matthiessen, 199.

26. Yinger, 65.

27. Matthiessen, 137.

28. Levy, 283.

29. Chávez reports that a preacher from a little church in Earlimart, when asked to preach at the mass during the fast, replied that he would be thrown out (he also worked for Schenley, one of the growers). "And when he came, I introduced him, gave the full name of his church and everything so there would be no doubt about where he came from. And he did it in great form and the people accepted him." Matthiessen, 186.

Chapter 11. Phillip E. Hammond.

1. Alexis de Tocqueville, *Democracy in America,* ed. J. P. Mayer, trans. George Lawrence (Garden City: Doubleday Anchor, 1969).

2. Seymour M. Lipset, *The First New Nation* (New York: Basic Books, 1963).

3. *Democracy in America,* p. 290.

4. Richard J. Neuhaus, The Naked Public Square (Grand Rapids: Wm. B. Eerdmans, 1984).

5. James A. Reichley, *Religion in American Public Life* (Washington, D.C.: The Brookings Institution, 1985).

6. See *Religion in American Public Life,* ch. 2, for Reichley's scheme and its analysis.

7. See Phillip E. Hammond, "The Courts and Secular Humanism," *Society* 21 (May/June 1984): 11–16, for a discussion of this point regarding the Supreme Court's choice of words in handing down church-state decisions.

8. Robert N. Bellah, "Civil Religion in America," *Daedalus* (Winter 1967): 1–21.

Chapter 12. Gustavo Benavides.

1. See Luis Guillermo Lumbreras, "El Perú prehispánico," in *Nueva historia general del Perú,* 4th ed. (Lima 1985) pp. 19–21; Richard W. Keatinge, "The Nature and Role of Religious Difussion in the Early Stages of State Formation: An Example from Peruvian History," in Grant. D. Jones and Robert R. Kautz, eds., *The Transition to Statehood in the New World* (Cambridge 1981), pp. 172–87.

2. Lumbreras, "El Perú prehispánico;" Maurice Godelier, "Le concept de 'formation économique et sociale': l'exemple des Incas," *Horizon, trajets marxistes en anthropologie*, vol. I (Paris 1977), pp. 177–87.

3. See particularly Juan Ginés de Sepúlpeda, *Apologia pro libro de justis belli causas,* first published in Rome in 1550 and now available in a bilingual Latin-Spanish edition as *Tratado sobre las justas causas de la guerra contra los indios* (Mexico 1941, repr. 1979). For a general overview and a bibliography see Gustavo Benavides, "Catholicism and Politics in Latin America," in Charles Fu and Gerhard Spiegler, eds., *Movements and Issues in World Religions,* vol. I; *Religion, Ideology, and Politics* (New York, Westport and London 1987), pp. 107–42.

4. On the *Taqi onqoy* see Luis Millones Santa Gadea, Un movimiento nativista del siglo XVI; el Taki Ongoy," and "Nuevos aspectos del Taki Ongoy," both reprinted in *Ideología mesiánica del mundo andino,* ed. Juan Ossio (Lima 1973), pp. 83–101; Nathan Wachtel, *La vision des vaincus, Les indiens du Pérou devant la Conquête espagnole 1530–1570* (Paris 1971), pp. 269ff., quoting Cristóbal de Molina, *Relación de las fábulas y ritos de los Incas (1575)* (Lima 1916), p. 98; Pierre Duviols, *"Religions et répression dans les Andes aux XVIe et XVIIe siècles,"* in Robert Jaulin, ed., *L'Ethnocide a travers les Amériques* (Paris 1972), pp. 93–105; Marco Curatola, "Mito y milenarismo en los Andes: del Taki Onqoy a Inkarrí," *Allpanchis* 10 (1977): 65–92; Alberto Flores Galindo, *Europa y el país de los Incas: la utopía andina* (Lima 1986), pp. 46–47.

5. Duviols, "Religions et répression," p. 97.

6. Of the vast literature on millennialism we have consulted the following: Norman Cohn, *The Pursuit of the Millennium* (New York 1961, rev. ed.); Peter Worsley, *The Trumpet Shall Sound, A Study of "Cargo" Cults in Melanesia* (New York 1968, ed ed.); Guglielmo Guariglia, *Prophetismus und Heilserwartungs-Bewegungen als völkerkundliches und religionsgeschicht- liches Problem* (Vienna 1959); E. J. Hobsbawm, *Primitive Rebels, Studies in Archaic Forms of Social Movements in the 19th and 20th Centuries* (New York 1959); Vittorio Lanternari, *Movimenti religiosi di libertà e di salvezza dei poppoli oppressi* (Milan 1974); Yonina Talmon, "Pursuit of the Millennium: The Relation Between Religious and Social Change," in *Archives européennes de sociologie* 3 (1962): 125–48; id., "Millenarian Movements," ibid. 7, (1966): 159–200; Maria Isaura Pereira de Queiroz, *Réforme et révolution dans les sociétés traditionnelles. Histoire et Ethnologie des movements messianiques* (paris 1968); id., *O messianismo no Brasil e no mundo* (São Paulo 1977); Kenelm Burridge, *New Heaven, New Earth. A Study of Millenarian Activities* (New York 1969); Bryan Wilson, *Magic and the Millennium. A Sociological Study of Movements of Protest among Tribal and Third World Peoples* (London 1973); Michael Adas, *Prophets of Rebellion, Millenarian Protest Movements against the European Colonial Order* (Chapel Hill 1979).

7. Cf. Marjorie Reeves, *Joachim of Fiore and the Prophetic Future* (New York 1977), pp. 128–29.

8. Cf. José Antonio Maravall, *Utopía y reformismo en la España de los Austrias* (Madrid 1982), pp. 85–86.

9. For this peculiar thesis see José Sánchez-Boudy, "La conquista española como obra mística," in *Santa Teresa y la literatura mística hispánica,* ed. Manual Criado de Val (Madrid 1984), pp. 715–20. Sánchez-Boudy's mystical version of what could be called "vulgar Weberianism" may appear as extreme but is not new; for an early twentieth-century example see the now almost forgotten Ernest Seillière, *Mysticisme et domination. Essais de critique imperialiste* (Paris 1913).

10. See Juan M. Ossio A., ed., *Ideología mesiánica del mundo andino* (Lima 1973). On pp. xxi–xxii of his Introduction to the volume Ossio writes: "... *al enfatizar la explicación ideológica, no negamos que la Conquista pudiese generar algunos efectos socio-económico desequilibradores para el hombre andino, que lo hubieran hecho sentir deprivado y estimulado a desarrollar movimientos mesiánicos sino sólo afirmamos que también hay factores ideológicos que se tienen que tomar en cuenta y que para el caso andion quizás sean los más inportantes.*" The anthology itself is quite useful; on the other hand, Ossio's is a rather inept attempt to rewrite in a "superstructural" manner and therefore to make inoffensive the tragic history of the destruction of the Inca empire and the exploitatin (that still continues) of "Andean man."

11. See Jürgen Golte, *Repartos y rebeliones. Túpac Amaru y las contradicciones de la economía colonial* (Lima 1980) (translation of *Warenverteilung und Bauernrebellionen im Vizekönigreich Peru [1751–1783]*, Berlin 1977), esp. pp. 150–52, 192ff. In "La revolución tupamarista y los pueblos andinos," *Allpanchis* 17/18 (1981): 253–65, Alberto Flores Galindo has criticized Golte's "structural" explanation, and emphasizes the role played by the revolutionaries as social agents (pp. 256–57). The disagreement between Flores Galindo and Golte parallels the (far less friendly) controversy between E. P. Thompson (*The Poverty of Theory* [London 1978]) and Perry Anderson (Arguments within English Marxism [London 1980]); in any case the positions defended by Flores Galindo and Golte are not entirely contradictory. For a discussion of structural explanations, which also takes into account the role of social agents and the uniqueness of historical events, see Philip Abrams, *Historical Sociology* (Ithaca 1982), esp. ch. 7. Abrams' investigation is indebted to Giddens' theory of structuration; see Anthony Giddens, *Central Problems in Social Theory* (Berkeley 1979), pp. 69–73 and *passim,* but also Derek Layder, *Structure, Interaction and Social Theory* (London 1981), esp. pp. 62–70.

12. On the existence of a contemporary utopian ideology in the Andes see Manuel Burga and Alberto Flores Galindo, "La utopía andina," *Allpanchis*

20 (1982): 85–101; Henrique Urbano, "Representaciones colectivas y arqueología mental en los Andes," ibid., pp. 33–83 (polemical and at times unclear); Alberto Flores Galindo, *Europa y el país de los Incas;* id., "¿Es posible la utopía?," *El Caballo Rojo,* 28 September 1986, pp. 4–5.

13. See Jan Szeminsi, *La utopía tupamarista* (Lima 1983), pp. 88–89.

14. Szeminski, pp. 127ff.

15. On the concept of *pachacuti* see Nathan Wachtel, *Sociedad e ideología* (Lima 1973), pp. 221–25; Szeminski, *La utopía tupamarista,* pp. 125–32; Flores Galindo, *Europa y el país de los incas,* pp. 41–46; "Mito y rito en la iconografía mochica," Entrevista de Alberto Flores Galindo y Manuel Burga a Anne Marie Hocquenghem, *Cultura popular* 13/14 (1984): 168–75. We have not been able to consult José Imbelloni, *Pachacuti IX* (Buenos Aires 1976).

16. See Flores Galindo, *Europa y el país de los Incas,* pp. 51–52, 70.

17. Several versions of the Inkarrí myth collected by José María Arguedas, Josafat Roel Pineda, and Alejandro Ortiz can be found in *Ideología mesiánica del mundo andino,* pp. 217–36; Alejandro Ortiz Rescaniere, *De Adaneva a Inkarrí. Una visión indígena del Perú* (Lima 1973). See also Franklin Pease, "El mito de Inkarrí y la visión de los vencidos," in *Ideología mesiánica,* pp. 439–58; id., "Las versiones del mito de Inkarrí," *Revista de la Universidad Católica* 2 (1977): 25–41.

18. On the *extirpación de idolatrías* see Pierre Duviols, *La destrucción de las religiones andinas* (Mexico 1977) (translation of *La lutte contre les religiones autochtones dans le Pérou colonial. L'extirpation de l'idolatrie entre 1532 et 1660* [Lima 1971]); id., "Religions et répression dans les Andes aux XVIe et XVIIe siècles"; Manuel Burga, "La crisis de las identidad andina. Mito, ritual y memoria en los Andes Centrales en el siglo XVII," ms. pp. 26–39.

19. Cf. Duviols, "Religions et répression," p. 103; *"On sait moins que les suicidés furent aussi très nombreux au Pérou. Matienzo s'étonnait du très grand nombre d'Indiens, très jeunes ou très vieux, qui se pendaient 'sans raison'; il attribuait ce phénomène à la coeuleur de leur peau!"*

20. Pease, "El mito de Inkarrí y la visión de los vencidos," p. 450.

21. On the persistence of rebellions against the Spaniards see Golte, *Repartos y rebeliones;* Flores Galindo, "La revolución tupamarista y los pueblos andinos (una crítica y un proyecto)," *Allpanchis* 17–18 (1981): 253–64.

22. For examples outside the Andean world involving the appropriation of Spanish Catholicism see David R. Sturtevant, *Popular Uprisings in the Philippines 1840–1940* (Ithaca 1976), pp. 83–95 and *passim;* Robert Wasserstrom, "Indian Uprisings under Spanish Colonialsim: Southern Mexico in 1712," in Robert P. Weller and Scott E. Guggenheim, eds., *Power and Protest in the Countryside* (Durham 1982), pp. 42–56, esp. p. 43; "[in the early

eighteenth century] a young Tzeltal girl—inspired, she claimed, by the Holy Virgin—informed her followers in the remote highland town of Cancuc that both God and the king had died. The time had come, she declared, for *naturales* to avenge their past sufferings and reestablish true religion." For examples involving slave rebellions see Eugene D. Genovese, *From Rebellion to Revolution* (New York 1981), pp. 32, 45–46. For a general discussion see James C. Scott, *The Moral Economy of the Peasant. Rebellion and Subsistence in Southeast Asia* (New Haven 1976), pp. 219–40; id., "Protest and Profanation. Agrarian Revolt and the Little Tradition," *Theory and Society* 4 (1977): 1–38, 211–46; id., "Hegemony and the Peasantry," *Politics and Society* 7 (1977): 267–96. See also notes 63–64 below.

23. See Michael Mann, *The Sources of Social Power* (Cambridge 1986), vol. 1, pp. 301–40.

24. See Alan Wardman, *Religion and Statecraft among the Romans* (Baltimore 1982), p. 138.

25. Eric Wolf, "The Virgin of Guadalupe: A Mexican National Symbol," *Journal of American Folklore* 71 (1958): 34–39, repr. in William A. Lessa and Evon Z. Vogt, eds., *Reader in Comparative Religion* (New York 1979, 4th ed.), pp. 112–15, (p. 115).

26. Ibid.

27. But see "Mito y rito en la iconografía mochica" (note 15 above) p. 169, where the possibility of the persistence of pre-Christian elements in the figure of *el Señor de los milagros* is discussed.

28. Which does not mean that the existence of a unified symbolic system (à la Parsons) or of a "civil religion" (American or otherwise), or of a "dominant ideology" should be taken for granted in the case of other societies. On this important problem one should consult the writings of Scott (note 22 above), and particularly Nicholas Abercrombie, Stephen Hill and Bryan S. Turner, *The Dominant Ideology Thesis* (London 1980), and Bryan S. Turner, *Religion and Social Theory. A Materialist Perspective* (London 1983).

29. Peru's defeat by Chile (functioning as a proxy for Britain) was due to a great extent to the fact that "Peru" hardly existed at the time. In "The Choreography of History in Andean Dance," to appear in *Andean Kaleidoscope*, ed. Billie Jean Isbell, Deborah A. Poole has studied the ways in which the war and the defeat were perceived by the various groups that constitute Peruvian society.

30. See note 71 below.

31. On Andean rituals and their persistence see Billie Jean Isbell, *To Defend Ourselves. Ecology and Ritual in an Andean Village* (Austin 1978), esp. pp. 117–65, 189–91, 197–220; Michael T. Taussig, *The Devil and Commodity Fetishism in South America* (Chapel Hill 1980), pp. 150–68, 214–22; Glynn

Custred, "The Place of Ritual in Andean Rural Society," in Benjamin S. Orlove and Glynn Custred, eds., *Land and Power in Latin America. Agrarian Economies and Social Processes in the Andes* (New York and London 1980), pp. 195–209; Henrique Urbano, "Representaciones colectivas," pp. 55–68.

32. See Isbell, *To Defend Ourselves,* pp. 198–99. For a general discussion of the role rituals play in ecological control see Roy A. Rappaport, *Ecology, Meaning, and Religion* (Richmond 1979), and id., *Pigs for the Ancestors. Ritual in the Ecology of a New Guinea people* (New Haven 1984) (2d ed.), particularly "Epilogue, 1984," pp. 299–496.

33. Manuel Burga, "La crisis de la identidan andina. Mito, ritual y memoria en los Andes Centrales en el siglo XVII," pp. 56–57.

34. Flores Galindo, *Europa y el país los Incas,* pp. 71–78.

35. See Roland L. Grimes, *Symbol and Conquest. Public Ritual and Drama in Santa Fe, New Mexico* (Ithaca 1976).

36. See Eva Hunt, "Ceremonies of Confrontation and Submission: The Symbolic Dimensions of Indian-Mexican Political Interactions," in Sally F. Moore and Barbara G. Myerhoff, eds., *Secular Ritual* (Assen and Amsterdam 1977), pp. 124–47.

37. Hunt, pp. 144–45; see also Charles A. Reilly, "Cultural Movements in Latin America: Sources of Political Change and Surrogates for Participation," Myron J. Aronoff, ed., *Culture and Political Change [Political Anthropology* vol. 2] (New Brunswick and London 1973), pp. 127–53, esp. 149–51.

38. On this issue, crucial in the formation and development of religions, see Abner Cohen, *Two-Dimensional Man. An Essay on the Anthropology of Power and Symbolism in Complex Society* (Berkeley 1974); id., "Drama and Politics in the Development of a London Carnival," *Culture and Political Change,* pp. 101–26; David I. Kertzer, "The Role of Ritual in Political Change," ibid., pp. 53–73. Birnbaum and Lukes have emphasized the role of rituals not in promoting value integration but as elements in the "mobilization of bias"; see Norman Birbaum, "Monarchs and Sociologists: A Reply to Professor Shils and Mr. Young," *The Sociological Review* 3 (1955), repr. in id., *Toward a Critical Sociology* (New York 1971), pp. 57–80; Steven Lukes, "Political Ritual and Social Integration," *Sociology* 9 (1975), repr. in id., *Essays in Social Theory* (New York 1977), pp. 52–73.

39. Discussed in Roberto Oliveros, *Liberación y teología. Génesis y crecimiento de una reflexión 1966–1976* (Lima 1980 2d ed.); Renato Poblete, S.J., "From Medellín to Puebla: Notes for Reflection" (apologetic and superficial) and Phillip Berryman, "What Happened at Puebla," both in Daniel H. Levine, ed., *Churches and Politics in Latin America* (Beverly Hills and London 1980), pp. 41–54, 55–86.

40. Gustavo Gutiérrez, *Teología de la liberación* (Lima 1971); Hugo Assmann, *Teología desde la praxis de la liberación* (Salamanca 1973); Juan Luis Segundo, *Liberación de la teología* (Buenos Aires 1975).

41. Overview and bibliography in Benavides, "Catholicism and Politics in Latin America" (note 3 above).

42. See Alberto Escobar, ed., *El reto del multilingüismo en el Perú* (Lima 1972); on the role of the Peruvian educational system in the preservation of these stereotypes see Roland G. Paulston, "Educational Stratification and Cultural Hegemony in Peru," *Journal of Developing areas* 5 (1971): 401–15, repr. in Jerome Karabel and A. H. Halsey, eds., *Power and Ideology in Education* (New York 1977, repr. 1979), pp. 412–23.

43. Alfredo Garland Barrón, *Como lobos rapaces* (Lima 1978).

44. See Roy Rappaport, "Ritual, Sanctity, and Cybernetics," *American Anthropologist* 73 (1971): 59–76, repr. in *Reader in Comparative Religion,* pp. 254–66, esp. pp. 264–66; id., "Sanctity and Lies in Evolution," in *Ecology, Meaning, and Religion,* pp. 223–46; Maurice Bloch, "Symbol, Song, Dance and Features of Articulation. Is Religion an Extreme Form of Traditional Authority?" *Archives européennes de sociologie* 15 (1974): 55–81.

45. Gustavo Gutiérrez, *A Theology of Liberation* (Maryknoll 1973), p. 153; the original (*Teología de la liberación,* p. 189) reads: *"no hay dos historias, una profana y otra sagrada 'yuxtapuestas' o 'estrechamente ligadas' sino un solo devenir humano asumido por Cristo, Señor de la historia."*

46. Segundo, *The Liberation of Theology,* pp. 156–70; we have not been able to consult the original Spanish edition.

47. For examples of similar condemnations of political activity, this time against those priets involved in the struggle against Spain, see Benavides "Catholicism and Politics in Latin America," p. 109.

48. *Instruction on Certain Aspects of the "Theology of Liberation,"* Sacred Congregation for the Doctrine of the Faith, 6 August 1984, p. 3.

49. *Instruction,* p. 8.

50. Ibid., p. 9.

51. Ibid., p. 11.

52. Ibid., p. 30.

53. See Joel Kovel, "The Vatican Strikes Back," *Monthly Review* 36, no. 11 (April 1985), repr. in William T. Kabb, ed., *Churches in Struggle* (New York 1986), pp. 172–84. The theologian who has explored from a theological perspective the issue of power in the church is Leonardo Boff; see his *Church: Charism and Power* (New York 1986) (translation of *Igreja: Carisma e Poder* [Petrópolis 1981], which was not consulted).

54. An English translation of *Liberation and the Gospel, Pastoral Message of the Peruvian Bishops* has appeared in *Origins, NC Documentary Service,* vol. 14, no. 31 (17 January 1985); the Spanish original was not consulted. See also Christine E. Gusdorf, "Ratzinger, Gutierrez, and the Bishops of Peru," *Commonweal* 8 (February 1985): 77–79.

55. English translations of the pope's messages have appeared in *Origins,* vol. 14, no. 35 (14 February 1985); the Spanish original versions were not consulted. The passage appears on p. 573.

56. Ibid., p. 575.

57. Ibid., p. 579.

58. See Gustavo Benavides, "The Discourse of Liberation Theology in Perspective," in M. Darrol Bryant and Rita H. Mataragnon, eds., *The Many Faces of Religion and Society* (New York 1985), pp. 122–34.

59. See Turner, *Religion and Social Theory,* ch. 6; Natalie Zemon Davis, "Some Tasks and Themes in the Study of Popular Religion," in Charles Trinkaus and Heiko A. Oberman, ed., *The Pursuit of Holiness in Late Medieval and Renaissance Religion* (Leiden 1974), 307–36; François-André Isambert, *Le sens du sacré. Fête et religion populaire* (Paris 1982). The most recent, and most lucid, discussion of this issue is Richard Trexler, "Reverence and Profanity in the Study of Early Modern Religion," in Kaspar von Greyerz, ed., *Religion and Society in Early Modern Europe 1500–1800,* London 1984, pp. 245–69.

60. This is argued in Benavides, "The Discourse of Liberation Theology in Perspective," pp. 127–29; see also Bloch, "Symbols, Song, Dance and Features of Articulation," esp. pp. 66–67.

61. Segundo, *The Liberation of Theology,* pp. 40–57 and *passim*; Assmann, "El cristianismo, su plusvalía ideológica y el costo social de la revolución socialista," "La función legitimadora de la religión para la dictadura brasileña," *Teología desde la praxis de la liberación,* pp. 171–202, 211–27.

62. Segundo, *Liberation,* pp. 7–39.

63. Cf. Worsley, *The Trumpet Shall Sound,* p. 43.

64. Ibid., pp. 137–38; see also note 22 above.

65. See Emilio Willems, "Protestantism and Culture Change in Brazil and Chile," in William D'Antonio and Frederick Pike, eds., *Religion, Revolution, and Reform. New Faces for Change in Latin America* (New York 1964), pp. 91–108, esp. p. 105. The recent study by Sheldon Annis, *God of Production in a Guatemalan Town,* Austin 1987, appeared too late to be incorporated in our discussion of conversion. Annis' study should be used as a model for research in other Latin American countries.

66. See Samuel L. Popkin, *The Rational Peasant. The Political Economy of Rural Society in Vietnam* (Berkeley 1979), pp. 188–93.

67. I wish to thank Carlos Iván Degregori for information about the *Israelitas del nuevo pacto;* on the physical appearance of Brazilian messiahs and their Iberian and Latin models see Pereira de Queiroz, *Réforme et révolution,* p. 110.

68. On *Sendero luminoso* see: Raúl González, "Ayacucho: por los caminos de Sendero," *Qué hacer* 19 (October 1982): 37–77; id., "Qué pasa con Sendero luminoso," ibid., 29 (June 1984): 34–38; id., ". . . Y ahora ¿qué?" ibid., 30 (August 1984): 6–29; id., "Sendero: cinco años después de Belaúnde," ibid., 36 (August/September 1985): 37–49; id., "Para entender a Sendero," ibid., 42 (August/September 1986): 28–48 (includes interviews with Luis Lumbreras [pp. 34–43] and Henri Favre [pp. 44–48]; id., "¿Qué pasa en Puno? El PUM, el PAP, Sendero y Alan García," ibid., 43 (October/November 1986): 41–51; id., "La cuarta plenaria del Comité Central de S. L.," ibid., 44 (December 1986/January 1987): 49–53; "Informe inglés sobre Sendero," *Oiga* 15 August 1983; Cynthia McClintock, "Sendero Luminoso: Peru's Maoist Guerrillas," *Problems of Communism* 32, no. 5 (September/October 1983): 19–34; id., "Why Peasants Rebel: The Case of Peru's Sendero Luminoso," *World Politics* 37 (October 1984): 48–84; David P. Werlich, "Peru: The Shadow of Shining Path," *Current History* 83 (February 1984): 78–82, 90; Henri Favre, "Pérou: Sentier lumineux et horizons obscurs," *Problèmes d'Amérique latine* 72 (2ᵉ trimestre 1984): 3–27 (there is a Spanish translation of pp. 15–25 of this article: "Perú: Sendero Luminoso y horizontes oscuros," *Qué hacer* 31 [October 1984]: 25–34); Jeanne DeQuine, "The Challenge of Shining Path," *The Nation* (8 December 1984): 610–13; Carlos Iván Degregori, *"Sendero Luminoso": I. Los hondos y mortales desencuentros. II. Lucha armada y utopía autoritaria* (Lima 1986); "Sendero espera el año dos mil," *Diario La República* 24 May 1987, 33–35. See also "Sendero Luminoso: A Bibliography," *Hispanic Focus* 3 (Library of Congress, Washington, D.C. 1985), compiled by Everette E. Larson, Hispanic Division.

69. Urban perceptions of the rural population go from the misconceived generalizations about an edenic "Andean cultural identity," found among some superstructural anthropologists to the undisguised contempt, combined with fear, found among the middle and upper classes. Examples of the former are Ossio, "La Creatividad del pensamiento andino," and Urbano, "Dogmas, bancarrotas y sistemas cognitivos," *La Revista* 4 (April 1981): 57–59 (these are responses the Golte, "Gregorio Condori Mamani o la bancarrota del sistema cognitivo andino," ibid., 3 (November 1980): 18–20; see also Golte's lucid response, "¿Qué es la cultura frente a la historia?" ibid., 4 (April 1981): 59–63; the attitude of the latter is not fundamentally different from the one expressed by a nineteenth-century Spanish official in the Philippines: ". . . the Indian is pacific, superstitious, indolent, respectful to authority, heedless, distrustful, and deceitful. . . . The natives are also spiteful and revengeful when they believe themselves offended; and at such times, hiding their [anger] under the veil of . . . humility, they await the opportunity for satisfying it and generally

give rein suddenly to their ill-will with perfidy and ferocity" (quoted by Sturtevant, *Popular Uprisings in the Philippines*, p. 78). On the violations of human rights in Peru see America's Watch, *Abdicating Democratic Authority. Human Rights in Peru*, 1984; id., *Derechos Humanos en el Perú. Primer año del presidente García* (Lima 1986) (Spanish transl.); Diego García S., Carlos Capelleti, Félix Gutiérrez, Javier Diez Canseco, "Derechos humanos y estado de emergencia en la sierra central y sur," *Mundo andino y región* (Lima 1984), pp. 31–44; Alberto Flores Galindo and Nelson Manrique, *Violencia y campesinado* (Lima 1986); Célula parlamentaria del Partido Unificado Mariateguista-IV, *Los sucesos en los penales. Acusación constitucional sobre un caso de genocidio* (Lima 1986); current information about human rights in Peru can be found in the reports of Amnesty International, (304 West 58th Street, New York, NY 10019) and Eco-Andes (198 Broadway, Rm. 302, New York, NY 10038), and in the issues of *Qué hacer* listed above.

70. *Sendero*'s violence and use of terror is beyond any doubt; information about it can be found in *Derechos humanos en el Perú*, pp. 43–51, and in the articles listed in note 68 above. Violence and use of terror against the terror of conquest and domination is not new in the Andes, having been an important component of, among others, the revolution led by Tupac Amaru; see Szeminski, *La utopía tupamarista*, pp. 45, 175–76, 256 (destruction of fields and killing of animals), 272, 281; Flores Galindo, "Ideología, democracia y violencia en la región central y sur andina," *Mundo andino y regin*, pp. 61–63. In "Mito y rito en la iconografía mochica," Flores Galindo and Anne Marie Hocquenghen discuss the importance of violence, authoritarianism and hierarchy in Andean societies as well as the role these elements could play in a revolution (which itself could be seen as a pachacuti). It should be pointed out, however, that violence and terror are common weapons in peasant rebellions and need not be explained in cultural-historical terms, but rather structurally (see, for example, Eric Wolf, *Peasants* [Englewood Cliffs 1966], p. 107; "The bloodiness and cruelty of these uprisings has often been remarked upon, and seems to in curious contradiction to the everyday life of the peasant. . . . Yet, seen from another perspective, such outbreaks are merely occasional manifestations of the latent opposition which divides the peasant from those who siphon off his surplus funds. . . . We must not forget that the peasant often idolozes, in song and story, figures who stand in open defiance of the social order which he supports with his labor.") One should also remember Gluckman's discussion of Mau Mau violence, which, he believes, "has been produced by the colonization of Africa, and not by indigenous Africa itself" (Max Gluckman, "The Magic of Despair," in *Order and Rebellion in Tribal Africa* (London 1963), pp. 137–45). An examination of the literature on peasant rebellions shows instances of violence which are remarkably similar to those committed by *Sendero*. In his study of the Vietnamese peasantry Popkin describes how the Viet Minh, "who wanted to isolate the cities and starve them out, while keeping the liberated areas autonomous, went so far as to kill ducklings and piglets in order to curtail trade. These measures only aroused

strong resentment and evasion. Eventually they had no choice but to allow the trade and relied instead on taxing it" (*The Rational Peasant*, p. 241). This is similar to the apparently senseless destruction on 3 August 1982 of Allpachaca, an animal husbandry center, part of Huamanga University, and the killing of valuable cattle by *Sendero*. It appears that peasant groups resort to violence when all other alternatives are closed; on this issue see Henry A. Landsberger, "The Role of Peasant Movements and Revolts in Development," in *Latin American Peasant Movements* (Ithaca 1966), pp. 1–61, est. p. 36; Jeffery M. Page, *Agrarian Revolution. Social Movements and Export Agriculture in the Underdeveloped World* (New York 1975), p. xi; Adas, *Prophets of Rebellion*, pp. 80–91.

71. Military expenditures almost tripled in real terms between 1971–1982 (McClintock, "Why Peasants Rebel," pp. 71–72; see also Werlich, "Peru: The Shadow of Shining Path, p. 79). In the 1985 budget, expenditures were as follows: 30%, service of debt; 20%, military; 4.1%, health; 9.6%, education; 0.1%, housing (Eco-Andes vol. 2, no. 1 [March 1985]). According to the SIPRI, military expenditures by Peru in U.S. dollars (in 1980 prices and exchange rates) were as follows: 1976: 771m; 1977: 1120m; 1978: 1850m; 1979: 667m; 1980: 980m*; 1981: 1211m*; 1982: 1217m*; 1983: 1293m*; 1984: 1290m**; 1985: 1202m**; according to the same source, military expenditures as percent of gross domestic product were as follows: 1976: 5.0; 1977: 7.3; 1978: 5.5; 1979: 3.9; 1980: 5.7*; 1981: 7.2*; 1982: 7.2*; 1983: 8.6*; 1984: 8.2**; 1985: no data available (* = uncertain data; ** = high degree of uncertainty; source: SIPRI, Stockholm International Peace Research Institute, *World Armaments and Disarmament* [Oxford and New York 1986], pp. 237 and 246).

72. Besides the studies dealing specifically with millenarian movements and with *Sendero luminoso* listed above, the following studies have been consulted; Barrington Moore, *Social Origins of Dictatorship and Democracy. Land and Peasant in the Modern World* (Boston 1966); Henry A. Landsberger, "The Role of Peasant Movememts and Rcvolts in Development"; id., "Peasant Unrest: Themes and Variations," in *Rural Protest: Peasant Movements and Social Change* (London 1974), pp. 1–64; Eric R. Wolf, *Peasant Wars in the Twentieth Century* (New York 1969); Gerrit Huizer, *The Revolutionary Potential of Peasants in Latin America* (Lexington 1972); Joel S. Migdal, *Peasants, Politics and Revolution. Pressures Toward Political and Social Change in the Third World* (Princeton 1974); Jeffery M. Paige, *Agrarian Revolution*; James C. Scott, *The Moral Economy of the Peasant*; Samuel L. Popkin, *The Rational Peasant*; Theda Skocpol, *States and Social Revolutions* (Cambridge 1979); Peter Singlemann, *Structures of Domination and Peasant Movements in Latin America* (Columbia and London 1981); John Walton, *Reluctant Rebels. Comparative Studies of Revolution and Underdevelopment* (New York 1984); Robert P. Weller and Scott E. Guggenheim, eds., *Power and Protest in the Countryside. Studies of Rural Unrest in Asia, Europe, and Latin America* (Durham 1982).

73. See Degregori, *Sendero Luminoso,* p. 21; González and Lumbreras, *Qué hacer* 42,p. 35; González and Favre, ibid., p. 44; McClintock, "Sendero Luminoso," p. 27; id., "Why Peasants Rebel," p. 76.

74. Cf. Wolf, *Peasant Wars,* p. 1969; for general discussions of the role of the market and of dependent capitalism see: Moore, *Social Origins,* pp. 470–71; Scott, *Moral Economy of the Peasant,* pp. 56–90, 196; Migdal, *Peasants, Politics, and Revolution,* pp. 230, 258; Guggenheim and Weller, "Moral Economy, Capitalism, and State Power in Rural Society," in Weller and Guggenheim, eds., *Power and Protest,* pp. 7–10; Sidney Mintz, "Peasantries and the Rural Sector," ibid., 183; Walton, *Reluctant Rebels,* pp. 29, 162–62, 202.

75. See Worsley, *The Trumpet Shall Sound,* pp. 39ff., 79ff., and *passim;* Hobsbawm, *Primitive Rebels,* pp. 67–80; Burridge, *New Heaven, New Earth,* p. 146; Adas, *Prophets of Rebellions,* pp. 15ff., 37ff., 64ff., and *passim.*

76. Degregori, *Sendero Luminoso,* pp. 24–25; Favre, "Pérou: Sentier lumineux et horizons obscurs," pp. 13–15; McClintock, "Why Peasants Rebel," pp. 50–51; González and Lumbreras, *Qué hacer* 42 (1986): 35ff; on the role of "culture brokers" see Wolf, *Peasant Wars,* pp. 288–89; Scott, "Protest and Profanation," p. 110 and note 87 below.

77. The need to analyze revolutions from a structural perspective, taking into account both domestic (regional, national) and international developments, as well as the role of the state is emphasized in Skocpol, *States and Social Revolutions,* pp. 5, 14; according to Skocpol, "Modern social revolutions have happened only in countries situated in disadvantaged positions within international arenas" (p. 23); see also id., "What Makes Peasants Revolutionary," in Weller and Guggenheim, *Power and Protest,* pp. 157–79, esp. pp. 178–79. For a criticism of Skocpol and Popkin, similar to Flores Galindo's criticism of Golte, see Walton, *Reluctant Rebels,* p. 156.

78. On the expectations raised and not fulfilled by the agrarian reform and by the electoral victories of the left see McClintock, "Sendero Luminoso," p. 29; id., "Why Peasants Rebel," p. 49; the effects of the cancellation of political gains is discussed by Huizer, *The Revolutionary Potential,* p. 181, and Walton, *Reluctant Rebels,* p. 29. On the revolutionary potential of sudden changes in the economy see Moore, *Social Origins,* p. 474; Migdal, *Peasants, Politics, and Revolution,* pp. 252–53; Scott, *Moral Economy of the Peasant,* p. 194; Adas, *Prophets of Rebellion,* p. 183; Walton, *Reluctant Rebels,* pp. 29, 152.

79. Cf. Favre, *Pérou,* pp. 13–14; this was stressed by Migdal in a book published when *Sendero* was still in its formative period; *Peasants, Politics, and Revolution,* pp. 262–64.

80. Degregori, *"Sendero Luminoso,",* pp. 8–9.

81. On the *desarraigados* see González and Favre, *Qué hacer,* 42 (1986): 44; Favre, ''Pérou: Sentier lumineux et horizons obscurs,'', p. 25. On the role played by the *mestizos,* the uprooted of the sixteenth and seventeenth centuries, in the generation of utopias see Flores Galindo, *Europa y el país de los Incas,* pp. 52–57.

82. Singelmann, *Structures of Domination and Peasant Movements in Latin America,* pp. 176–77, 205.

83. González and Favre, *Qué hacer,* p. 47.

84. Adas, *Prophets of Rebellion,* p. 92.

85. The relative rationality and creativity of millenarian movements is discussed in Worsley, *The Trumpet Shall Sound,* pp. lxvi–lxix, 267–71; Pereira de Queiroz, *Réforme et révolution,* pp. 268, 373; Adas, *Prophets of Rebellion,* pp. 160–64.

86. In ''Pérou: Sentier lumineux et horizons obscurs,'' Favre writes that *Sendero*'s lack of use of the mass media, *''qui n'est sans doute pas sans rapport avec la culture encore imprégnée de tradition orale dans laquelle baigne Sentier,''* could have been compensated by the use of symbolic language which could have endowed the movement with *''une forte expressivité.''* However, he maintains that this is not the case, and that *''les sentiéristes manipulent une gamme restreinte de symboles dont la plupart sont d'ailleurs d'un hermétisme déconcertant''* (p. 15). It is certainly possible that the range of symbols accessible to *Sendero* may be limited; nevertheless, Favre himself has described how young members of the movement take part in the agricultural and religious activities of their communities, and how the leaders ''étaient les moins occidentalisés, les plus provinciaux, les plus andins de tous les membres de l'intelligentsia locale'' (p. 14). Furthermore, it must be remembered that some of the punishments used by *Sendero* against abusive local authorities are the same ones that have been traditionally used in the Andes and are therefore endowed with symbolic meaning; likewise, the revolutionary hymns taught to students in the areas controlled by *Sendero* are sung using the melodies of traditional religious songs and of *huaynos* (pp. 18–19). This confluence between the language of a secular revolutionary ideology and the symbolic universe available to a community does not prove *Sendero*'s access to a rich symbolic language but it points in that direction.

87. Favre describes *Sendero* as the result of the encounter of a lumpen intelligentsia and an uprooted, ''ex-Indian'' milieu (*''Sentier résulte de la rencontre détonnante d'une lumpen intelligentsia et d'une milieu cholo qui, majoritairement, ne se résout pas à devoir rester dans les marges du corps social''* p. 24). Millenarian movements and their leaders have emerged precisely as the result of the encounter of, on the one hand, a lumpen intelligentsia (or members of the lower clergy, members of colonized groups who have close contact with the colonizers, literate individuals in an illiterate milieu, lower

nobility, déclassé individuals) and, on the other, groups occupying an uncertain position in the social structure. On the ambiguous social position of leaders of millenarian rebellions see Pereira de Queiroz, *Réforme et révolution,* p. 52; Adas, *Prophets of Rebellion,* pp. 118–19 and notes 76 and 81 above.

88. Cf. Werlich, "Peru: The Shadow of Shining Path," pp. 80–81.

89. The notion of a world turned upside down—a *pachacuti* in Andean terms—is discussed in Wolf, *Peasant Wars,* p. 295, and particularly in Scott, *The Moral Economy of the Peasant,* pp 237–40; "Protest and Profanation," pp. 4–5, 19–20, 224, 241; "Hegemony and the Peasantry," p. 284.

90. *Poemas—Tiempos de Guerra* (Peru: Ediciones Ayacucho, n.d.), p. 1; *"El trabajo se limitó a seleccionar los pensamientos más altos, colocarlos en forma de poema y darles estructura, ordenamiento y ritmo poético. Es preciso señalarlo, que no se contribuyó a enriquecer el texto, ni siquiere con una sola palabra."* According to Murinache, these poems force us to recognize in Guzmán not only a great politico-military strategist but also a great poet, and the publication of this book constitutes a rupture in the history of Peruvian literature: *"Considero que nada será igual en la literatura peruana después de la publicación de este desconcertante libro de poemas. Se constituirá, definitivamente, en una línea que marcará lo anterior y lo posterior a él"* (p. 2).

91. On the mythical components of Marxism see Ernst Topitsch, "Marxismus und Gnosis," and "Entfremdung und Ideologie," in *Sozialphilosophie zwischen Ideologie und Wissenschaft* (Darmstadt 1971, 3d ed.), pp. 261–96, 297–327. The possibility of a confluence of millenarian expectations and political organization has been emphasized by Flores Galindo in "¿Es posible la utopía?" and in "Mito y rito en la iconografía andina." Journalistic accounts of *Sendero* contain references to the use of the notion of *pachacuti* by members and sympathizers of the movement; see "Informe inglés sobre Sendero," *Oiga* 15 (August 1983): 36, and Jeanne DeQuine, "The Challenge of Shining Path," *The Nation* 8 December 1984, p. 613.

92. See Emanuel Sarkisyanz, *Russland und der Messianismus des Orients. Sendunbgsbewusstsein und politischer Chiliasmus des Ostens,* Tübingen 1955, pp. 269–70.

93. *Anglo-Russian News* 88, no. 18 (January 1929): 2, quoted in Sarkisyanz, pp. 385–86.

Note. Since the completion of this article two important studies on Andean utopian ideologies have been published: Alberto Flores Galindo, *Buscando un Inca: Identidad y utopía en los andes* (Lima 1988; originally published in La Habana, 1986); Manuel Burga, *Nacimiento de una utopía. Muerte y resurrección de los incas* (Lima 1988).

Contributors

Gustavo Benavides (Ph.D. Temple University), teaches religious studies at Villanova University. He has contributed chapters to *Buddhist and Western Philosophy* (Delhi 1981); *Buddhist and Western Psychology* (Boulder 1983); *Sein und Nichts in der abendländischen Mystik* (Freiburg 1984); *The Many Faces of Religion and Society* (New York 1985); *Movements and Issues in World Religions* (New York 1987); *Dossier Eckhart* (Lausanne [forthcoming]). He is currently working on a study of mysticism.

M. W. Daly (Ph.D. University of London), teaches history at Memphis State University. He is the author of *British Administration and the Northern Sudan* (Leiden 1980); *The History of the Sudan, From the Coming of Islam to the Present Day* (with P.M. Holt), London 1980; *Sudan* (Oxford and Santa Barbara 1983); and *Empire on the Nile* (Cambridge 1986); and has edited *The Road to Shakyan* (Durham 1983); *Al-Majdhubiyya and al-Mikashfiyya, two Sufi Tariqas in the Sudan* (Khartoum 1985), and *Modernization in the Sudan* (New York 1986).

William M. Batkay (Ph.D. Columbia University), chairs the department of political science at Montclair College. He is the author of *Authoritarian Politics in a Transitional State* (Boulder 1982).

Spencer C. Bennett (Ph.D. Case Western Reserve University), chairs the history department at Siena Heights College in Michigan. He is currently working on a book on minority civil religion in America, and has contributed to *Icons of Popular Culture* (1970).

Alexandre Bennigsen is director of studies at the Ecole des Hautes Etudes en Sciences Sociales, Paris. He is the author of numerous books on Islam in the Soviet Union; they include *Les mouvements nationaux chez les musulmans de Russie* (Paris-La Haye 1960); *The Evolution of the Muslim Nationalities of*

233

the USSR and their Linguistic Problems (London 1961); *Islam in the Soviet Union (with Chantal Quelquejay), New York 1967; Muslim National Communism in the Soviet Union* (with S. Enders Wimbush), Chicago 1979; *Sufis and Commissars. Sufism in the USSR* (with S.E. Wimbush), Berkeley 1986.

Stephan Feuchtwang (Ph.D. University of London), is senior Lecturer in Sociology at the City University, London. He is the co-editor of *The Chinese Economic Reforms* (London 1983), and of *Transforming China's Economy in the Eighties* (London 1987); he has contributed chapters to *Religion and Ritual in Chinese Society* (Stanford 1974); *The Chinese City Between Two Worlds* (Stanford 1974); *The City in Late Imperial China* (Stanford 1977); *The Re-Emergence of the Chinese Peasantry* (London 1987).

Shahin Gerami (Ph.D. University of Oklahoma), teaches at Southwest Missouri State University. She has contributed articles to *Social Science Quarterly* and *Western Sociological Review.* Her "Iranian Revolution from the World-System Perspective" will appear in the forthcoming *Counter Modernization Movements in Less Developed Countries.*

Lina Gupta (Ph.D. Claremont), teaches in the department of religious studies at the California State University, Northridge. She is currently doing research in the area of religion and politics.

Phillip E. Hammond is professor of religious studies and sociology and chairman of the department of religious studies, University of California, Santa Barbara. He is the author of, among others, *Religion in Social Context* (with N.J. Demerath), New York 1968; *The Role of Ideology in Church Participation* (New York 1980); *Varieties of Civil Religion* (with Robert Bellah), New York 1980; and he has edited *Sociologists at Work* (New York 1964); *American Mosaic* (New York 1970); *Beyond the Classics?* (with C. Y. Glock), New York 1973; *The Sacred in a Secular Age* (Berkeley 1985).

Ninian Smart is professor of religious studies, University of California, Santa Barbara and University of Lancaster. His publications on the history and philosophy of religion include *The Philosophy of Religion* (New York 1970); *The Science of Religion and the*

Sociology of Knowledge (Princeton 1973); *The Long Search* (New York 1978); *The Phenomenon of Christianity* (London 1979); *Beyond Ideology* (San Francisco 1981); *Worldviews* (New York 1983); *Nineteenth Century Religious Thought in the West* (co-edited). Cambridge 1985.

Warren L. Vinz (Ph.D. University of Utah), teaches history at Boise State University. He has contributed articles on religion and politics to *Continuum, Journal of Church and State,* and *Foundations,* and has contributed three chapters to the forthcoming *The Conservative Press in America.*

Index